Th

# Clinical Psychology Since 1917

*Science, Practice, and Organization*

# APPLIED CLINICAL PSYCHOLOGY

Series Editors:
Alan S. Bellack, *Medical College of Pennsylvania at EPPI, Philadelphia, Pennsylvania,*
and Michel Hersen, *Nova University School of Psychology, Fort Lauderdale, Florida*

A Continuation Order Plan is available for this series. A continuation order will bring delivery of each new volume immediately upon publication. Volumes are billed only upon actual shipment. For further information please contact the publisher.

# Clinical Psychology
# Since 1917

*Science, Practice, and Organization*

## Donald K. Routh
*University of Miami*
*Coral Gables, Florida*

PLENUM PRESS • NEW YORK AND LONDON

Routh, Donald K.
    Clinical psychology since 1917 : science, practice, and
organization / Donald K. Routh.
        p.   cm. -- (Applied clinical psychology)
    Includes bibliographical references and index.
    ISBN 0-306-44452-6
    1. Clinical psychology--United States--History. 2. American
Psychological Association. Division of Clinical Psychology-
-History.   I. Title.  II. Series.
    [DNLM: 1. Psychology, Clinical--history--United States.
2. Organizations--history--United States.   WM 11 AA1 R86c 1994]
RC466.8.R68   1994
150'.973--dc20
DNLM/DLC
for Library of Congress                                    93-50551
                                                              CIP

ISBN 0-306-44452-6

© 1994 Plenum Press, New York
A Division of Plenum Publishing Corporation
233 Spring Street, New York, N.Y. 10013

Printed in the United States of America

To Marion W. Routh

# Preface

This book is dedicated to my wife, Marion W. Routh. In her way, she has been informally involved in clinical psychology organizations for as many years as I have. She has also served for many years as the first reader of almost all manuscripts I have written, including the one for this book. I can always depend on her to tell me straight out what she thinks. When she found out I was writing this book, she was afraid that the mass of detailed factual information I was gathering would be dull to read. Therefore, when I actually started writing, I laid aside all notes and just told the story in a way that flowed as freely as possible. (I went back later to fill in the documentation and to correct factual errors that had crept in.) When she looked over the first draft of the book, her comment was, "It is not as boring as I thought it would be." Her frankness is so dependable that I knew from these words that there was hope, but that I had my work cut out for me in the revision process. By the middle of the second draft, she grudgingly had to admit that she was getting hooked on the book and kept asking where the next chapter was. I hoped that others will find the book equally interesting to read; however, I still doubted that it would ever be the book selected to read beside the swimming pool. It was therefore a welcome surprise to receive, in September 1992, the comments of David Barlow on a draft of the entire manuscript. Barlow, at that time president-elect of Division 12, was on sabbatical in Nantucket and indeed took this book to the beach with him during a weekend. Perhaps he was just trying to say something nice, but he claimed that he was literally unable to put it down.

A number of books have been written by others about the history of clinical psychology (Napoli, 1981; Reisman, 1991; Walker, 1991). As far as I know, this is the first one about the history of clinical psychology *organizations*. My interest in the organizational side of clinical psychology began when I was a psychology intern in the Department of Psychiatry and Behavioral Sciences at the University of Oklahoma Medical School. My supervisor, Logan Wright, was active in the Division of Clinical Psychology (Division 12) of the American Psychological Association and was one of the founders of what became one of the sections of the division, the Society of Pediatric Psychology (later Section 5, Division 12). Not long after I received my PhD, I participated in a symposium at the 1969 APA convention in Washington, DC, sponsored by the society. Logan asked me to write an article for one of the first issues of the newsletter, *Pediatric Psychology*, that Gail Gardner had started editing. In 1970, I was asked to allow my name to be placed on the ballot for secretary-treasurer of the society. I did not realize it at the time, but I had stepped onto a sort of organizational escalator where (if you don't do something that makes you fall off) you just keep moving upward.

These events were thus only the beginning of a lifetime of involvement with the Society of Pediatric Psychology, the Section on Clinical Child Psychology (Section 1, Division 12), and eventually Division 12 itself. Regardless of where I might be employed in the United States (Iowa, Ohio, North Carolina, and Florida), these organizations provided a national network of friends and colleagues with whom to compare notes on the passing scene. These sections and this division came to serve as my main reference group not just in my professional life but, I must admit, in my personal life as well. It has been important to have the support provided by these colleagues in withstanding pressures to become, in effect, just another experimental psychologist within an academic department where clinicians were often regarded as second-class citizens. Similarly, when working in a medical school setting where behavioral science personnel were often considered inferior to physicians, it was helpful to have the reassurance of colleagues that it was okay to be a *psychologist.* This includes having meetings at which to present pediatric psychology research findings to colleagues, and psychological journals in which to publish research on the psychological aspects of physical illness in children.

I have come to realize all over again in writing this book that clinical psychology has been for me a very personal enterprise. Like many other people in the world over the past half-century, I had grandparents, parents, and siblings who moved around quite a lot. It did not matter whether my relatives were going west trying to escape the Dust Bowl, working for the Southern Baptist church, the U.S. Army, a newspaper, a group of doctors, a hospital, a bar, IBM or Exxon, or a university. We all moved quite often, and it meant that we did not get to see each other face to face very often. Thus, the people I see every year at the APA convention and at various executive committee meetings during the rest of the year have come to be like a dependable extended family group. In fact, I know them a lot better and can depend on them at least as much as many people I encounter only at a family reunion. (I am told a Dutch proverb says that a nearby friend is better than a faraway relative.) I realize that this does not make for the greatest objectivity in a historian, but I may as well be frank about my favorable bias.

The approach of the 1992 centennial year of the American Psychological Association brought with it the request that each division write its history in recognition of this occasion. I agreed to become Division 12's historian but then found that the task was much more demanding of time than it appeared to be at first. Thus, when I applied for a sabbatical leave from the University of Miami in the spring 1992 semester, I specified the writing of Division 12's history as my sabbatical project. Fortunately, my chairman, Herbert Quay, and the Dean of Arts and Sciences, Ross Murfin, agreed, and this freed up the time needed. The dean, being himself a professor of English literature, probably considers it important to write books (I should probably be glad that in this instance the dean was not an academic psychologist).

The collection of the newsletters of Division 12, which I thought would be the prime source of information in writing its history, goes back only to 1947. The division had its official origin in 1945 as a part of the reorganized, post–World War II APA. However, I soon learned that the organization was considerably older than that. It is the direct descendant of three previous organizations; the American Association of Clinical Psychologists (AACP), founded on December 28, 1917; the Clinical Section of the American Psychological Association, which existed from 1919 to 1937; and the Clinical Section of the American Association for Applied Psychology (AAAP), which existed from 1937 to 1945. Thus, instead of being 47 years old, organized clinical psychology on December 28, 1992, celebrated its 75th birthday. Despite being listed within APA as Division "number 12," it is actually the oldest of them all, and it is about time that it had its history written.

The division's newsletters and the publication called *The Clinical Psychologist* that developed from them contain the minutes of executive committees, board meetings, and committee reports; the records of convention programs; and various articles by psychologists associated with the division. In writing this history, I read through this collection of newsletters repeatedly. It became clear that though they were a necessary source of information, the newsletters required abundant supplementation. As it developed, my approach to writing the history first involved searching out the successive versions of the division's bylaws and a list of the names of psychologists who had been importantly involved with the division, its precedessors, and its various sections. These included at a minimum the elected officers, the editors of newsletters and journals, and persons who have been the recipients of various awards. Appendix

A traces some of the changes in organizational bylaws over time. Appendix B provides a list of the officers and editors of the AACP, the APA Clinical Section, the AAAP Clinical Section, and Division 12 and its sections. Appendix C provides a list of those who have received awards from each of these organizations. Finally, Appendix D contains the names from Appendixes B and C listed in alphabetical order with certain specific information about each one—date of birth (and death); highest degree; area of training within psychology; university and year of graduation; and information about licensure, diplomate status, and fellow status in the division or in APA.

Even in order to arrive at the information given in Appendixes A–D, I had to go well beyond the newsletters. As already noted, the newsletters do not really begin until 1947, and the story I wished to tell begins in 1917. The earlier minutes of the APA appear in the *Psychological Review* and later in the *Psychological Bulletin*. The minutes of the AAAP are in the *Journal of Consulting Psychology*. The minutes of the APA Council and Board of Directors after World War II are in the *American Psychologist*, which also attempts to publish a complete list of the elected officers of its various divisions each year. When there was disagreement between sources as to who was an officer at a given point, I tended to err on the side of overinclusion, even if it meant listing more than the legal number of representatives to or from the division.

The names listed in Appendixes B, C, and D are thus the people who have been most involved with clinical psychology organizations. An underlying premise of this book is the idea that much can be learned about the nature of an organization by looking at the persons elected to positions of leadership or given honorary awards by it. My next step was thus to become familiar with who these people were and their views and accomplishments, especially as these relate to the larger goals of the organization. In general, it was relatively easy to find information about them. Clinical psychologists are a highly articulate and literate group, and many of them leave long paper trails. I searched the electronic catalogs of several libraries for books written by these individuals. Similarly, I traced their writings in professional journals through *Psychological Abstracts*, including the most recent *Psychlit* computer ROM disks. Some have written autobiographical chapters or books or have been the subject of published biographies. For those who have won awards, the award citations are an excellent source of peer judgments as to what their most important accomplishments were. For those whose lives have been completed, there are often published obituaries, for example, in *The New York Times*, the *American Psychologist*, or the *American Journal of Psychology*. Personal papers and letters in the Archives at Akron or the Library of Congress Manuscript Division filled in many details.

I believe that any organization, by the people it elects or appoints to office and chooses for its awards, makes a statement about itself and its aspirations. Getting to know who these people were and what they did seems to be the best way of decoding what that "statement" says.

# Acknowledgments

Many persons and organizations were helpful to me in writing this book. Judy Wilson, the administrative officer of the Division of Clinical Psychology, made available the division's almost-complete file of its newsletters. Thomas Oltmanns sent me a prepublication copy of his history of Section 3, the Society for a Science of Clinical Psychology, and Richard Bootzin provided a list of officers and awardees of Section 3. Carole Rayburn loaned me the newsletter collection of Section 4, the Clinical Psychology of Women. Michael C. Roberts added significantly to my information and corrected some errors concerning Section 5, Pediatric Psychology. Diane J. Willis and Russell T. Jones shared with me their perspectives concerning Section 6, Ethnic Minority Clinical Psychology. Among the many libraries I used were the Arthur W. Melton Library of the American Psychological Association; the U.S. Library of Congress (including its Manuscript Division); and the libraries of American University, Florida International University, the University of Miami, and Vanderbilt University. I also consulted the Archives of the History of American Psychology at the University of Akron, where Director John Popplestone, Associate Director Marion White McPherson, and archivist John Miller were most hospitable.

Eric Vernberg served as the first psychologist colleague to read and comment on the entire text, and Paul Blaney soon followed as the second one. Others who made helpful comments included George Stricker and Judy Wilson. I especially appreciated the willingness of John M. Reisman, the historian of clinical psychology, to comment on this book. I thank Julia Frank-McNeil and Ted Baroody of the American Psychological Association and their staff for their suggesting how the book could be organized in a more logical way. Robert Freire served as the book's production editor. Finally, I thank Eliot Werner, my editor at Plenum Press, for his advice on this book—he chose its present title (and this is not the first book of mine on which he has provided help). None of these people, of course, is responsible for any errors or infelicities of expression that remain; these are my own responsibility.

# Contents

## II. ISSUES AND PERSONALITIES

### III. SUMMING UP

### APPENDIXES

# I

# Chronological Narrative

# 1

# Introduction

## The Founding of Clinical Psychology (1896) and Some Important Early Developments

Clinical psychology is one of the newest professions, built upon a discipline that is itself hardly more than a century old (the conventional date for the founding of modern psychology, that is, Wundt's laboratory in Leipzig, is 1879). The essential elements of clinical psychology are considered to be science and practice. In the view of most of those in the field, these two are inseparably linked to each other and make up a whole that is larger than the sum of its parts. If there were no science, the practitioner would have little credibility. If practitioners did not actually help their clients, the public would have less reason to underwrite research and professional education. This book also deals with the role played by scientific, professional, or "guild" organizations in the historical development of the field. (In clinical psychology, certain credentials such as a doctoral degree, supervised experience, and a license by the state or province have come to be regarded as necessary for full participation in the profession. These make up the profession's "union card." Advocacy by persons associated with the organizations played a significant part in making these credentials a reality.) This book tells the story of the series of a series of organizations within the profession of clinical psychology in the United States: the American Association of Clinical Psychologists (1917–1919), the Clinical Section of the American Psychological Association (1919–1937), the Clinical Section of the American Association for Applied Psychology (1937–1945), the Division of Clinical Psychology of the American Psychological Association (1945–present), and the various sections of Division 12 (1962–present).

The "narrow" history of any such organization covers such relatively mundane matters as the development of its bylaws (see Appendix A), the officers it elected or appointed (see Appendix B), its committees and their activities, its publications, and the awards it gave (see Appendix C). It is difficult to put this kind of factual information into a coherent narrative that one would stay awake to read. However, the broader history of these organizations and the people in them makes a fascinating story. It is intertwined with the development of the profession it serves.

This book thus begins with a chronological narrative of the above clinical psychology organizations. It then continues with a discussion of certain issues and personalities related to the organizations.

## MAJOR DEVELOPMENTS

The major developments that have occurred in the field over the last century were not the doings of any clinical psychology organization as such. The organizations were involved only indirectly. Nevertheless, it is worthwhile at the beginning to try to list some of these larger developments:

1. The development of new psychological knowledge relevant to psychopathology and other clinical issues, for example about the development of children's attachment to parents (John Bowlby and Mary Ainsworth), internal vs. external locus of control (Julian Rotter), risk and protective factors (Norman Garmezy), or trait vs. state anxiety (Charles Spielberger). This includes the development of professional and scientific publications sponsored by various organizations: newsletters and journals (for example, the founding of the *Journal of Abnormal Psychology* by Morton Prince and of the *Journal of Consulting Psychology* by Johnnie Symonds).
2. The idea of mental testing (Francis Galton [1978/1869], James McK. Cattell). The creation and validation of intelligence tests: the Binet-Simon (1905) test, the Stanford-Binet (L. M. Terman); subsequently the Wechsler tests.
3. The emergence of personality assessment, as exemplified by the Rorschach test, the Thematic Apperception Test (Henry Murray), and the Minnesota Multiphasic Personality Inventory (Starke Hathaway and J. C. McKinley).
4. The emergence of a form of outpatient psychotherapy that was sought by patients worldwide: Sigmund Freud's psychoanalysis.
5. The development of empirical research on psychotherapy, as exemplified by the work of Carl Rogers and Hans Strupp.

6. The emergence of behavior therapy and its challenges to more traditional therapies, as exemplified by the work of Mary Cover Jones, O. Hobart Mowrer, Hans Eysenck, and Joseph Wolpe.

7. The development and differentiation of formal graduate training programs in clinical psychology, as described and legitimated at the Boulder and Vail Conferences (among others) and of schools of professional psychology.

8. The development of the American Board of Professional Psychology, certification, licensure, the National Register of Health Providers in Psychology, and other such forms of recognition and regulation of individual psychologists' competence to offer services to the public.

9. The inclusion of clinical psychologists in the health care system, in terms of membership on hospital staffs and eligibility for third-party payments from government or private insurance.

It would be inaccurate to suggest that clinical psychology organizations caused most of these things to happen. First of all, many of these developments occurred outside the United States or were due to the influence of individuals who were foreigners, nonpsychologists, or both. Binet was a Frenchman, Rorschach a Swiss, Freud a Viennese, Eysenck an expatriate German, Wolpe a South African, and Galton and Bowlby were English. Rorschach, Freud, McKinley, Murray, Prince, and Wolpe were physicians. Research is done by individuals or by teams organized for the purpose, not by committees set up by professional organizations. Training programs are developed in universities and community agencies and are only secondarily ratified by organizations. Licensing and certification are generally carried out by state and provincial governments, and legislation concerning them must be the concern of state and provincial professional organizations rather than national ones. Lobbying the federal government regarding the health care system is best done by the agents of larger organizations than APA divisions. Certainly, it would be difficult to find examples where such an APA division or its committees had actually helped any clients, developed any new knowledge, or gotten any new law passed by a legislature. Yet a large organization such as an APA division or section can in certain ways facilitate such developments. It can provide a context for discussion and the presentation of scientific findings. It can sponsor workshops and symposia to facilitate continuing education and the communication of professionals with each other. It can help maintain the morale of persons who ultimately do the work that will achieve the division's goals. It can recognize significant accomplishments. So in this history an attempt was made to address the activities of the organization and those most highly involved in attaining such goals.

## THE FOUNDING OF CLINICAL PSYCHOLOGY

As is well known, the founder of clinical psychology was Lightner Witmer, a professor in the Department of Psychology of the University of Pennsylvania (Brotemarkle, 1931; Watson, 1956). Witmer first presented some of his ideas for a profession of clinical psychology at the meeting of the American Psychological Association on December 29, 1896 (Witmer, 1897). However, there is little evidence that his audience was responsive to this presentation. The APA was, after all, explicitly founded in order to advance psychology "as a science," and the proposal that the principles of psychology should be used to help people individually did not seem to square very well with that objective. The same point has no doubt been made many times in faculty meetings in various universities.[1] Traditional academic departments wish to train scientists but so far have little interest in training practitioners. So the resistance to Witmer's ideas is of contemporary as well as historic significance.

In any case, Witmer did not just talk about the possibility of clinical psychology in the abstract. In the spring of 1896 (well before his APA talk in December), he actually founded a psychological clinic at the University of Pennsylvania that is still in existence. His first case was reportedly a child with spelling difficulty—he reasoned that if there was anything to this new science, it should be able to contribute something to the understanding of such practical problems. As it developed, Witmer's clinic was especially concerned with children and with problems of mental and academic development, especially mental retardation (not what we would at present think of as the typical concerns of the clinical psychologist). Its interventions were often carried out by teachers. The assessment procedures were not static; at times trying to teach a child something served as an important part of the assessment procedure.

A third contribution to clinical psychology made by Witmer was the development of a program for training graduate students as professionals in this field. Some of the trainees indeed stayed on at the University of Pennsylvania and themselves became directors of the original Psychology

---

[1] I often heard such discussions over the years at faculty meetings in the Department of Psychology at the University of Iowa. Its goal has long been to produce scientists, not practitioners, and in fact about half of its doctoral graduates in clinical psychology have gone on to significant scientific careers (Routh, 1982).

Clinic. For example, Edwin B. Twitmyer, whose doctoral dissertation on the kneejerk reflex anticipated Pavlov's work on conditioned reflexes, went on to become one of the founders of the related field of speech pathology (e.g., Twitmyer & Nathanson, 1932). Edward Viteles, another of the early directors of the University of Pennsylvania clinic, became a pioneer in the study of vocational assessment and in industrial psychology (e.g., Viteles, 1932). Robert A. Brotemarkle, a subsequent clinic director and department chair at the University of Pennsylvania, was an expert in personnel psychology. Other Witmer trainees were pioneers in the field in other ways. David Mitchell became perhaps the first clinical psychologist in independent practice, in New York (Mitchell, 1931). Reuel Sylvester went off to found the first psychology clinic in one midwestern state in 1913 (Routh, 1984).

Still another contribution of Witmer to clinical psychology was a professional journal, the *Psychological Clinic*, which he founded in 1907 and personally edited through Volume 23 (when the journal terminated publication). This publication featured mostly detailed case studies and program descriptions. From our present perspective, it contained little that could be described as scientific research. The conclusions reached by some of Witmer's own articles in this journal appear today to be rather dubious, for example, the favorable effect of removal of a child's adenoids upon academic performance. Witmer tried to donate the journal to the American Association for Applied Psychology in 1937 to assure its continued publication, but they already had started one of their own, the *Journal of Consulting Psychology*, and did not choose to continue to publish the one Witmer began.

What about Witmer's contributions to clinical psychology organizations? As far can be determined, participation in such organizations did not seem to be his forte. In the American Psychological Association, Witmer was known as a rather critical and even cranky person. He was bold enough—or foolhardy enough—to criticize William James in 1908 as "the spoiled child of American Psychology" (McReynolds, 1987, p. 295) and to point out that James was primarily a writer rather than an active researcher. This brought disapproval upon Witmer from psychologists without doing any harm to James. Second, Witmer did not seem eager to join clinical psychology organizations. He was asked to join the original American Association of Clinical Psychologists but did not do so. He ultimately became a member of the APA Clinical Section and its successors but never was elected to any office in these national organizations. His only active participation in a clinical organization as far as can be determined was his presidency from 1934 to 1936 of the newly formed Pennsylvania Association of Clinical Psychologists, the precursor of the Pennsylvania Psychological Association. Witmer retired in 1937. He set up a "Witmer School" after his retirement, but it was an actual school for handicapped children, and certainly not a school of thought in psychology. One of his memorials is an award for early career contributions—but in school psychology, not clinical—offered by APA Division 16, the Division of School Psychology. Witmer's contributions were actually broader than either clinical psychology or school psychology as these are presently defined. John M. Reisman, the well-known historian of clinical psychology, pointed out in a letter to the author in 1992 that Witmer was quite committed to treatment (which he referred to as "orthogenics"). Witmer also urged clinicians to interest themselves in neurophysiology, prevention, and social action, among other matters.

## OTHER PRE-1917 CONTRIBUTIONS TO THE DEVELOPMENT OF CLINICAL PSYCHOLOGY

As is well known, Alfred Binet and Theophile Simon developed in 1905 the "intelligence test" that was empirically valid in the sense of identifying mentally retarded children as such and predicting academic performance, vocational performance, and related criteria. At the time this test was developed, the field of clinical psychology in the American sense had not yet developed in France. The Binet-Simon test utilized items that were considerably more complex in their demands than the sensory and motor tasks previously used by Frances Galton, James McKeen Cattell, and others. Binet-Simon items were chosen on the basis of ease of administration, the fact that they showed an increase in percentage passing with the age of the child tested, and their internal consistency.

The person who was responsible for bringing the Binet test to the United States was H. H. Goddard, who in 1905 became the first director of research at the Vineland, New Jersey, Training School, a private institution for the feebleminded. He was largely responsible for bringing the Binet-Simon to the United States in 1908 (Burtt & Pressey, 1957). Goddard discovered an unexpectedly large number of "morons" (a word he invented) in the population. Many of these may have been people with low intelligence test scores but at least minimally adequate social functioning. Such persons would not officially qualify as mentally retarded today in terms of the concept of adaptive behavior resulting from Edgar Doll's work. Goddard believed that mental retardation was mainly due to genetic factors and later became notorious because of what we now view as his flawed study of retardation in the Kallikak family in New Jersey (Goddard, 1912).

Goddard was the developer of what was evidently the first formal 1-year internship program in clinical psychology, at Vineland, in 1908. In terms of curent ideas about how psychology interns should occupy themselves, it is interesting that interns who worked with Goddard (and Doll) usually did some research as well as clinical activities (Doll, 1946). Perhaps their whole program deserves a further look. After he left Vineland, Goddard became a professor at Ohio State University in 1922, and was one of the early graduate educators of clinical psychologists.

The Binet scale was further standardized by L. M. Terman at Stanford University and was provided with much more elaborate norms than had previously been available. The competent administration of the Stanford-Binet scale became a skill that was universal among early clinical psychologists. Like Goddard's early activities, Terman's work on the Stanford-Binet began during the time before there were was any clinical psychology organization. Later Terman used the Stanford-Binet to define and study a large cohort of "gifted" children over time (Terman, 1925). Terman was eventually elected a member of the National Academy of Sciences.

By this time, the reader may be getting the idea that in its early days, clinical psychology was mainly concerned with mental testing. This is not far wrong. One of the well-known figures at this time was Guy M. Whipple. He was originally trained at Cornell University, but his interest was viewed negatively by Edward Titchener, the most influential figure in experimental psychology at the time. Whipple soon went elsewhere (Ruckmick, 1942). While still at Cornell, Whipple did supervise the senior honors thesis of a promising young man named Edgar A. Doll. Actually, it has been stated that Whipple's manual of mental tests (Whipple, 1910) did the same thing for applied psychology that Titchener's laboratory manual did for the experimental psychology of the day—it was in nearly universal use. In any case, Whipple's manual was widely used and admired. One of Whipple's claims to fame as a clinical psychologist was that he sponsored a resolution passed by APA in 1915 as follows:

> Whereas: Psychological diagnosis requires thorough technical training in all phases of mental testing, thorough acquaintance with the facts of mental development and with various degrees of mental retardation. And whereas: There is evident a tendency to appoint for this work persons whose training in clinical psychology is inadequate; Be it resolved: That this Association discourages the use of mental tests for practical psychological diagnosis by individuals psychologically unqualified for the work. (Fernberger, 1932, p. 46)

Although Whipple introduced the above resolution, J. E. W. Wallin (1966) states that he, not Whipple, was the one who wrote it. There is also some confusion as to whether Whipple was a member of the founding group of the American Association of Clinical Psychologists (see next chapter). The minutes in the Manuscript Division of the Library of Congress list him as being there, but Wallin's (1966) article does not.

Whipple later moved in the direction of education, becoming one of the founders of the *Journal of Educational Psychology* and the long-term editor of the Yearbooks of the National Society for the Study of Education.

## THE FOUNDING OF THE *JOURNAL OF ABNORMAL PSYCHOLOGY* AND OF THE HARVARD PSYCHOLOGICAL CLINIC

The first important journal in the field of clinical psychology was the *Journal of Abnormal Psychology*, founded by Morton Prince in 1906. Prince was a physician, not a psychologist. At the time this journal was founded, no clinical psychology organization yet existed. Nevertheless, the development of this journal needs to be described because it has long been the principal outlet for research by psychologists on psychopathology. This journal provides a key bit of context for the development of all later publications by clinical psychology organizations.

Morton Prince practiced medicine in Boston and originally taught at Tufts University Medical School. He was particularly influenced by Pierre Janet, and was famous for his published description of Sally Beauchamp, a case of multiple personality (Prince, 1906). He edited the *Journal of Abnormal Psychology* for many years and in 1926 gave it to the American Psychological Association, which still publishes it. Prince was also the founder of the American Psychopathological Association, an interdisciplinary group (mostly psychiatrists, actually) that holds scientific meetings and publishes edited volumes on various topics based on its proceedings.

Although Prince read Freud's writings with great interest, he did not become committed to psychoanalysis. Rather, he remained neutral in his views. He did agree with Freud's view that psychopathology was more properly a part of psychology than of medicine and (with an anonymous endowment provided by his brother, a wealthy Boston lawyer), founded the Harvard Psychological Clinic. This clinic was part of the psychology program on the arts and sciences campus of Harvard rather than at the Medical School. Beginning in 1926, Prince hired as his assistant a most interesting person named Henry Murray, about whom more will be said in a later chapter.

## EARLY DEVELOPMENTS IN PSYCHOANALYSIS AND PSYCHOTHERAPY

The first influential form of psychotherapy was Freudian psychoanalysis. Therefore, in order to discuss the role of clinical psychology organizations in therapeutic intervention, it is necessary to provide some general background, beginning with Sigmund Freud and his influence on the entire mental health field.

Freud's famous book with Breuer on the treatment of hysteria by psychological means appeared in 1885 and his book on the interpretation of dreams in 1900. Freud had studied with Charcot in Paris and was knowledgable concerning hypnotic treatment methods but rejected them in favor of having his patients free associate (Gay, 1988). Freud came to America in 1909 to speak at a conference at Clark University, a meeting arranged by G. Stanley Hall and attended by the leading American psychologists of the day, including William James and Edward Titchener (in fact, Freud's papers make it clear that on that occasion he regarded Titchener and by extension the academic psychologist as "der Gegner," the opponent).

Before Freud's visit, considerable activity had already occurred in the United States—particularly in Boston—in the field of psychotherapy, mostly by physicians (Hale, 1971). Some members of the clergy were also interested in mental healing, for example, Mary Baker Eddy and her Christian Science Church, and an activity within Protestant churches known as the Emmanual Movement. But, to use the metaphor of physician Morton Prince:

> Freudian psychology had flooded the field like a full rising tide and the
> rest of us were left submerged like clams in the sands at low water.
> (quoted by Hale, 1971b, p. 434)

By 1911 the Freudians were already referring to themselves as "psychoanalysts," implying that they were practitioners of a profession not identical with other ones such as neurology, psychiatry, psychology, or social work.

In Europe, it was (and is) possible to become a psychoanalyst without a medical degree, indeed without any other conventional graduate or professional training, a famous example being Anna Freud (Sigmund's daughter). The pattern of training developed by Max Eitingon at the Berlin Psychoanalytic Institute and required internationally since 1922 involved three components: a personal psychoanalysis, theoretical or didactic training provided by classes at an institute, and a "control" or supervised analysis of a patient. In one famous European legal case, Theodore Reik, a PhD, was arrested and tried in 1926 for practicing medicine without a license, that is, engaging in psychoanalysis without medical training. Exhibit A in his trial was Freud's statement—published in 1927 as *The Problem of Lay Analysis*—that psychoanalysis was a part of psychology rather than a part of medicine, and that for this reason medical training was not required. However, the American Psychoanalytic Association in 1938 decided otherwise, and officially forbid the training of nonmedical individuals as psychoanalysts (Fine, 1990). Naturally, at the time this attitude discouraged American clinical psychologists from trying to become psychoanalysts. To the extent that they saw psychoanalysis as the premier variety of psychotherapy, they might have been at least temporarily discouraged from becoming psychotherapists as well.

# 2

# The American Association of Clinical Psychologists, 1917–1919

On December 28, 1917, a group of eight psychologists got together at the American Psychological Association meeting in Pittsburgh (on the campus of Carnegie Institute of Technology) and formed an independent organization, the American Association of Clinical Psychologists (AACP). They elected as their chair J. E. Wallace Wallin and as their secretary Leta S. Hollingworth. The others in the group were Francis N. Maxfield, James B. Miner, David Mitchell, Rudolf Pintner, Clara Schmitt, and Guy M. Whipple. The purposes of the organization (see Appendix A) were basically twofold: to increase the morale and espirit de corps of clinical psychologists by raising professional standards, and to encourage research in clinical psychology. It was the first aim, the professional one, that seemed to conflict with the purpose of the American Psychological Association (APA). (According to its bylaws, the APA officially had only one objective, to advance psychology as a science.) These eight founders tentatively chose 48 individuals as prospective members of this organization, 46 of whom subsequently confirmed that they wished to be members (see Table 2–1). All but one had PhD degrees. William Healy had an MD but not a PhD, and five people had both MD and PhD degrees (Bruner, Dearborn, Gesell, Haines, and Stevens).

Of the 46 AACP members, the 1918 APA *Yearbook* lists 22 as being associated with universities, 10 as employed by public school systems, and two each as employed by the juvenile courts, institutions for the mentally retarded, and by psychiatric hospitals. One worked for a children's hospital. Several of the AACP members were not listed in this yearbook. Recall that the APA itself had relatively few members at that time and had begun in 1892 (25 years before) with only 31 members (Fernberger, 1932).

13

TABLE 2-1. *Membership of the American Association of Clinical Psychologists (1917–1919)*

| | | |
|---|---|---|
| Bird T. Baldwin | William Healy | H. C. Stevens |
| Gardner C. Bassett | Samuel B. Heckman | Arthur H. Sutherland |
| Charles S. Berry | David S. Hill | Reuel H. Sylvester |
| Augusta F. Bronner | Leta S. Hollingworth | L. M. Terman |
| Frank G. Bruner | Buford J. Johnson | Clara H. Town |
| Harry W. Crane | Frederic Kuhlmann | J. E. Wallace Wallin |
| Josephine Curtis | Florence E. Matteer | Jean Weidensall |
| Walter F. Dearborn | Francis E. Maxfield | F. L. Wells |
| Grace M. Fernald | James B. Miner | Guy M. Whipple |
| Mabel R. Fernald | David Mitchell | S. Harold Williams |
| S. I. Franz | George Ordahl | Elizabeth Woods |
| Robert H. Gault | Rudolf Pintner | Helen T. Woolley |
| Arnold L. Gesell | W. H. Pyle | Robert M. Yerkes |
| Henry H. Goddard | Clara Schmitt | Herman H. Young |
| Thomas H. Haines | Stevenson Smith | |
| Mary Hayes | Lorle Stecher [Weeber] | |

*Source:* Manuscript Division, U.S. Library of Congress.

## MOTIVES OF THE "FOUNDERS"

What were the motives of the people who formed the new organization? J. E. Wallace Wallin has written extensively on this question (e.g., Wallin, 1966). In some ways he seems like the Rodney Dangerfield of clinical psychology, a man who was concerned because he got "no respect" for what he considered his valuable professional activities. Wallin got his PhD from Yale University. He subsequently complained that Yale was not very supportive of its former students because the psychology laboratory there had fallen apart, with George T. Ladd retiring and Edward Scripture leaving for Europe. Wallin first became concerned in 1910 about the issues that led him to form the AACP when training some school teachers as "Binet testers" (as he called them). Wallin found that these individuals could certainly learn the mechanics of giving and scoring the tests but lacked the depth of background in psychology needed to interpret the results properly. Yet the public readily began to label such teachers as "psychologists." Similarly, in Wallin's opinion, psychologists with PhD degrees and solid academic training were not thereby qualified to administer and interpret such tests, either. In order to do so, they would need to add appropriate practical experience to their academic background. Wallin felt that somehow there should be a way to make it clear to the public who the qualified clinical psychologists were.

A second experience Wallin had that led up to his involvement in forming the AACP was his employment in 1910 for 8 months at the New Jersey Village for Epileptics at Skillman (David, 1962; Wallin, 1955). (The present name of this facility is the New Jersey Neuropsychiatric Institute.) There, Wallin felt that he was mistreated by the physician–superintendent of the institution. His main objection was that he was not treated as a professional. Thus, he was expected to give one Binet test after another, day after day. He was not permitted to go into the patients' cottages without the superintendent's permission. He was not permitted to give a scientific paper without the superintendent's name on it. He was not even allowed to leave the grounds of the institution without the superintendent's permission.

Others writing about the AACP have claimed that its founding was related in some way to World War I. After all, the organization was founded in 1917. However, Wallin subsequently denied that any of the founders were in any way connected with the military, even though many of the original 46 members were involved in the war effort. Wallin was not being entirely candid in these statements. His papers in the Archives of the History of American Psychology at Akron show that during World War I he wrote to President Woodrow Wilson to volunteer his services to examine military recruits. In these communications, Wallin criticized Robert Yerkes, then President of the American Psychological Association, who was heading up many of the activities of psychology in the military, because Yerkes included, as examiners, some experimental psychologists with no clinical training. As Wallin said in a subsequent letter dated November 1, 1917 to Wilson's Secretary of War:

> Men have been appointed to diagnose mental defectives who have utterly no clinical experience and whose practical acquaintance with mental deficiency is limited to the academic armchair, while persons who have spent all their time for years in the examination of mental defectives and in administration of work for them, have been entirely ignored.

In 1918, Wallin got official letters September 13 and September 26 from Major Robert M. Yerkes informing him that his application to serve the military as a psychological examiner was declined. In response to Wallin's request to explain why, Yerkes went so far as to say that Wallin had been found "unfit for military service" on the basis of his problems with personal relationships. This must have been a blow to Wallin's professional self-esteem, to say the least. Similarly, Carl Seashore had written Wallin on September 4, 1917, that Wallin had been among those considered for the position of director of the new Iowa Child Welfare Research Station but was not selected because the job required someone with good public relations skills. Indeed, Wallin's career contained a remarkably high number of job changes. He left in his papers an unpublished manuscript, "How to Lose Your Job Once You Have Found One," and seems to have known what he was talking about on that topic. Wallin's own view of his career, in contrast to the rather negative words of Yerkes and Seashore, may have been revealed by the working title of unpublished autobiographical papers, "Genius Unfolding: Markings in the Pioneer Career of J. E. Wallace Wallin."

One might well ask whether Wallin got some respect, so to speak, from his activities in founding the AACP. He did keep coming to meetings of the organization and its successors for many years, often being mentioned in organizational newsletter articles and described (often rather vaguely) as one of the early leaders in clinical psychology. He later served on the Executive Committee of the Clinical Section of the American Association for Applied Psychology (AAAP, not to be confused with the earlier AACP) in 1940–41. He also wrote several articles about the founding of the AACP, stating in one of these that the date December 28, 1917, should be regarded as a "red-letter day" in APA history (Wallin, 1966). Incidentally, it is interesting that the APA as a whole was founded on December 27 (1892) and the AACP on the next day of the month, December 28, 25 years later (1917). However, clinical psychology organizations have not yet chosen to honor the date (or Wallin's role as a "founder"). To this day, Wallin is probably better known as a special educator than as a psychologist (just as Lightner Witmer is more honored by school psychologists than by clinicians). Wallin went on to receive an honorary LLD from Upsala College (in New Jersey) in 1958. With funds provided by Wallin himself, the Council for Exceptional Children established a J. E. Wallace Wallin Award in 1963, for significant contributions to the education of handicapped children, which it still bestows (*Exceptional Children*, 1963, *20*, p. 51). Perhaps the greatest tribute to Wallin was provided in a special issue of the *Journal of Education* edited by his friend, Burton Blatt (1968). Blatt pointed out in his introduction to this issue that Wallin wrote the first state regulations (in Missouri) requiring provision of special classes for severely retarded children, that is, what is now called a "no-push-out" policy. Thus, Wallin was a pioneer in the delivery of services to a much neglected group, long before the parent advocacy in a Pennsylvania case and other events led up to the U.S. Education of All Handicapped Children Act of 1974.

John M. Reisman, the historian of clinical psychology, made some interesting comments about Wallin in a letter to the author (August 11, 1992):[1]

> Unfortunately, Wallin was not unique in feeling that he was underappreciated and "got no respect." Among those with similar feelings were Witmer, James, Freud, Maslow, and Rogers. So ... I felt [that] comparing Wallin to Rodney Dangerfield created an association—sweating, beefy, comic, coarse—that didn't give Wallin the respect that is his due.

The other main founder of the AACP, Leta S. Hollingworth, has perhaps received more recognition within psychology than Wallin did, but so far mostly as a feminist pioneer rather than as a clinician (Shields, 1975). She actually worked as a clinical psychologist for only about 2 years, beginning in 1914. Her extremely high scores on the New York City civil service examination evidently helped get her a position doing testing at Bellevue Hospital. In 1916 she moved on to a position as a faculty member at Teachers College, Columbia University, but continued to be a strong supporter of clinical psychology right up until her untimely death at age 53. For example, at the request of the Clinical Section of APA, she did a survey of each state's criteria for expert testimony concerning mental retardation. Also, as A. T. Poffenberger (1940) states:

> She vigorously defended the cause of clinical psychologists and was a leading spirit in building their professional organization and raising the standards of mental examiners in universities and the civil service. She did not hesitate to appear before school boards and state legislatures to plead her cause. (p. 300)

As noted already, Hollingworth was a recognized pioneer feminist. She did systematic research on the (lack of a) role of the menstrual cycle in female intellectual efficiency and fought other stereotypes of females of the time. She participated in the suffragist battle for the vote for women (achieved in 1920). Her principal interest in the last years of her life was gifted children. She was among those who established a special school for

---

[1] In response to Reisman's insightful remarks, I have to admit that I also have had the feeling, myself, that as a clinical psychologist I did not get enough respect—from the public, from physicians, and from experimental psychologist colleagues. That was no doubt among my own motivations for being involved in clinical psychology organizations for so many years. They can provide a powerful antidote to such feelings. Therefore, perhaps I should not have singled out Wallin but should have squarely faced the fact that clinical psychology has been a sort of Rodney Dangerfield among the professions, as perhaps psychology itself has been among the biological sciences.

both dull and gifted children in the New York City system. It was known as Public School 500, or the Speyer School.

## APA'S REACTION

As Wallin (1961) recalled it many years later, the founding of the AACP caused a storm within the APA:

> The decision reached in the evening of December 28 to form a new association spread rapidly and became the topic of consuming conversation in cloakrooms and corridors. Soon a blackboard notice appeared calling a rump meeting of the APA which attracted a large attendance, twice as many as the room would accommodate in the available seats. The meeting was characterized by a rather acrimonious debate, the majority of the speakers being bitterly opposed to the formation of another association, which they regarded as separatistic in nature and a threat to the prosperity of the parent association. (p. 257)

The AACP actually had a very short life, 2 years. Its major activity during this time was to schedule a symposium on clinical psychology during the APA meeting in 1918. So many people came to its second meeting and the discussion was so heated that there was never time to present this symposium orally, but the papers that had been prepared for it were published the next year (i.e., 1919) in the *Journal of Applied Psychology*. In one of these papers, Arnold Gesell presented the view that there needed to be some profession that combined the expertise of the clinical psychologist with that of the pediatrician. In the other papers, there was an early discussion of the difficulty of defining clinical psychology—a recurring theme in the field.

In the APA Council meeting in 1918 (as reported in the *Psychological Bulletin*, 1919, 16, p. 34), Robert M. Yerkes said rather prophetically that he thought "certain educational institutions should specialize in applied psychology and that others should continue with general instruction." E. L. Thorndike replied, saying "he believed that in 20 years there would be as many 'doing' as teaching psychology, but that both groups must be scientific. He saw no reason why the PhD in psychology should not represent both types."

# The Clinical Section of the American Psychological Association, 1919–1937

In 1919, the AACP dissolved itself, and a Clinical Section was begun within the American Psychological Association. The person who may have been most responsible for this merger was Robert M. Yerkes. Yerkes had been the President of APA in 1917 when the AACP was founded. He is best known as a comparative psychologist. For example, he was the author of a famous book, *The Dancing Mouse* (Yerkes, 1907). He stated the principle now known as the Yerkes–Dodson Law (Yerkes & Dodson, 1908). Eventually the Yerkes Laboratories of Primate Biology, now in Atlanta, Georgia, were named after him. In addition, in the era before and during World War I, Yerkes also had excellent credentials as a clinical psychologist. He worked extensively at the Boston Psychopathic Hospital with the psychiatrist E. E. Southard. He also worked with clinical psychologist Edmund B. Huey, a pioneer researcher on reading and reading disabilities. Yerkes and his colleagues (Yerkes, Bridges, & Hardwick, 1915) devised a scale of intelligence. The APA Committee on Psychological Examination of Recruits (accepted in November, 1917, as a subcommittee of the Psychology Committee of the National Research Council) met initially at Vineland, New Jersey, on May 28, 1917, for a period of about 6 weeks. The members of it who were later affiliated with clinical psychology organizations in some way included Edgar A. Doll, Henry H. Goddard, Thomas H. Haines, Lewis M. Terman, F. L. Wells, Guy M. Whipple, and Robert M. Yerkes, chair. During World War I, Yerkes' committee developed Army Alpha and the Army Beta tests and evaluated 1,700,000 officers and enlisted personnel (Elliott, 1956).

Yerkes did not, himself, attend the organizing meeting of the AACP, though he was evidently well aware of it. He was one of the individuals invited to join the splinter group (the AACP), and did so (see Table 2–1), but as APA president he had responsibilities to the larger organization, and evidently took immediate steps to heal the breach that some considered to threaten the unity of American psychology. Bird T. Baldwin on behalf of the APA and Arnold Gesell on behalf of the AACP negotiated the compromise in which the AACP would be replaced by the Clinical Section, whose members would be identified in the APA Yearbook as being members of the section. (It was thus the first section or division of APA—now there are almost 50 of them.) In addition, APA agreed to set up a mechanism by which "consulting psychologists" could be certified as competent to offer their services to the public.

## ROLE OF EARLY CHILD DEVELOPMENT RESEARCHERS IN THE CLINICAL SECTION

Baldwin, the psychologist who represented APA in the negotiations, was at that time a member of the U.S. Army and was involved in the psychological testing program headed by Yerkes. He became better known subsequently as the first director of the Iowa Child Welfare Research Station, founded in 1917 with $25,000 in state funds as the first of the university child development research institutes. Recall that this was the position that Carl Seashore did *not* offer to Wallin. It is interesting that in those days what we now label as developmental psychology was seen as a part of applied psychology, indeed of clinical psychology. Not only Bird T. Baldwin but other prominent child researchers such as John E. Anderson (the first director of the University of Minnesota Institute of Child Development), Jean W. Macfarlane, Florence Goodenough, Myrtle McGraw, and others were members of the clinical psychology organization. Arnold Gesell, who negotiated on behalf of AACP in the above compromise agreement, originally received his PhD in psychology under G. Stanley Hall at Clark University. He later completed his MD at Yale and served as a faculty member for many years in both education and medicine there. He also served as the first "school psychologist" for the State of Connecticut. Gesell also at this time very clearly identified himself as a "clinical psychologist."

Another child development expert who was prominent in the Clinical Section of APA (though few people know his name today) was Martin L. Reymert. He served as the head of what were called the Mooseheart Laboratories of Child Development in Mooseheart, Illinois. This organization came into existence as part of a charitable venture run by the International Order of the Moose. It was an orphanage, open to children whose parents were members of the Moose lodge but who because of death or incapacity could not care for their children. It was natural for research on psychological development to go on in places such as this where children were found. For good reasons, such institutions are far less common today, and I think this may be taken as some evidence of progress, based in part on the knowledge obtained through research in the behavioral sciences.

To anticipate the story a bit, one of the researchers in developmental psychology most highly honored by Division 12 was Jean W. Macfarlane. She served as president of the division and later received one of its awards for contributions to the science and profession of clinical psychology. Macfarlane was a faculty member for many years at the University of California, Berkeley. She began at one point to carry out research on the efficacy of child guidance on a group of children there (Macfarlane, 1938)— in fact it was referred to as the Berkeley Guidance Study. The results were negative as far as the effects of guidance were concerned, perhaps because the staff could not seem to refrain from offering guidance to the control subjects as well as the intervention group. However, Macfarlane reoriented the study and turned it into one of the classic longitudinal investigations of human development. She and her coworkers (including, for example, Erik Erikson) followed these children into adolescence, adulthood, and even into old age. The data of this study are in an archive and are still being subjected by other researchers to secondary analyses, some with obvious clinical relevance. It is therefore not surprising that the visitor to the University of California today will find a street sign saying "Jean W. Macfarlane Lane."

## ACTIVITIES OF THE APA CLINICAL SECTION

As the title of this chapter indicates, the APA Clinical Section existed for approximately 18 years, from 1919 to 1937. Its major function during that time seemed to be to serve as a sponsor for programs of interest to its members as part of the annual APA convention. At the 1922 APA meeting in Cambridge, Massachusetts:

> The sessions were held in Emerson Hall, with the exception of the session of the Section on Clinical Psychology on Friday afternoon, which was held at the Boston Psychopathic Hospital.... This arrangement made it possible for persons interested only in clinical psychology to come late to the meeting and for persons whose interest was only in theoretical and experimental psychology to leave early. (*Psychological Bulletin*, 1923, 20, pp. 161–162)

The chair of the Clinical Section during its first 3 years was Francis N. Maxfield. He had received his PhD under Witmer at Pennsylvania, worked for a time in state government, and finally became professor of clinical psychology at Ohio State University. There he taught Marie Skodak (who was later an officer of the Clinical Section of the AAAP) as an undergraduate about the hereditary nature of mental retardation. She later repudiated this view after participation in the "Iowa Studies" (e.g., Skodak, 1939), showing that orphanage children thrived intellectually when given environmental stimulation. Maxfield also served later as the first chair of the Clinical Section of the American Association for Applied Psychology in 1937–1938.

The Clinical Section evidently met only at the APA convention each year—actually, there were two years when it did not meet because of the illness of Herman H. Young, the Indiana University clinical psychologist who was supposed to have planned the meetings (he caught pneumonia and died suddenly at the age of 43; Hearst & Capshew, 1988). The section elected new officers each year. On at least two occasions it published single-issue newsletters.

## THE APA CLINICAL SECTION AND THE CHILD GUIDANCE MOVEMENT

In 1926 the chair of the Clinical Section was Augusta F. Bronner. Of all the early clinical psychologists, her name may be the one most firmly associated with the development of the child guidance movement. The concept of child guidance was crucial to the way in which clinical psychology developed. One can hardly think of Bronner without also thinking of the man who worked with her so long and who married her after his first wife died, the psychiatrist William Healy.

In 1907 William Healy had been the founder of the Juvenile Psychopathic Institute (later called the Institute for Juvenile Research) in Chicago, the first child guidance clinic in the United States Healy had been an undergraduate at Harvard, where he knew William James and received an excellent background in psychology. He later received his MD from Rush Medical College in Chicago. The child guidance center he founded was closely connected with the juvenile court in Chicago and was supported by influential persons in the private sector as well. The aims of child guidance were partly to evaluate children and teenagers being seen in court, but also to intervene early to prevent delinquency. It was there that the model of the mental health team emerged, including the psychiatrist, psychologist, and social worker. The activities of the team were, however, more concerned with evaluation than with treatment, because in the juvenile courts the main agents of intervention were probation officers. The first psychologist to work with Healy was Grace Fernald. However, she left and went to California, where she later made substantial contributions to remedial work for children with reading disabilities. (She founded what is now called the Fernald School on the UCLA campus.) In Chicago, Fernald was replaced by Augusta Bronner as Healy's chief psychologist.

In 1917 William Healy and Augusta Bronner moved to Boston, where they set up the Judge Baker Guidance Center, one of the best known of the child guidance clinics even today. In 1921 the Commonwealth Fund initiated a program financing demonstration child guidance clinics all over the country. There were seven clinics by the end of 1921 and 102 by 1927 (Stevenson & Smith, 1934). Both Healy and Bronner were charter members of the American Association of Clinical Psychologists and of the Clinical Section of the APA. Besides his work as a psychiatrist, Healy made significant contributions to clinical psychology through developing "performance" tests such as the Healy Picture Completion Test (Healy, 1914), a forerunner of one of the Wechsler subtests. Healy was also one of the founders and served as the first president of the American Orthopsychiatric Association, founded in 1924. This became the principal interdisciplinary mental health organization and welcomed psychologists, social workers, and others as well as physicians into membership. Until fairly recently it was common for a clinical psychology organization such as APA Division 12 to have its midyear board of directors meeting at the time and place of the "Ortho" meeting. Augusta Bronner herself served as the president of "Ortho" in later years. In terms of their theoretical orientation, both Healy and Bronner (1926) appeared to start out with their own, somewhat eclectic views, focusing for example on the psychological and social origins of juvenile delinquency (detailed case histories were a key part of their method). Over time, they appeared to move steadily in the direction of the psychoanalytic viewpoint that was typical of the times among most mental health workers.

## CERTIFYING "CONSULTING PSYCHOLOGISTS"

As already stated, when it approved the existence of a Clinical Section in 1919, the APA had agreed to devise a system of "certifying" individuals who were qualified to offer psychological services to the public, to be known as "consulting psychologists." The original scheme specified that APA members who were already in the Clinical Section could simply pay $35 and be certified (this was obviously a "grandparent" clause), whereas others would also have to undergo an examination of their professional credentials. F. L. Wells was appointed by APA as the executive officer of the Standing Committee on the Certification of Consulting Psychologists. This certification plan, unfortunately, proved to be stillborn. Great frustration is evident in F. L. Wells' committee report to APA in 1926:

> The constituted objects of the Association are scientific, and this places it at a partial disadvantage in the maintenance of professional standards. Scientific men are predominantly schizoid, and while commonly energetic and at times heroic in the pursuit of personal aims and ideals, seldom exhibit the capacity for resolute common action which is observable in professional and more markedly in industrial groups. It is an open question whether the corporate resolution of a scientific group such as this one, without strong personal or professional interests at stake, can be counted on for effective opposition to the energy and resources which would be mustered by a colleague charged with misconduct and his professional life to fight for. One can see in this an argument for the organization of the psychological profession into a group distinct from the present one. (Committee on Certification, 1927, p. 149)

Only 25 psychologists were ever certified under the committee's rules, and in 1927 APA gave up the effort to continue the process. In retrospect it is difficult to see what would motivate would-be practitioners to seek this kind of certification from an organization, because it had no legal force behind it and was not well known to the public. For the historic record, it may be of interest to list the 25 individuals who were certified as consulting psychologists (see Table 3–1). Some of their names have become quite familiar to us. Seventeen of them had been original members of the AACP.

According to their listings in the 1925 APA *Yearbook*, these 25 psychologists included 17 who were associated with universities, four who were employed by public school systems, one who worked in a psychiatric hospital, and only three who appeared to be in independent practice: Gardner C. Bassett, of Charlotte, NC; Lillien J. Martin, of San Francisco; and David Mitchell, of New York City.

After 1927 the Clinical Section served purely as an interest group, and membership in it was not supposed to be used as evidence of clinical competence. Not unexpectedly, at least one member was reprimanded for trying to use membership in this way. In 1934 a certain consulting psychologist sent out a circular containing the words: "My work is fully accredited by the American Psychological Association and by the Clinical Section." According to the *Psychological Bulletin* (Vol. 31, p. 655), this statement was protested both by the APA Council and by the Clinical Section because

TABLE 3-1. *"Consulting Psychologists" Certified by APA as of 1927*

| | | |
|---|---|---|
| Gardner C. Bassett | Leta S. Hollingworth | William T. Root |
| Charles S. Berry | Buford J. Johnson | Benjamin R. Simpson |
| Harry W. Crane | Bertha M. Luckey | Arthur H. Sutherland |
| Walter F. Dearborn | Lillien J. Martin | Reuel H. Sylvester |
| June E. Downey | James B. Miner | L. M. Terman |
| Mabel R. Fernald | David Mitchell | F. L. Wells |
| Arnold Gesell | Garry C. Myers | Helen T. Woolley |
| Samuel B. Heckman | Rudolf Pintner | Herman H. Young |
| | Louise E. Poull | |

*Source*: Fernberger, 1932, p. 51.

neither the association nor the section had a mechanism for such accreditation.

In 1927 the Clinical Section approved new bylaws that were more explicitly professional than its original 1919 ones had been (see Appendix A). However, apparently inadvertently, these new bylaws were not immediately shown to the officials in charge of APA as a whole. When the section's new bylaws did come to the attention of APA, they were considered to be unsatisfactory, and in 1935 were approved only in an amended form that left the group with the single function of providing a forum for scientific results (see Appendix A). Thus, the section was criticized by many of its members because (unlike the AACP), it was only a paper-reading group.

In fact, the APA as a whole was growing more research oriented and less practice oriented at this time. In 1927, a bylaws amendment was passed requiring "acceptable published research of a psychological character beyond the doctoral dissertation" (*Psychological Bulletin*, Vol. 24, p. 143) for membership in the APA. This change would of course exclude many clinical practitioners whose positions did not require such research. At the 1928 APA meeting, an additional bylaws amendment was passed stating "that no person may be an associate of the Section of Clinical Psychology who is not also an associate of the American Psychological Association" (*Psychological Bulletin*, 1929, Vol. 26, p. 128). That closed one more door to some in clinical practice, it would seem. As late as 1941, the APA passed the following statement:

> Resolved, that organized blocs, electioneering, or caucasing are inappropriate in a scientific association such as the American Psychological Association. (*Psychological Bulletin*, Vol. 38, p. 830)

Psychologists were evidently to be chosen for office solely on the basis of their visibility as scientists. Such rules are more appropriate to a learned society than to a professional organization.

## EARLY LEADERS OF THE APA CLINICAL SECTION

Who were some of the psychologists active in the Clinical Section of the APA? One well-known figure who was a leader in the section and its successors for many years was Edgar A. Doll. Doll's best known role in psychology was that of research director at the private institution for the mentally retarded at Vineland, New Jersey (from 1925 to 1949). In 1961, Doll was involved with the Kennedy administration's efforts to breathe life into mental retardation research and services. The following letter, written by Doll on November 29, 1961, to Darrell J. Mase, may have been one of the seeds for the concept of a University Affiliated Facility the government later endorsed:

> As opposed to the centralized congregate institution out in the country, I think we need an administrative, classification, and research center (near a university center) with decentralized small branch institutions scattered regionally around the state. (Archives of the History of American Psychology, Akron)

Doll was later honored for such innovations not only by the clinical psychology division but also by the newer APA Division on Mental Retardation and Developmental Disabilities (Division 33), which gives an annual "Edgar A. Doll Award" for outstanding contributions to the field.

The officers of Clinical Section did not seem to feel the need to publish even its minutes and proceedings, which can therefore be found only in the Manuscript Collections of the U.S. Library of Congress.

# 4

# The Clinical Section of the American Association for Applied Psychology, 1937–1945

## THE ASSOCIATION OF CONSULTING PSYCHOLOGISTS

As suggested in the previous chapter, the clinical psychologists in the late 1920s and early 1930s were relatively unhappy with the restrictions placed on their Section by the larger APA, but such dissatisfaction often does not lead to action unless there is some alternative. In this case, the alternative developed out of various organizations of psychologists at the state level. For the most part, state and local organizations of psychologists have always been formed by practitioners and other people with applied interests rather than by academics (Hamlin & Habbe, 1946). These groups usually began with names that reveal this origin, such as the Pennsylvania Association of Clinical Psychologists, or (even more specific) the Los Angeles Society of Clinical Psychologists in Private Practice. Subsequently, many of these groups changed their names to reflect a more inclusive self-definition, but that did not greatly change the nature of their membership. Even today, state and local psychological associations are dominated by practitioners.

In 1921, the Notes section of the *Psychological Bulletin* (Vol. 18) reported the following:

> The New York State Association of Consulting Psychologists has been organized for the purposes of: "The promotion of high standards of professional qualifications for consulting psychologists" and "stimulating research work in the field of psychological analysis and

evaluation." Membership is limited to those who have the minimum requirements of two years graduate work in psychology. The Executive Committee for the current year are: D. Mitchell, President; L. A. Pechstein, Vice-president; E. A. Walsh, Secretary-treasurer; E. E. Farrell; S. B. Heckman; L. S. Hollingworth; and R. S. Woodworth. (p. 439)

(Perhaps the only surprising name in this group is that of Robert S. Woodworth, who was associated with the Department of Psychology of Columbia University and was the coauthor of a famous textbook in experimental psychology.) All during the 1920s many such organizations began to form, and because New York had the largest group, it was natural for the others to form coalitions with its organization, which eventually became known in 1930 as the Association of Consulting Psychologists (ACP). Other labels were considered for this group, but "clinical" was considered too narrow a term for what they had in mind. As noted previously, a "consulting" psychologist was understood to be one who was qualified to engage in independent practice, whether the nature of the practice be clinical, industrial, educational, or some combination of these. The person who emerged as the early leader of the New York group and eventually of the national group that formed around it was David Mitchell. He has already been mentioned as a University of Pennsylvania PhD in clinical psychology who was in private practice in New York City—perhaps the first successful private practitioner in the field. Hyman Meltzer (1966) later wrote concerning him:

> When I started practice in 1934 ... to my knowledge there was only one full time psychologist making a living out of it and that was Dr. David Mitchell in New York City, a student of Witmer from whom I took a course in clinical psychology at Teachers College. (p. 465)

Mitchell was also at one point the chair of the Clinical Section of APA. Perhaps ahead of his time, Mitchell (1919) considered that "the field of clinical psychology is that of individual diagnosis and treatment" (p. 325). Mitchell may be seen as the prototype of practitioners who were active in local and state matters and also in national leadership positions (examples of more recent individuals with similar histories of involvement in Division 12 and local/state groups include Max Siegel, Jules Barron, and Rogers Wright).

In the 1930s, the Association of Consulting Psychologists began a newsletter, *The Consulting Psychologist*, edited by Johnnie Symonds, that was lively and interesting. This newsletter subsequently developed into the *Journal of Consulting Psychology* (now the *Journal of Consulting and Clinical Psychology*), which Symonds edited under the sponsorship of the American Association of Applied Psychology for about 10 years. Under Symonds's editorship, this journal published news, the official minutes of meetings of the different sections of the AAAP, and professionally oriented articles, but not empirical research. It may be seen as the forerunner of several later publications, including the *American Psychologist*, published by the reorganized APA beginning in 1946, and the *Clinical Psychologist*, published by Division 12 since 1966.

Another person who was active in both the Association of Consulting Psychologists and in the Clinical Section of the APA was Gertrude Hildreth. She seems to have been a talented organizer. According to Johnnie Symonds (1946), at the 1936 APA meeting in Hanover, New Hampshire, there was a dinner sponsored by the Association of Consulting Psychologists attended by 76 persons. At this meeting, Gertrude Hildreth, who was then President of the ACP, appointed a committee to plan a national federation. It was known as the National Committee on Federation and Affiliation of Applied Psychologists. Hildreth was associated with Teachers College, Columbia University, and worked at the Lincoln School there. She wrote what was perhaps the earliest book on the topic of school psychology (Hildreth, 1930) and is today regarded as a pioneer school psychologist. At the time under discussion, there was of course little meaningful distinction between clinical and school psychology. There is one other point that should be made about Gertrude Hildreth for any readers who might have unwarranted associations to the name "Gertrude" (for example, of a somewhat frumpy, middle-aged female). There is a portrait of Gertrude Hildreth in one of the early issues of *The Consulting Psychologist* (published by the Association of Consulting Psychologists), and she was a strikingly attractive young woman. From a historian's point of view, this may not have been unrelated to her social effectiveness.

## THE AMERICAN ASSOCIATION FOR APPLIED PSYCHOLOGY

In 1937, the Association of Consulting Psychologists got together with various fledgling state psychological associations to form the American Association for Applied Psychology (AAAP; not to be confused with the AACP, the original psychology spinoff group). In a well-coordinated move, the Clinical Section of the APA dissolved itself and encouraged its members to join the new Clinical Section of the AAAP, which also had other sections devoted to Consulting Psychology, Educational Psychology, and the like. The chair of each section of the AAAP was considered a Vice-President of the parent organization, and each section sent representatives to the Governing Board of the AAAP, to its Board of Affiliates (the affiliates were the state psychological associations previously mentioned), and to the Board of Editors of its publication, the *Journal of Consulting Psychology*. In addition to the official ties the AAAP Clinical Section had with its association's journal, it did publish at least two newsletter issues on its own on a sporadic basis. The AAAP existed from 1937 to 1945, when it merged with the old APA to form the present (reorganized) American Psychological Association. In effect, the AAAP thus formed the model for the way APA was reorganized, with the AAAP sections later becoming APA divisions.

In understanding the relationship between the APA and the AAAP, it is important to recognize that although they were separate organizations, they were still in many ways symbiotic. The applied psychologists who joined the AAAP, and there were several hundred of them at its peak, generally continued to belong to APA. In all except 1 year of their existence, the two groups met at the same place and at about the same time. In 1939, the AAAP met separately from the APA because APA met in Palo Alto.

> The center of population for the [AAAP] lies too far away [from Palo Alto], and members not in academic positions are unable to get the needed time. (*Journal of Consulting Psychology*, 1939, 3, p. 96)

The AAAP met in Washington, DC in December, instead. It thus had to plan its own entire program, a task previously shared with APA. On this occasion, the AAAP found that it had not developed a very efficient system for reviewing research papers that were submitted for presentation. This was because the APA had always handled the research papers before, even those with content relating to clinical psychology. The AAAP had not had to worry about research papers in its program and could therefore concentrate strictly on the professional issues, using formats such as round-table discussions and invited symposia.

Another important point is that the AAAP had been in existence only a short time when the plans began to be made for the two organizations to merge (*Psychological Bulletin*, 1940, 37, p. 738). The atmosphere of the whole country at that time was dominated by the gathering clouds of war in Europe, and it was easy to see that psychologists were going to have to cooperate with each other in order to help meet this challenge. In other words, the need to confront Hitler loomed much larger than differences between academic and clinical psychologists.

The most prominent person in the Clinical Section of the AAAP was Carl Rogers. At one point he was vice president (chair) of the section and later was president of the AAAP and indeed subsequently of the APA as well. It could be argued that Rogers was the best-known clinical psychologist so far. He was a pioneer in many ways. For example, he served as the director of a child guidance clinic, showing that it was not necessary to have a medical degree to be the leader of the mental health team. (His administrative role was, however, opposed by some members of the Board of the Rochester Child Guidance Clinic.)

Carl Rogers said that at one point in his career he had begun to wonder if he was still a psychologist at all, because the meetings he went to and the journals he read were as likely to appeal to social workers or medical people as to his supposed colleagues. Then, with the emergence of the AAAP and the reorganized APA, Rogers achieved strong recognition from psychologist colleagues. For example, he was one of the first persons to receive one of APA's awards for distinguished scientific contributions.

Later in his life, however, it must be admitted that Rogers went well beyond his identification with the field of clinical psychology. Together with several other psychologists, Abraham Maslow, Rollo May, and Charlotte Buhler, he founded the humanistic psychology movement. As a part of these developments, he also came to question whether formal professional training was really necessary or helpful in making a person into an effective psychotherapist—this view naturally clashed with the guild interest of professional psychology. Also, participation in scientific research seemed to become of lesser importance to Rogers later in his career. Humanistic values seemed uppermost to him, scientific and professional ones of lesser importance.

Incidentally, one of Rogers' best-known students, Victor Raimy, wrote an influential dissertation at Ohio State on self-concept and later served as the chair of the Boulder Conference (to be discussed in a later chapter).

The first person to serve as secretary of the Clinical Section of the AAAP and a person who was deeply involved in running the overall Association was C. M. "Mac" Louttit. He directed the psychology clinic at Indiana University for a number of years before World War II. Today he is probably best remembered as the author of a book published in 1936 with the title *Clinical Psychology: A Handbook of Children's Behavior Problems*. The existence of this well-written volume now seems to be used most commonly to provide evidence of how much clinical psychology has changed. Before World War II the field was concerned mostly with children, whereas after that it veered strongly toward a greater emphasis on working with adults (right after the war, the emphasis was even more specific—working with adult males, i.e., veterans). By that time, the AAAP and its Clinical Section were but a memory.

# The Division of Clinical and Abnormal Psychology/Division of Clinical Psychology (Division 12), 1945–

## YERKES'S ROLE

The object of the reorganized APA, as stated in its bylaws, was to advance psychology not only as a science but also as a profession and, in addition, as a means of promoting human welfare. The person most responsible for the successful merger of the APA and the AAAP was Robert M. Yerkes. As stated in the *Psychological Bulletin* in 1945 (Vol. 42):

> Resolved: that the Board of Governors of the AAAP, the retiring Council and new Board of Directors of the APA express to Dr. R. M. Yerkes their appreciation of his initiative, vision, and persistent constructive endeavor in bringing about at this highly opportune time the merger of the various psychological organizations previously existing into a new structure of new and great potentialities for the development of the future of our science. (p. 713)

It is interesting to note that Yerkes had played a similar role as president of APA in 1917, in unifying the AACP and the old APA. The reorganized APA was so large that after 1946 it had to hold its conventions in large city hotels rather than on university campuses. (The AAAP had pioneered the practice of meeting in such hotels in Washington in 1940; *Journal of Consulting Psychology*, 1940, 4, p. 19.) This change seems to have some symbolic significance as well, distancing the organization a bit from the university campus. Psychology had literally outgrown its university origins.

## ORIGIN OF DIVISION 12

When the AAAP and the APA were merged, 19 divisions were proposed. Purely on the basis of historical precedent, the clinical division should have been given the designation of "Number 1" but a different, logical scheme prevailed in which Division 1 was General Psychology. The more scientifically oriented divisions were given lower numerals and the more practice-oriented divisions larger ones. Initially in this tentative arrangement, Division 11 was called the Division of Abnormal Psychology and Psychotherapy. Divison 12, Clinical Psychology, was to have been the direct continuation of the AAAP Clinical Section. A letter from Laurance F. Shaffer to David Rapaport in 1945 (now in the Manuscript Division of the Library of Congress) suggests that Division 12 was to have been an organization concerned purely with the professional aspects of clinical psychology, whereas Division 11 was to have dealt only with its scientific side. It was apparent to the organizers of these two proposed divisions that their membership overlapped heavily and so they immediately decided to join together. In terms of the overall theme of the present book, this was an important decision in the sense that it kept what we are calling science and practice together as a unity. The name of the combined organization was Division 12, "The Division of Clinical and Abnormal Psychology." In 1955, the name was shortened to "The Division of Clinical Psychology."

## FAMILIAR LEADERS AND NEW ONES

The leadership of the new division included many persons who have already become familiar in this narrative, including Edgar A. Doll and Carl Rogers. In the second postwar year, the president of Division 12 was Laurance F. Shaffer. He was an important person in the domain of training, because he was chair of a department of Teachers College, Columbia University. As has already become evident, in the early years Columbia University exceeded even the University of Pennsylvania as the most frequent educational origin for clinical psychologists. And as the Department of Psychology at Columbia phased itself out of clinical training, Teachers College took over this task. Besides his importance as a clinical psychology educator, Laurance Shaffer served as the first newly appointed editor of the *Journal of Consulting Psychology* after it was taken over by APA. He set this journal on the path toward its place today as the *Journal of Consulting and Clinical Psychology*, a major peer-reviewed research journal in clinical psychology. Shaffer also served as President of the APA in the postwar period.

The next president of Division 12 after Shaffer was David Shakow, the key figure in setting up modern clinical psychology training (see Chapter 17). Shakow had been a doctoral student in psychology at Harvard University in the 1930s, working with E. G. Boring (Garmezy & Holzman, 1984). A pilot study for Shakow's dissertation produced null results, and he did not at the time have the funds to continue in graduate school. Instead, he took a position at Worcester State Hospital where he was to learn almost everything he knew about clinical work, including clinical research. His own clinical training included being psychoanalyzed. Shakow ultimately produced a series of studies on the reaction time of schizophrenic patients showing the importance of their difficulty in maintaining preparatory set—an elegant experimental illustration of the attentional problems that seem inherent in schizophrenia.

In 1948, Shakow moved on from the Worcester State Hospital to the Department of Psychiatry and the University of Illinois and in 1954 to the Laboratory of Psychology at the National Institute of Mental Health, where he truly was clinical psychology's main representative for many years. He was, in fact, an excellent example of the scientist–practitioner and was one of the few persons to receive both APA's distinguished scientific contribution award and its distinguished professional contribution award. He also received public recognition from the medical community, being made an honorary member of the Washington Psychoanalytic Society in 1955 and an honorary Fellow of the American Psychiatric Association in 1969. Beginning in 1994, Division 12 will begin an early-career award called the David Shakow Award, given to a person who has made contributions to both the science and the practice of clinical psychology.

The postwar period was a time of relatively good relationships between psychology and psychiatry. The Army's chief psychiatrist in World War II, William Menninger, was an important friend of psychology, as was psychiatrist Robert Felix, the first director of the National Institute of Mental Health in 1946. An example of an MD–PhD who got along with colleagues in both fields was James G. Miller, who served as president of Division 12 in 1958–1959. Miller had been educated at Harvard and during the war worked with Henry Murray on the Office of Strategic Services's assessment project. After the war, Miller was chairman of both the Department of Psychiatry and the Department of Psychology at the University of Chicago, then headed the University of Michigan's Institute of Mental Health. His principal scientific interest, fittingly for such a capable administrator, was in general systems theory (Miller, 1978).

Very soon a new group of clinical psychologists were elected to leadership in Divison 12 who were associated with the Menninger Clinic and with a psychoanalytic point of view. The intellectual leader of this group was no doubt David Rapaport, who began as secretary of the division in 1946–1947, began Division 12's *Newsletter* in 1947–1948, and was a Representative to Council for several years. The Menninger colleagues of Rapaport who served on the Divison 12 Board during the 1940s, 1950s, and into the early 1960s included Margaret Brenman, Robert C. Challman, Robert R. Holt, George S. Klein, Roy Schafer, and Helen D. Sargent.

The presidents of the division during these same three decades were almost without exception distinguished academics or researchers who were clinical psychologists. In this era the only practitioners elected president were Florence C. Halpern, of New York, in 1967–1968, and Theodore H. Blau, of Tampa, Florida, in 1973–1974.

In more recent years, the top officials of the division have tended to alternate between highly visible academic researchers and practitioners who had become well known both within large state associations and practitioner-oriented divisions of APA such as Division 29. It became more and more difficult for face-to-face meetings to occur between the leadership and the rank and file of the division, and thus an important part of the story shifts to the smaller subgroups of the division known as sections, which are the theme of the following narrative chapters.

## CONVENTION PROGRAMS

A traditional purpose of scientific meetings is to provide members the opportunity to present their research findings to colleagues. A more or less rigorous process may be used to review papers and select those with the highest merit for presentation. Academic department chairs sometimes reimburse convention expenses only for faculty or graduate students who present such papers. Clinical psychology organizations from the beginning have usually abided by this tradition, and certainly Division 12 has always done so.

However, practitioners have limited interest in hearing about various small-scale research projects of uncertain relevance to their work. They prefer and will pay extra to attend workshops that are more comprehensive and aimed at helping them to update their clinical skills and learn new ones. Division 12 has tried to meet this need especially with its annual Post Doctoral Institutes.

Both academics and practitioners generally enjoy hearing invited addresses by well-known psychologists. But the differences between the interests of academics and practitioners can make them strange bedfellows at the national APA convention. A classic, hilarious account of what it is like to be Division 12 program chair ("On Being a Divisional Program

Chairperson, or I Loved You Long Distance, Junie Moon") was written by Stephen Goldstein (1975). Goldstein was a promising clinical psychologist who unfortunately died young, before he could fully express his potential as a scientist, practitioner, and humorist.

## PUBLICATIONS

Division 12 began to publish a newsletter relatively regularly beginning in 1947, shortly after the division had been organized, with each president and secretary in turn serving as coeditors. This newsletter appeared irregularly (as needed) with up to seven issues per year. The division's newsletter first acquired an independent editor, Elizabeth B. Wolf, of Cleveland, Ohio, with Volume 10, in 1956–1957. Its second editor, D. Craig Affleck, of the University of Nebraska Medical Center, took over in 1959–1960. Leonard Haber became the next editor in 1960–1962—he no doubt became best known in subsequent years as the Mayor of Miami Beach, Florida. The transition of the newsletter to the more formal publication known as the *Clinical Psychologist* came with Donald K. Freedheim in 1966–1967 (Volume 20). The *Clinical Psychologist* moved away from the newsletter format. Although it still published archival minutes, committee reports, and a president's message, the *Clinical Psychologist* also solicited other brief artlcles from the membership. These were generally professionally oriented articles rather than representing empirical research. The *Clinical Psychologist* spun off the APA journal, *Professional Psychology*, under Freedheim's leadership in 1968. This "spinoff" in effect left Division 12 without a journal, so in 1969 it began to publish the *Clinical Psychologist* again separately. The editors of the *Clinical Psychologist* since that time (as indicated in Appendix B) have included Norman Milgram, Jerome H. Resnick, Sandra Harris, Samuel Turner, Lawrence Cohen, Gerald Koocher, Ronald Blount, and Lawrence Siegel.

A bold (but, as it turned out, temporary) venture for Division 12 was its sponsorship of a journal, the *Clinical Psychology Review*, coedited by Alan Bellack and Michel Hersen, from 1988 to 1992 (Volumes 8–12). The initial negotiations with the journal's publisher, Pergamon Press, were led by George Stricker for Division 12. Although the division's affiliation with this journal was not free of controversy, it did seem to be the factor most responsible for causing the division's membership to approve a dues increase in 1988, after previously rejecting it. During the 5 years of the partnership, the *Clinical Psychology Review* incorporated the *Clinical Psychologist* (under its own distinct editor) as a separate set of pages within its covers. This caused problems in publishing time-sensitive material on schedule, most notably getting the division's convention program into the hands of members before they left home for the annual convention. The problem was solved temporarily by the publication of a separate newsletter, the *Clinical Psychology Bulletin*, used strictly for such time-sensitive material. A second problem was the limited number of pages that, by contract, could be published per year by the *Clinical Psychologist*. The masthead alone (listing the editor and various divisional officers and committee chairs) took up quite a significant amount of space because of the six issues per year in which the *Clinical Psychologist* now had to be published. After necessary archival material was added, there was little room for other articles. Finally, the *Clinical Psychologist* was in effect "buried" in the back of the issues of the *Clinical Psychology Review* rather than being published between its own covers. This unusual arrangement proved to be confusing to readers and reduced the overall visibility of the *Clinical Psychologist* from 1988 to 1992. On the positive side of the ledger was the fact that since the *Clinical Psychology Review* was collected and bound by many libraries, the *Clinical Psychologist* was more available as an archival publication than its predecessors for the few years of the joint publishing arrangement. Michel Hersen and Alan Bellack were not specifically chosen as editors of the *Clinical Psychology Review* by Division 12 but rather "came with the package" when the division began to sponsor this journal. They were both better known among research/academic clinical psychologists than to Division 12 members-at-large but had done much to build a strong review journal from its beginnings.

# Growth of Division 12 and the Origins of the Section on Clinical Child Psychology (Section 1), 1962–

## THE IDEA OF SECTIONS WITHIN THE DIVISION

In his article in the symposium that was supposed to have been presented to the American Association of Clinical Psychologists in 1918, J. E. Wallace Wallin (1919) speculated that in the future, clinical psychology would probably have to be divided up into various "sections" because it was so diverse. When the sections of Division 12 began to be formed in the 1960s, no one seemed to remember Wallin's words, but he was certainly among the earliest to recognize the heterogeneity of the profession. In a way, Division 12's present six sections (Clinical Child Psychology, Clinical Geropsychology, Science of Clinical Psychology, Clinical Psychology of Women, Pediatric Psychology, and Ethnic Minority Issues) are in some ways analogous to APA's nearly 50 divisions—a way to acknowledge the diverse groups of people the organization is trying to serve.

As shown by Table 6–1, even by the 1950s, Division 12 had well over 1,000 members. It became so large that its officers were beginning to feel that they were losing touch with the rank-and-file membership (Macfarland, 1955). No doubt the members were feeling even more isolated from the leaders. In his president's message in a 1960 issue of the *Newsletter*, E. Lowell Kelly proposed that Division 12 allow sections to be formed within the division to cope with the heterogeneity of its membership. A survey of the membership the same year showed that about two-thirds of the members thought that such "sections" were a good idea. The particular

TABLE 6-1. *Growth of the Membership of Clinical Psychology Organizations since 1917*

| Year | Name of organization | Total membership |
|------|----------------------|------------------|
| 1917 | American Association of Clinical Psychologists | 46 |
| 1924 | Clinical Section, American Psychological Association | 62 |
| 1935 | | 291 |
| 1937 | Clinical Section, American Association for Applied Psychology | 229 |
| 1948 | Division 12, American Psychological Association | 482 |
| 1951 | | 1,289 |
| 1957 | | 1,907 |
| 1960 | | 2,376 |
| 1970 | | 3,662 |
| 1981 | | 4,579 |
| 1992 | | 6,417 |
| 1993 | | 6,470 |

*Sources*: Manuscript Division, U.S. Library of Congress; APA *Yearbook*; *Journal of Consulting Psychology*; APA *Biographical Directories*.

types of sections most often mentioned were "psychotherapy" and "private practice" (both were areas subsequently represented by entire APA divisions). The next president of the division, Nicholas Hobbs, did two things that importantly influenced the way in which sections developed. First, he emphasized the profession's heritage of clinical work with children. This foreshadowed the development of clinical child psychology as the first section. The second thing he did was to organize the so-called Corresponding Committee of Fifty (discussed in Chapter 8).

Of course, encouraging sections to form hardly stopped the growth of the Division. On the contrary, it kept getting larger and larger, as shown in Table 6–1. At these words are written, there are well over 6,000 members in the division (over 7,000, counting students). One other change that eventually had to be made in response to the increasing size and complexity of the division was to establish an office and hire permanent staff. Division 12 established its Central Office in 1988, with Judy Wilson as its Executive Officer. Wilson was not a psychologist but had previously worked under the direction of one of the division's elected secretaries, Russell Adams. In the view of subsequent boards of directors of the division, the organization would have proved impossible to run any longer merely with volunteer effort.

## THE DEVELOPMENT OF SECTION 1

Perhaps the first clinical child psychologist in terms of our contemporary understanding of the term was C. M. Louttit (1936). He wrote the book previously mentioned, *Clinical Psychology: A Handbook of Children's Behavior Problems*. Witmer, Doll, and others with their interests might today be more likely to be considered school psychologists or specialists on mental retardation and developmental disabilities.

Clinical psychologists who worked with children did not change their activities drastically from before to after World War II. However, a new field of clinical psychology, involved in projective testing and psychotherapy with adults, grew up around them.

Like the whole field, child clinicians were also affected by new European influences. Some of the European refugees who arrived were interested in clinical work with children, not just with adults. According to the *Psychological Bulletin* (1941, Vol. 38, p. 777), Charlotte Buhler, formerly of the University of Vienna, began to offer instruction in "clinical child psychology" at Clark University in Worcester, Massachusetts, in 1941. Buhler later settled in Los Angeles, where she engaged in clinical work with children. In Europe, she had been known mainly as a researcher in developmental psychology and had the support of the Rockefeller Foundation for her work. Eventually, in the United States, she became one of the founders of humanistic psychology (Buhler, 1971; Gardner & Stevens, 1992).

Another influential refugee was Bruno Bettelheim, the founder of the Sonia Shankman Orthogenic School at the University of Chicago. Bettelheim treated autistic and psychotic children and wrote a number of influential popular books about his work (e.g., Bettelheim, 1967). Although honored by Division 12 and others, Bettelheim also drew criticism because of his harsh attitudes toward parents. Hare-Mustin (1987), for example, commented that "we were all terrorized by Bettelheim. I think he liked kids but he did not really like parents" (p. 45). More recently, his credentials as a psychologist have been questioned (Gardner & Stevens, 1992).

Boyd McCandless was a developmentalist, a clinician, and a school psychologist as well. In 1955 he was president of the APA Division of Developmental Psychology (Division 7) and voiced concern about the apparent neglect of training in clinical psychology for work with children.

He appointed a joint committee to look into this. All members of it were psychologists who belonged to both Division 7 and Division 12: Joseph E. Brewer (chair), Liselotte K. Fischer, Max Levin, and L. Joseph Stone. The committee discussed the child development training needed for all clinicians, the special training needed by child clinicians, and whether there should be such a specialty. Unfortunately, nothing lasting came of this particular committee's work. The same thing can be said of a similar committee appointed 2 years later to look into the psychologists' activities in pediatrics departments (see Chapter 11).

One early form of organization of psychologists working in child guidance clinics was an interdisciplinary group called the American Association of Psychiatric Clinics for Children, later called the American Association of Psychiatric Services for Children (AAPSC). The psychologists in this group eventually got AAPSC to come up with accreditation criteria for internship programs in clinical psychology with children. Psychologists such as Loretta Cass, of the St. Louis Child Guidance Center, were very involved in this effort, as was Albert Cain of the University of Michigan (Cass, Cain, & Waite, 1970).

The founder of Division 12's Section on Clinical Child Psychology was Alan Ross, at the time a psychologist at the Pittsburgh Child Guidance Center. In 1959, Ross published a book, *The Practice of Clinical Child Psychology*. This rather traditionally psychodynamic book became a natural rallying point for clinical child psychologists. As Ross describes it, Section 1 had its origins in a meeting in 1961 of a group of psychologists at a 7th Avenue delicatessen in New York. All of them were attending the meeting of the American Orthopsychiatric Association there. Together they first formed the Interest Group in Clinical Child Psychology and petitioned Division 12 to become a section.

At about this same time, J. McV. Hunt, a future president of Division 12, gave strong impetus to the national Head Start program and all that went with it by his book, *Intelligence and Experience* (Hunt, 1961). He endorsed a Piagetian viewpoint and interpreted this as favoring the positive effects of early cognitive intervention on disadvantaged children's lives.

In 1962, Clinical Child Psychology became the first section of Division 12, and Alan Ross became its first chair. It originally had 166 members. Allan Barclay became the first editor of the section's *Newsletter*. His performance as a section newsletter editor brought him to the attention of his colleagues. He was subsequently a Division 12 president and still later served as editor the the APA journal, *Professional Psychology*. Throughout his career, Barclay has retained an interest in the provision of clinical services to the mentally retarded child.

Alan Ross later went on to become a president of Division 12 and a recipient of its award for distinguished professional and scientific contributions to clinical psychology. It is interesting to report that Ross was undergoing some changes in his own professional life at this time. He experienced a "conversion" from a Freudian to a behavioral viewpoint, left the child guidance center to become a professor in the Department of Psychology at the State University of New York at Stony Brook, and eventually terminated his involvement in training clinical psychologists altogether. The example he set as a behaviorist has not been as influential within Section 1 as perhaps in other groups, for example, the Society of Pediatric Psychology (which has always been more behaviorally oriented than Section 1). But after Ross it certainly has been OK to be a behaviorally oriented child clinician.

In a sense the "godfather" of Section 1 was Nicholas Hobbs, who had been president of the division when the idea of sections was emerging. When Section 1 began to give a "Distinguished Professional Contribution Award," Hobbs was the first to receive it. The criteria for this award included (a) work history with children, (b) creative or innovative concepts or programs for the solution of clinical child problems, and (c) research or other efforts to implement the concepts or programs for the benefit of children. (In 1986 a student award was also established by Section 1.)

## OTHER EARLY LEADERS OF SECTION 1

Lovick C. Miller, the second chair of Section 1, was also involved in the AAPSC clinical child psychology group that developed standards for internships. To this day, he works in a setting that combines a child guidance center with a university program in child psychiatry and has continued to be involved in research. He was the main developer of the Louisville Behavior Checklist for Children, one of the earliest standardized scales of its kind. He and his colleagues carried out one of the earliest controlled psychotherapy studies with children, though it unfortunately had null findings (Miller, Barrett, Hampe, & Noble, 1972). The young phobic children he worked with recovered too speedily on their own for therapy to make any additional difference.

Other child clinicians identified with psychoanalytic ego psychology or object relations approaches. An example is Albert C. Cain, of the University of Michigan's Children's Psychiatric Hospital and later chair of Michigan's Department of Psychology. Cain's work on children's reactions to the death of a sibling (Cain, Fast, & Erickson, 1964) and the risk inherent in the situation of the "replacement child" remain well known. Another example is Sebastiano Santostefano, an early Section 1 president, who is now the chief child psychologist at McLean Hospital. This is a psychoanalytically oriented hospital in Belmont, Massachusetts, affiliated with Harvard University. Santostefano (1978) is known for procedures he developed to assess and treat children's ego functioning.

Several other prominent early leaders of Section 1, though clinically active and respected by colleagues for their skill in working with children and families, did not engage in many nationally visible activities. To give an example, Marilee Fredericks, president of Section 1 in 1973–1974, was Director of the Des Moines Child Guidance Center, helped establish an APA-approved internship there, and was active and well known in the affairs of her community. She was also active in the AAPSC.

Even by the early 1960s, Section 1 established a life of its own, somewhat apart from Division 12. One interesting provision of the division's new bylaws was that they allowed sections to accept members who did not belong to the division, so long as the proportion of such members did not exceed 50%. Thus, Section 1 from its beginning served as a professional home for others such as developmental or school psychologists without formal "clinical" training who identified with its purposes. In 1965 the section reported that it had 425 members, 52% of them being also members of Division 12.

## THE JOURNAL OF CLINICAL CHILD PSYCHOLOGY

The next major development in Section 1 was its journal, with its emphasis on child advocacy. The section had several newsletter editors. The third of these, Gertrude J. "Trudy" Williams, published the first issue of the *Journal of Clinical Child Psychology*, on December 12, 1971. Williams was a memorable figure in the development of Section 1 as well. She did not establish the usual peer review system for evaluating manuscripts. Her interest was child advocacy, and she published articles on topics such as child abuse, the plight of the mentally retarded, and the need of children and teenagers for better sex education. She was also willing to print articles written by parents and the children themselves: poetry, essays, and the like. She used abundant illustrations, not just graphs reporting research findings. It would be hard to find a more free-wheeling journal than Williams produced—in the author's experience only the journal *Voices*, published by the American Academy of Psychotherapists, comes close. She also pushed the section in the direction of an emphasis on advocacy and was one of the strongest supporters of a new APA division, Children, Youth, and Families (Division 37), that was to be advocacy oriented. Indeed, this division came into existence, and its emphasis has continued to be as she would have wished it. Division 37 is an advocacy-oriented collection of "child" people from diverse backgrounds, including developmental psychology, clinical child and pediatric psychology, school psychology, and people with an interest in law and psychology.

A colleague whose advocacy efforts were exactly in line with these values was Sol Gordon, who chaired Section 1 in 1970–1971. Gordon (1973) championed the cause of sex education for children and teenagers and helped to develop vivid comic-book type materials for this purpose. Gordon's research, demonstrations, and advocacy in this area has continued to the present, despite the continued resistance of more conservative religious and political forces.

Section 1 has also kept an emphasis on child advocacy. But it has not lost its specific commitment to the professional clinical child approach and to clinical research, which Division 37 does not have. Gertrude Williams's colleague in the forefront of organizing Division 37 was Milton F. Shore, who also served as president of Section 1 of Division 12 in 1974–1975 and later won its award and that of Section 5. Shore was the author of an influential book published by the government on the psychological aspects of the medical hospitalization of children, called *Red Is the Color of Hurting*. He also coauthored a series of controlled studies on the effects of comprehensive vocationally oriented therapy for delinquent boys. Not only was this treatment effective in the short term but it continued to be so upon follow-up over a remarkable number of years. Shore was also subsequently president of the American Orthopsychiatric Association and editor of the *American Journal of Orthopsychiatry*.

The person who replaced Williams as the editor of the *Journal of Clinical Child Psychology*, Diane J. Willis, has also had a significant impact on the section and on the field, although her approach is more low-key. Before she took over this journal, Willis had previously served as the founding editor of the *Journal of Pediatric Psychology*, bringing it along from newsletter to journal status before turning it over to its next editor. She was editor of the *Journal of Clinical Child Psychology* longer than anyone else—6 years—and was Williams's choice for the position. Indeed, she maintained the advocacy emphasis and sponsored many guest-edited special issues. However, she also rather quietly introduced a peer-review process. This started the journal on its way to scientific respectability. This was necessary if the journal was to keep getting articles from academic child clinicians, who had to worry about the acceptability of their publications to tenure and grant committees. Willis also became involved in a wider net of advocacy-oriented activities such as chairing the Association for the Advancement of Psychology and serving as a Division 12 Council Representative. Thus she was able to combine a professional emphasis with a concern about public policy issues. As a part-Kiowa Indian, Willis was also able to combine her other areas of emphasis with a steady pressure on colleagues to remain concerned with ethnic minority issues. Willis seems to have come by her political skills naturally enough, because her father was at one time Speaker of the Oklahoma House of Representatives.

June M. Tuma followed Willis as editor of the *Journal of Clinical Child Psychology*. During her editorship (from 1982 to 1986), the journal began to be published by Lawrence Erlbaum and Associates rather than by local printers and went from three issues per year to a quarterly.

## THE HILTON HEAD TRAINING CONFERENCE

Tuma also made an impact on Section 1 and on the division. Her particular interest was training. For many years she published a directory of internship and postdoctoral programs in clinical child and pediatric psychology. When she was the president of Section 1, she formed a committee to sponsor a national training conference. (This had once been a plan of Nicholas Hobbs, but it was never carried out.) APA supported this idea financially, but NIMH demurred, out of concern that the conference might go in an "elitist" direction. For example, if such a conference endorsed postdoctoral training for child clinicians, this might conflict with the public sector's lack of funds to pay for such specialized services. In the end, the participants paid their own way to the training conference—held in Hilton Head, South Carolina, in 1985. The NIMH need not have worried about elitism. The main recommendation of the conference was for required training in child development for all professional psychologists, not for further specialization.

## SOME OTHER SECTION 1 LEADERS

Paul Wohlford, who was president of Section 1 in 1977–1978, is presently a grants administrator with the National Institute of Mental Health. He has been involved in a number of national conferences of psychologists helping to set a new NIMH training agenda, emphasizing the needs of underserved populations. These include disadvantaged ethnic minority persons, the severely and persistently mentally ill, and children with severe emotional disturbances (SED). As described in a later chapter, SED children are often the concern of multiple systems in the public sector: juvenile justice, mental health, child welfare, and special education. The

NIMH no longer has the mandate of providing funding for mental health services to such populations, but it has tried to use its leverage with the state mental health systems, for example, in the Child and Adolescent Service System Program (CASSP) and its training funds, to help others provide such services. Thus, for example, a university wishing to`receive NIMH graduate student stipends for students in a program with a clinical child emphasis, would have to show that it could forge linkages with the public mental health sector serving SED children. The program would also have to show that its graduates continued to be employed in such public sector activities. This is a far cry from earlier days when most graduate programs in clinical psychology could get federal training money without changing their priorities. The current NIMH training priorities are clearly demanding more detailed accountability from the programs they fund.

Lenore Behar, Section 1 president in 1984, is an example of a child clinician who has worked effectively within the framework of state government. She was involved with the notable Willie M. case. In this case, the court mandated the state of North Carolina to provide appropriate mental health services not only to Willie M. but to all other violent youth similarly situated: a landmark in the legal literature on the "right to treatment."

Sheila Eyberg, who has served as president of both Sections 1 and 5, is known for her development of parent and teacher report measures of externalizing behavior problems in children (e.g., Eyberg, 1978). She has also by her systematic research helped develop parent-training methods that have become among the best standardized ones used by child clinicians.

The author's own 5-year term as editor of the *Journal of Clinical Child Psychology* began in 1987 (he had served as secretary and then as president of Section 1 several years earlier). At first the goal during this editorial term was to try to build the scientific reputation of the journal and to encourage clinical child psychology researchers to choose it as the place to send their best work. As time went on, the need became evident for the journal also to maintain a balance among research, practitioner interest, and child advocacy, while maintaining strict peer review.

Richard R. Abidin, president of Section 1 in 1989, is as far as can be determined the first one fully trained as a school psychologist as well as a child clinician. The doctoral program Abidin directs at the University of Virginia routinely trains its students to a professional level in both areas and has a stong emphasis on family therapy and family systems. Abidin's best known research is on the measure he developed, the Parental Stress Inventory (PSI), which attempts to tap interactive difficulties as well as child and parent psychopathology (Loyd & Abidin, 1985).

Jan L. Culbertson, president of Section 1 in 1990 and the present editor of the *Journal of Clinical Child Psychology*, followed Abidin's precedent in that her doctoral training was in school psychology. She did not, however, have formal training in clinical psychology and is thus not a member of Division 12. Culbertson is remarkable for her devotion to child advocacy (as former editor of Division 37's *Quarterly* and as guest editor of a special issue of the *Journal of Clinical Child Psychology* before she took over as its regular editor). Recall that the only section officers who are required by the division's bylaws to be members of Division 12 are section representatives to the division.

Thomas Ollendick, president of Section 1 in 1991, is a behavior therapist who has done extensive research on anxiety in children and adolescents. He and a colleague have recently taken over as editors of a series of books published by Plenum Press, *Advances in Clinical Child Psychology*, now in Volume 16.

## SOME RECIPIENTS OF SECTION 1'S AWARD

It was mentioned above that Nicholas Hobbs was the first to win Section 1's award. The second to do so was Lee Salk. Although it is true that Salk was once president of Section 1, he is no doubt better known as one of the founders of Section 5, the Society of Pediatric Psychology, and still better known as a popular author of books and articles for parents. In a sense "Dr. Salk" was psychology's answer to medicine's "Dr. Spock." Not incidentally, at least to the readers of the New York newspapers, he became known for the case of *Salk v. Salk*, arguing for the custody of his own children in a divorce case and successfully maintaining the view that mothers should not receive any preference merely because of their gender. It is also of interest that Salk made a number of contributions to clinical psychology organizations even though he never joined Division 12. He identified himself as a child clinician and pediatric psychologist without ever wishing to align himself with the division (though as a University of Michigan PhD in clinical psychology, he certainly could have done so).

Ann Magaret Garner, another winner of Section 1's award, probably has more longevity in relation to clinical psychology organizations than anyone else in Section 1's history. In a much earlier era she was secretary of Division 12. At that time she was a coauthor of an influential psychopathology textbook with Norman Cameron (Cameron & Magaret, 1957). She served as the mentor to promising researchers such as Leonard Eron. Then, as women of an earlier era often did, she got married and raised her family, more or less going underground professionally. Later on, her family raised,

she began to be professionally visible again. She directed a child development unit and internship program at the University of Oregon Health
Sciences University. She did research on the behavioral aspects of diabetes
in children and adolescents. She helped to train a later generation of clinical
scientists such as Russell A. Barkley and Eric Mash.

Herbert E. Rie received Section 1's award posthumously in 1982. The
latter part of his life was devoted to a sort of crusade against the legitimacy
of the concept of "minimal brain dysfunction" (MBD) and the wholesale
use of stimulant drugs such as Ritalin by physicians. Indeed Rie and
like-minded professionals appear to have succeeded in almost stomping
out the term MBD (Rie & Rie, 1980). Subsequent research has also tended
to confirm Rie's view that stimulants have little or no lasting effect on
children's academic performance, only a temporary and reversible effect
on attention. Rie also opposed the creation of Division 37. He feared that
the division would destroy Section 1's focus on *clinical* child psychology.
Rie was wrong about the threat. Section 1 has survived despite the overlap
with Division 37.

Gerald Koocher, another Section 1 president and awardee, is known
for his early research on the dying child's conception of death, on parent–
child relationships in children with cancer, and on the "Damocles" syndrome in children who have survived cancer (Koocher & O'Malley, 1981).
More recently, Koocher seems to be on the verge of stepping into Nicholas
Hobbs's shoes as psychology's expert on ethical issues. Koocher has helped
to train such experts as Gary Melton in the law, ethics, and psychology field.
He is currently editing a new journal of ethics and the behavioral sciences.

Charles Wenar, also honored by Section 1's award, is an example of
a developmental psychologist turned child clinician. Wenar received his
PhD from the University of Iowa Child Welfare Research Station and then
worked for many years as a researcher and clinician at the Illinois Institute
of Juvenile Research (the original court-related child guidance center) in
Chicago. He then moved to Ohio State University to teach clinical child
psychology to graduate students. However, he did this within the developmental psychology program rather than alongside the "regular" [adult]
clinical psychology faculty. A group of Wenar's former students nominated
him for Section 1's award; upon receiving it, he naturally chose to speak on
the importance of the developmental approach to clinical work with children. As Wenar always emphasized, why is it when a child is brought in
to the clinic we immediately ask, "How old is the child?" It is because we
cannot evaluate the appropriateness of the child's behavior without putting
it into developmental context (Wenar, 1982). In all candor, it should be said
that this unusual clinical-developmental program once got Ohio State on

probation with the APA accreditation committee. It has not been influential as a training model.

In its elections and awards process, Section 1 did not just recognize child advocates, book writers, and "media stars" but also maintained a healthy respect for psychological researchers. Another awardee was Herbert C. Quay, the founding editor of the *Journal of Abnormal Child Psychology* and the editor of several rigorous books on child psychopathology and juvenile delinquency. He was a codeveloper of the widely used Revised Behavior Problem Checklist. Quay was the person who applied Jeffrey Gray's physiological theory of psychopathology to conduct disorder in children. He was also a founder and the first president of the Society for Research on Child and Adolescent Psychopathology.

A systematic study of the content of the section's *Journal of Clinical Child Psychology* across its first 18 years by Routh, Patton, and Sanfilippo (1991) indicated that, regardless of the particular editor, the journal moved steadily toward a higher and higher proportion of articles by authors working in academic psychology departments reporting empirical research, until by the end of 1990 such articles had almost driven out papers by practitioners or those devoted to child advocacy. However, at that point a self-conscious effort was begun to redress the balance somewhat, beginning with a special issue devoted to child advocacy that would undoubtedly have pleased Gertrude Williams. The interesting thing in comparing, say, 1970s advocacy articles with ones written in the 1990s is that the latter seemed to have a better database upon which to build. In other words, in the meantime a rather respectable scientific literature had begun to develop in such areas as child maltreatment. This is an encouraging development.

# Psychologists Interested in the Advancement of Psychotherapy (Section 2), 1963–1967

After World War II, a situation existed for clinical psychologists in which psychotherapy training was highly desirable but difficult to obtain. It has already been noted that David Rapaport said he found "no paved way" to learn psychotherapy. If he had trouble doing this in the relatively benign atmosphere of the Menninger Foundation, imagine how difficult it must have been for other clinical psychologists. Strupp (1991) has pointed out that in the early 1950s psychology departments, even if they had APA-approved PhD programs in clinical psychology, cautiously labeled what they taught as "counseling" rather than "psychotherapy."

It is thus easy to understand why Carl Rogers became such a hero to many clinical psychologists at this time. Rogers was a psychotherapist of acknowledged competence who did not work under the domination or supervision of any physician—in fact, Rogers was himself the director of a child guidance center in Rochester, before becoming a professor at Ohio State University. Not only that, but Rogers demonstrated that an American psychologist could develop his own system of psychotherapy with credibility (Rogers, 1942) and could even do research on it. Regardless of what a psychologist might think about Rogers's particular ideas about therapy or about his research findings, Rogers's professional accomplishments made him a highly visible role model. Thus, Rogers served successively as the chair or president of the AAAP Clinical Section, the entire AAAP, the new APA Division 12, and the whole APA. He not only received Division 12's highest award but was one of the first recipients of the APA's Distinguished Scientific Contribution Award.

Rogers had obtained much of his training as a therapist from Jessie Taft, who had been trained by Otto Rank, a Freudian "irregular" affiliated with a Philadelphia school for social work (Fine, 1982). Other clinical psychologists of the time obtained their training through either regular or dissident Freudian organizations. One of these rebellious organizations was Theodor Reik's National Psychological Association for Psychoanalysis (NPAP) founded in 1948. (The New York Psychoanalytic Association had outraged Reik by refusing to admit him unless he agreed not to train anyone, so he founded his own organization.) Another source of training for psychologists was the William Alanson White Institute in New York, which had a Sullivanian or interpersonal orientation. (Division 12 later honored Erich Fromm, who in 1943 was one of the founders of this training institute. The Institute offered low-cost psychoanalysis as well as training opportunities.) The didactic instruction of psychoanalytic institutes was generally carried on through part-time instruction in the evening, because so many students were employed during regular daytime hours. Sometimes psychologists who sought such instruction were asked to sign a statement that if they received it, they would never use it to begin to practice psychoanalysis. Psychologists could undergo personal psychoanalysis without restrictions if they could find the funds to do so (and, in fact, mental health professionals seem to have made up an appreciable proportion of the population of "analysands" then and now). Getting psychoanalytic supervision was sometimes more difficult, and often such supervision was carried out sub rosa by members of the American Psychoanalytic Association against its regulations. (Now two universities in New York, Adelphi and NYU, offer postdoctoral training in psychoanalysis to psychologists.)

One can also cite the career of Hans Strupp as a paradigm for psychologists interested in psychotherapy and psychoanalysis. Strupp was originally trained as a social psychologist at George Washington University, a school that did not at the time have a clinical training program. As he stated in an autobiographical chapter, Strupp (1991) became involved in psychotherapy first as the recipient of therapy himself (as have so many other mental health professionals). He began his research on psychotherapy with the blessings of psychiatrists with whom he dealt, and in fact soon with NIMH grant support. Although he was well regarded in the psychiatric community for his research—he was hired and eventually promoted to professor by the Department of Psychiatry at the University of North Carolina at Chapel Hill—he was rebuffed in his attempts to join psychoanalytic organizations. He stated that he left Chapel Hill for the Vanderbilt Psychology Department in 1966 in part because he was tired of being treated like a second-class citizen by psychiatrists. If a therapist and therapy researcher of Strupp's eminence felt such disrespect, one has to wonder what the ordinary clinical psychologist's chances were for any kind of egalitarian relationship with the medical profession. Witkin, Mensh, and

Cates (1972) stated that the greatest expansion of psychology into medical schools occurred in the 1950s and 1960s—fewer than a third of the schools in their survey employed any full-time psychologists before 1950. "The overwhelming complaint about a psychologist's life in medical schools ... was the sense of second-class citizenship, in some variation or other" (p. 439). It is thus pleasing to report that Strupp received a Distinguished Career Contribution Award from the Society for Psychotherapy Research in 1986, and also an honorary MD degree from the University of Ulm the same year.

## PSYCHOLOGISTS INTERESTED IN THE ADVANCEMENT OF PSYCHOTHERAPY (PIAP)

Recall that in the original plan for the reorganization of APA in 1945, there was to have been a "Division 11" called the "Division of Abnormal Psychology and Psychotherapy," but its prospective officers (including Carl Rogers) and members immediately joined Division 12, the "Division of Clinical and Abnormal Psychology," instead. Thus, without any elaborate rationale, the term *psychotherapy* was dropped from the title of the merged division. Perhaps the organizers of Division 12 should have kept this term in the division's title. In any case, a separate interest group known as Psychologists for the Advancement of Psychotherapy (PIAP) formed in the late 1940s and began meeting at the APA convention each year, soon expanding into symposia and workshops. In 1951, in his presidential address to Division 12, Carl Rogers already spoke of the possibility of a new division of psychotherapy (Rogers, 1951). In 1958 the first APA-sponsored conference on Research and Psychotherapy was held in Washington, DC. Its proceedings were published by APA the next year (Rubenstein & Parloff, 1959). The second such conference on research in psychotherapy was held in Chapel Hill in 1961 (Strupp & Luborsky, 1962). The early leaders of PIAP soon discussed the question of becoming an APA division but feared this idea because it would seem to be throwing down the gauntlet to psychiatry and inviting legal action or other retaliation. Pearson (1961), in a letter to the Division 12 *Newsletter* editor, spoke of "the questionable wisdom of having an official division with the bald title of 'psychotherapy' which might incur the wrath of organized medicine" (p. 15). After all, at the time, practicing psychotherapy was considered by many psychologists as well as by psychiatrists to amount to practicing medicine without a license. Gordon Derner's program at Adelphi in New York fought (and won) just such a legal battle with the Nassau County Medical Society.

So PIAP considered becoming a section of Division 12 instead, and in 1963 did so. Because PIAP had been meeting for many years as an ad hoc interest group, it had a larger membership at the outset than any subsequent Division 12 section did, and also a highly differentiated organizational structure, including a president, secretary-treasurer, and executive board. Beginning in August, 1963, PIAP published a journal, *Psychotherapy: Theory, Research, and Practice*, with Eugene Gendlin as editor. (Gendlin had been a student of Carl Rogers at the University of Chicago and was later associated with Rogers's schizophrenia psychotherapy research project in Wisconsin.) The lead article in the first issue of this journal was by Hans Strupp (1963) and concerned psychotherapy outcome research. The journal strove from its beginnings to be open to all theoretical viewpoints and methodological approaches. Thus the journal not only published conventional empirical research but also reviews, case histories, studies using qualitative approaches, and thoughtful essays of various kinds. Beginning in 1947, long before it started its journal, PIAP published a newsletter with Vin Rosenthal as the editor.

And PIAP had a high level of energy! In 1962, PIAP sponsored 10 symposia and 10 conversation hours at the APA meeting (*PIAP Newsletter* 1962, 15, 10–11). By 1965, PIAP reported a membership of about 1,500 (*PIAP Newsletter*, 1965, 18, No. 4).[1]

However, PIAP lasted only for a short time as a Division 12 section, from 1963 to 1967. In 1967, APA Division 29, the Division of Psychotherapy, was approved by the APA Council, and Division 12, Section 2 ceased to exist. In retrospect, the development of Division 29 hardly seems surprising. As already noted, PIAP members had considered becoming a division even before they decided to seek section status. As a section, PIAP also pressed hard for many of the prerogatives of a division. They wanted their membership to be identified in the APA Directory as being in their section as well as in Division 12, and for a time beginning in 1966 the APA Directory actually did identify the members of all Division 12 sections as such in its listings. Section 2 asked the APA office of governance services to put their section offices on the official APA ballot but did not succeed. Section 2 members chafed at the political restrictions on them, for example, the fact that their section could not elect an APA Council representative. In many ways, the relation of APA to its component organizations seems to be

---

[1] I can recall the first APA meeting I went to just out of graduate school in 1968. Posters announcing PIAP symposia, workshops, and conversation hours seemed to be everywhere, and many PIAP members wore large buttons reminiscent of political campaigns. Many of these psychologists were excited about being (or becoming) psychotherapists, and it showed.

patterned after the relation of the federal government to state and local governments. In this case, the various APA divisions correspond to "states" and the sections to "cities" or perhaps just "municipalities."

Obviously, the existence of Division 29 solved such status problems: Its members are listed as such in the APA Directory; the division elects as many Council Representatives as the strength of its membership dictates, and so on.

By any conventional criteria, one has to judge Division 29 as a success. The journal that PIAP started before it became a division is now in Volume 30 (it is presently under the editorship of Donald K. Freedheim). Division 29 has over 5,000 members. It is influential in APA politics. Theodore H. Blau, a private practititioner in Tampa, Florida, who was active in PIAP, served as president of Division 12 in 1973–1974. In 1977 he became the first (but hardly the last) such practitioner to be elected president of the APA.[2] Many Division 29 presidents such as Max Siegel, Gordon Derner, Jules Barron, Norman Abeles, and Gerald Koocher have either simultaneously been or have gone on to become presidents of the larger Division 12, and sometimes of APA as well. It is curious that Section 2 did not survive within Division 12 after Division 29 formed. Several other sections of Division 12 have continued despite the existence of other APA divisions related to their constituencies, but this one did not do so. Certainly, many members of Division 12 continue to do therapy and to study it. For example, Sol L. Garfield, strongly identified with Division 12, has become known as an author and editor of books tracking the progress of research on psychotherapy and other types of behavior change (e.g., Garfield & Bergin, 1978). Division 29 is the most frequent other APA division to which Division 12 members belong.

Many persons in PIAP and later in Division 12 were of a Freudian persuasion and no doubt did not see a division labeled *psychotherapy* to be sufficiently expressive of their own theoretical orientation. Reuben Fine, one of the presidents of Section 2 (and later of Division 29), went on to participate in another ad hoc interest group called Psychologists Interested in the Study of Psychoanalysis (with the unfortunate acronym PISP). Under Fine's leadership, this group went on to form the nucleus of APA Division 39 (Psychoanalysis), though it did not consider it necessary to become a section of Division 12 on its way to becoming a division. As one might expect, Fine's view was that there is only one science of psychology, with

---

[2] However, at least one research-oriented clinical psychologist I know quit APA specifically in response to what she regarded as the poor scientific quality of Blau's APA presidential address.

psychoanalysis as its heart. He utterly rejected behavior therapy, for example, and no doubt viewed the psychotherapy division as a rather watered-down version of what to him was the genuine article. Although not all clinical psychologists revere Freud, certainly most would agree that psychoanalysis has made important contributions to clinical psychology. Among the persons selected for Division 12's highest award was Erik Erikson, in 1979. Many observers may consider that the division was more honored by his acceptance of this award than he was in receiving it. His writings (e.g., Erikson, 1950) are certainly widely influential. On the other hand, it is unfortunate that psychoanalysis has never been able to develop conventional ties to the university or to the research community. As Holt (1985) puts it, "No career lines exist for anyone who might have the fantasy of becoming a psychoanalytic scientist" (p. 311).

The rapprochement between psychoanalysis and clinical psychology was no doubt improved by recent the successful lawsuit by the APA and Division 39 against the American Psychoanalytic Association for the refusal of the latter to consider psychologists on an equal basis with physicians for standard psychoanalytic training.

# The Corresponding Committee of Fifty, 1961–1971, and the Section on Continuing Professional Education (Section 2), 1971–1986

## THE CORRESPONDING COMMITTEE OF FIFTY

As Division 12 president in 1961, Nicholas Hobbs appointed what was called the Corresponding Committee of Fifty (CCF). This committee was intended as a way of getting younger people involved in the division's activities and thus increasing communication between the leadership and the membership of the division. To recruit for CCF, Hobbs asked the chairs of various psychology departments with APA-approved clinical training programs to nominate their most outstanding clinical psychology graduates of the last 5 years. These individuals were then contacted and asked to form CCF.

Such organizations of "young turks" have often provided a helpful mechanism by which to encourage young persons to become involved professionally. For example, in reaction to the restrictive membership policies of the Society of Experimental Psychologists, an organization of young experimentalists (under age 40) was formed in 1936, called the Psychological Round Table (Benjamin, 1977). The midwestern version of this organization had the comical German name of the Gesellschaft über Versuchen (GUV). Many groups of this kind have a rule that persons over 40 must leave the group. James Hinrichs, a former member of GUV, told the author that when he got to be 40, GUV presented him with a tiny rocking chair as a souvenir and told him he was now good for nothing but to be a department chair. However, such a "40-and-out" rule does not seem to have been strictly observed in the case of CCF. (Perhaps with such a rule the fate of the organization would have been different.)

When prospective CCF members were contacted, they were not necessarily members of Divison 12. Therefore, in order to participate, they first had to join the division, and then begin to attend CCF meetings. In retrospect, it is apparent that the rather elitist nomination mechanism for CCF introduced ethnic and gender bias. The young psychologists nominated were almost always male (49 out of the original 53 members of the group) and rarely of minority background. Many years later the author heard Karen Calhoun jokingly refer to the CCF as "50 white males." In justice to Nicholas Hobbs, the biased nature of the group seemed to be inadvertent rather than intentional.

In any case, the CCF did get itself together, elect a chair, start a newsletter, and begin to operate. At the time the group started, what became the Chicago conference on graduate training in clinical psychology was getting organized, and CCF took on the job of helping to plan the conference.

The correspondents writing in the CCF *Newsletter* raised several points in their continuing dialogue with their elders in the division leadership. For example, C. Eugene Walker, one of the most active participants in CCF, criticized the lack of evidence for the validity of the ABPP examination. This drew some rather defensive sounding responses from various ABPP officials. Other correspondents criticized the practice of academic departments of hiring clinical faculty members whose only intense clinical experience was their internship. In the view of these writers, this practice could serve to perpetuate a pattern of clinical training by the clinically naive.

At least in its early days, CCF did not have an effective mechanism for replacing its own members or people in leadership positions. At its high point, this committee of "50" had 92 psychologists who were members. Certain names kept turning up again, year after year, in the role of chair, representative to Division 12, or newsletter editor (see Appendix B). Another difficulty was that certain persons who were nominated to CCF turned out not to be interested in it. In response to this problem, Division 12 in 1965 began to let prospective members of CCF apply on their own rather than being nominated by the chair of the department from which they had graduated. As a way of assuring the serious interest of the applicants to CCF, prospective members had to submit essays with their applications stating why they were interested in being involved.

Eventually, as a result of the slump in interest in CCF following the Chicago conference, it was apparent to the leadership that the model of a "young turks" organization was not working. Therefore, after 10 years of its existence, CCF enclosed with its newsletter a petition for section status in Division 12. The new Section 2, to be called the Section on Continuing Professional Education, was approved by the Division Board of Directors in 1971, and CCF dissolved.

## THE SECTION ON CONTINUING PROFESSIONAL EDUCATION (SECTION 2)

The focus on continuing professional education of the new Section 2 had not been a major theme of CCF. The major continuing education activity of the division, the Post Doctoral Institutes (PDIs) at the APA convention, had begun in 1948 by a committee chaired by Anne Roe (Division 12 *Newsletter*, 1948, 2, p. 5). The PDIs had their beginnings as a group of "refresher courses" offered during the week before the convention. The original format was a set of intensive courses at an advanced level, limited to small groups. At first, only Division 12 members could attend PDIs, but in later years qualified nonmembers were also admitted. PDIs have always been popular with practitioners. They have generally proved to be financially self-supporting if not actually producing a profit. Section 2 did take over administering the PDIs for the division for a time and in this way served a useful function. The Section on Continuing Professional Education had 526 members at its highest point.

In other ways, the choice of continuing education as the focus of Section 2 was not successful. Continuing education opportunities were increasingly provided by the APA at large, by state and provincial psychological associations, and by private individuals, business organizations, and universities.

Finally, there was the ill-starred pamphlet on clinical psychology produced by Section 2 beginning in 1975. This was developed largely under the leadership of Larry Beutler, one of the presidents of Section 2, with financial support initially promised by the division. The title of the pamphlet was "Careers in Clinical Psychology: Is There a Place for Me?" It turned out that some division board members did not like this pamphlet. Today it seems difficult for former Section 2 officers even to recall why the pamphlet was so objectionable. Tom Patterson told the author in a telephone interview in 1992 that he remembered Max Siegel as the main critic, primarily on the grounds that a section should not be trying to speak for the whole division in such a publication. At the 1992 APA meeting, Eugene Walker told the author that for one thing, the pamphlet mentioned in a single paragraph the fact that some psychologists with master's degrees deliver clinical services, and this was felt to go against the division's emphasis on the doctoral degree as a prerequisite for clinical practice. In any case, the money to pay for the pamphlet was not provided by the board as had been agreed. The subject of the money for the pamphlet was a divisive one for about 10 years, right up until the time when Section 2 voted to disband after a poll of its membership in 1986 (Schroeder & Fish, 1987).

Of the various officers of CCF and the second Section 2, perhaps the best known were C. Eugene Walker, George Albee, and Larry Beutler. Interestingly, none of them is particularly associated with continuing education activities at this time. Walker, who was president of Section 5 (Pediatric Psychology) in 1987, directs a pediatric psychology internship and postdoctoral program at the University of Oklahoma Health Sciences Center that has been underway for over 25 years. He is also editor of a book series, *A History of Clinical Psychology in Autobiography*, that was an important source of information for the present book. George Albee is discussed at length in a subsequent chapter.

Larry Beutler, the author of the infamous Section 2 pamphlet, is a psychotherapy outcome researcher who focuses on an "integrative" approach to therapy, trying to discover the basic commonalities of all therapies that account for their effectiveness (Beutler, 1979, 1983). He is now the editor of the *Journal of Consulting and Clinical Psychology*, the premier APA journal for such research on psychological intervention.

# 9

# The Section for Clinical Psychology as an Experimental–Behavioral Science/Society for a Science of Clinical Psychology (Section 3), 1966–

In a way, an important forebear of Section 3 was Morton Prince, the physician who founded the *Journal of Abnormal Psychology* in 1906 and later gave his journal to APA. This journal has always fostered the kind of rigorous approach to research in psychopathology Section 3 tries to encourage. As noted previously, Prince was also the founder of the Harvard Psychology Clinic and a champion of psychopathology as a liberal arts subject rather than a strictly medical one.

There is also a long tradition of the psychological study of schizophrenia and other severe forms of psychopathology, including David Shakow, Loren and Jean Chapman, Rue Cromwell, Sarnoff Mednick, Kurt Salzinger, and others, that served as part of the "prologue" to Section 3.

Like the study of human brain–behavior relationships, the behavior modification techniques that were associated with the immediate origins of Section 3 of also have a long prehistory. For example, in 1924, Mary Cover Jones published her famous paper on desensitizing fear of furry animals of a toddler named Peter. Her supervisor in this research was John B. Watson, the founder of behaviorism, at that time in academic disgrace but working successfully in the advertising business in New York. Mary Cover Jones

(1975) commented in retrospect that she simply was not able to foresee the major practical implications of her research on overcoming a child's fearfulness. Nevertheless this early research has led some to consider her to be "the mother of behavior therapy" (Mussen & Eichorn, 1988). She became involved instead in her well known longitudinal studies of psychological development in collaboration with her husband and colleague Harold Jones. Her subsequent research on the psychological consequences of early vs. late puberty and on the developmental antecedents of drinking behavior are also highly clinically relevant. Another early clinical study in this tradition was Mowrer and Mowrer's (1938) work on the "bell and pad" device for treating childhood bedwetting.

Despite the presence in the American psychology literature of pioneering studies such as those by Jones and the Mowrers just mentioned, much of the impetus for the development of the behavior modification movement (and for Division 12's Section 3) came from abroad, most notably from Eysenck (1949) and Wolpe (1959). Hans Eysenck, who had been trained in psychometrics and experimental psychology at the University of London, headed up the psychology department at the Maudsley Hospital, Institute of Psychiatry (Gibson, 1981). Eysenck did not deal with patients except in terms of collecting data from them for research projects. Nevertheless, he had been hired at the Maudsley by psychiatrist Aubrey Lewis with the goal of creating a graduate training program in clinical psychology, the first one in the United Kingdom. Eysenck came to the United States in 1949 (to the University of Pennsylvania) to learn about related developments in this country. Before his trip to the United States, Eysenck had agreed with Lewis that the proper roles of psychologists in mental health settings included research and psychological assessment, not treatment (Eysenck, 1949). Eysenck's American experience changed his mind about the role of the clinical psychologist as a therapist. But that did not mean Eysenck accepted the psychoanalytic therapy typical of the United States— far from it. Instead, Eysenck thought that psychologists should develop their own treatments, based on the principles being developed by scientific (academic) psychology. In fact, Eysenck (1952) later became infamous among traditional clinicians—psychiatrists as well as psychologists—for his view that psychotherapy was no more effective than the spontaneous remission rate in dealing with neurotic problems. Together with colleagues such as Gwynne Jones and Stanley Rachman, Eysenck went on to defy Aubrey Lewis and to develop clinical psychology at the Institute of Psychiatry in London as a field involving behavior therapy as well as research and assessment.

Joseph Wolpe was a psychiatrist whose work with phobic human patients was presaged by considerable research on cats applying the behavior theory of Clark Hull as well as the examples of John Watson and Rosalie Rayner (1920) and Mary Cover Jones (1924). Wolpe developed the procedure of systematic desensitization of phobias by combining the use of Jacobson's (1929) relaxation training with the creation of a hierarchy of imagined scenes varying in their ability to evoke fear in the patient. Wolpe, who emigrated from South Africa to Charlottesville, Virginia (and later moved on to Philadelphia), claimed an impressive 90% success rate using such approaches to treatment.

An influential behavior modification conference was held in Charlottesville, Virginia, in 1962. Out of this developed the variegated behavior therapy movement in this country. The first of the behavior therapy journals, *Behaviour Reseach and Therapy*, began publication in 1963 and is presently edited by S. J. "Jack" Rachman, an Eysenck student who is at the University of British Columbia. Rachman is an expert on such topics as fear, phobias, and obsessive-compulsive disorders.

One strand of this movement, "applied behavior analysis," is rather purely "Skinnerian" in its orientation, whereas another strand, under the label of "behavior therapy," is more eclectic and open to other influences. Applied behavior analysis, as might be expected, grew out of "behavioral analysis," the preferred self-label for Skinnerian experimental psychologists. These individuals might be members of the Society for the Experimental Analysis of Behavior (founded in 1958), of APA Division 25, or of the independent organization called the Association for Behavior Analysis. Skinnerian experimental psychologists split off from their fellow animal behaviorists, for example, because of their preference for examining the cumulative records of individual animals (often pigeons rather than rats) rather than applying complex statistical analysis to group experiments. Similarly, applied behavior analysts preferred to study individual human subjects (often children or the mentally retarded) intensively. They used strictly behavioral measures and rejected the use of indirect or inferential measures such as personality inventories or (certainly) projective tests. Many did not like intelligence testing, either.

The behavior therapists (the more moderate group ideologically) in 1966 formed the interdisciplinary group now known as Association for the Advancement of Behavior Therapy (AABT). This association, in which clinical psychologists are perhaps numerically the dominant element, does contain many members who are practitioners as well as the academics, and hence has been subjected to some of the same science vs. practitioner cross-currents as Division 12. Since 1970, the AABT has published the influential journal, *Behavior Therapy*. It holds annual meetings including workshops as well as research presentations, and in general serves as a sort of behavioral alternative to the American Orthopsychiatric Association. Its membership and officers overlap heavily with those of Division 12, Section 3. Alan Kazdin (1978, 1979) has detailed the history of behavior modification. He has commented on the "spectrum" of behavioral approaches that appear to run from applied behavior analysis through behavior therapy to the most recent offshoot, cognitive behavior therapy.

## THE FOUNDING OF SECTION 3

So far, this chapter has presented the "prologue" to the development of Section 3. It is time to proceed with the section's actual history. Section 3 was founded in 1966 by Leonard Krasner, a behaviorally oriented clinical psychologist who was trained at Stanford University and who was among the founders of the Department of Psychology at the (then) new State University of New York at Stony Brook. The organizing committee of Section 3 included Albert Bandura, Cyril Franks, Arnold Goldstein, Frederick Kanfer, Leonard Krasner, Peter Lang, Robert Rosenthal, Kurt Salzinger, and Irwin Sarason. Section 3 was originally called the Section for the Development of Clinical Psychology as an Experimental–Behavioral Science. Krasner was also an early president of AABT. Leonard Ullman and Leonard Krasner (1965) edited an influential book not long before the section was founded featuring case studies in behavior modification and also one of the early behaviorally oriented textbooks of abnormal psychology ("behavior disorders"). The Department of Psychology at Stony Brook sponsored an internship program and a clinical postdoctoral fellowship as well as a doctoral program in clinical psychology (Davison, Goldfried, & Krasner, 1970). Thus, this department and others met the need for advanced clinical training that was analogous to that met by National Psychological Association for Psychoanalysis and similar organizations for therapists of a more Freudian viewpoint.

The degree to which organizations outside Division 12 served as the main focus of behaviorally oriented clinicians' professional activities meant that there was relatively little for Section 3 to do. In fact at one point a Section 3 president threatened to take his election as a purely honorary one and not bother to plan a convention program. Section 3 did have a newsletter, with Stanley Feldstein as its first editor, but there was relatively little news to report, certainly less than was the case in Sections 1 and in PIAP (Section 2) at a similar point in their history. For a long time, Section 3's major activity seemed to be that of electing its officers, sponsoring a presidential address, and providing presidential messages to the membership in the newsletter. Even though the author has been a member of Section 3 for many years, he has never been an officer of it, and therefore this story of its development is necessarily more of an "outsider's view" than are are the narratives about Sections 1 and 5.

An additional focus for Section 3 then developed, that of naming a person each year as Distinguished Scientist. The first one to win this award was David Shakow: a noncontroversial choice, because no better example could have been found of a person who represented the science as well as the professional side of clinical psychology. A subsequent Section 3 award winner who followed Shakow's scientific footsteps, studying information processing in schizophrenia, was John M. Neale.

Several other individuals chosen as Distinguished Scientist by Section 3 have been more one-sided representatives of research-oriented academic settings, with little involvement in the professional side of the field. The first one of these was Albert Bandura. It is true that Bandura was trained in an APA-approved clinical psychology PhD program (at the University of Iowa), took a similarly approved internship (Wichita, Kansas), but since that time Bandura has taught in the Department of Psychology at Stanford University, which long ago dropped its APA-approved clinical program.

One other characteristic of Section 3 is that practically all persons elected to its executive board and certainly its presidents are visible nationally as scientific researchers. Thus it is convenient to discuss a few of its presidents simply in chronological order. Several other Section 3 leaders and awardees are discussed in subsequent chapters on the research contributions of clinical psychologists.

David Barlow was president of Section 3 in 1977–1978, won its Distinguished Scientist Award in 1989, and is president of Division 12 in 1993. He directed a behaviorally oriented, scientifically productive psychology internship program at the University of Mississippi Medical School, did the same sort of thing at Brown, and then moved to the Department of Psychology Department at the State University of New York at Albany. He is known as an expert on anxiety and on the behavioral treatment of sexual disorders (e.g., Barlow, 1986).

K. Daniel O'Leary, who was president of Section 3 in 1978–1979, has had in a sense two careers as a behavior therapy researcher. In the first of these he dealt mostly with children with conduct disorders and hyperactivity, often in collaboration with his psychologist wife, Susan O'Leary. When she came up for academic tenure at Stony Brook and the independence of her research contributions was questioned, Daniel O'Leary stopped doing child research (while Susan continued it, now unquestionably independently, and got tenure). He moved into the study of marital relationships (e.g., O'Leary & Smith, 1991), especially marital violence, and has become known as one of the foremost researchers in this area. O'Leary won Division 12's Award for Distinguished Scientific Contributions to Clinical Psychology in 1993.

Rosemery O. Nelson, president of Section 3 in 1979–1980, had been a graduate student under Alan Ross (who was Section 3 president the next year). She established herself as an expert in behavioral assessment (Nelson, 1983), doing some classic experiments demonstrating the reactive effects of observation or self-monitoring on the frequency of different behaviors. When people know they are being observed or are keeping track of their own behaviors, positively valued behaviors tend to become more frequent and negatively valued ones less so. Thus, the generality of "social desirability" responding was shown for behavioral measures like that seen with self-report questionnaires.

Richard McFall, president of Section 3 in 1989–1990, is a prolific researcher on topics such as the use of role playing to evaluate clincally significant aspects of social behavior. As president of the section and subsequently, he has repeatedly presented the argument that *every* clinical psychologist should be a scientist. He means by this that clinicians should be able to present a research-based rationale for every clinical activity in which they are engaged. When listening to McFall presenting different versions of this basic talk, the author has sometimes wished for the presence of his polar opposites in Division 12's ideological spectrum to make it a debate. For example, what if McFall and Harold L. Raush were to engage in a public conversation (Raush tends to question whether the usual academic research has *any* relevance to the practitioner). Would they be able to communicate with each other?

Another project that Section 3 developed that has been of great interest to its members is its annual student research award. As one might expect, given the focus of this section on science, the criteria for this award are rigorous. First of all, only doctoral dissertations are eligible. Second, before it is considered, the dissertation must have already been published in some highly selective journal such as the *Journal of Abnormal Psychology* or the *Journal of Consulting and Clinical Psychology*. This guarantees that the award-winning project has survived review by experts on its particular topic. Thus, perhaps student research projects selected for Section 3's award are particularly likely to have high impact on the field.

In recent years, Section 3 seems to have become somewhat more active than at any time since its origins. The reason may be that the Division 12 board and all the section boards now meet at midyear, usually over the Martin Luther King weekend. As part of this activity, the Section 3 board was more or less forced to meet apart from the APA convention, and its members were thrown together for several days in the absence of many competing activities. Perhaps the work of the section expanded to fill the time available. One concrete result is Section 3's new name, the Society for a Science of Clinical Psychology.

A related matter is that at least one threat has emerged to the status of Division 12 as the sole national representative of clinical psychology. The American Psychological Society, beginning in 1988, presented itself as a sort of scientific alternative to APA (VandenBos, 1989). A group known as the American Association for Applied and Preventive Psychology (AAAPP) has developed featuring a number of prominent academic/research clinical psychologists on its board. This group, with former Division 12 (and APA) president Logan Wright as its executive director, has been meeting annually in June in conjunction with the convention of the larger APS. It has also recently developed its own journal—with Logan Wright as managing editor. These developments are no doubt being watched by many members of Divison 12, especially by Section 3. In this regard it is interesting that members of the AAAPP leadership (such as Logan Wright, George Albee, and Bonnie Strickland) have chosen to retain their membership in Division 12 and in the APA.

# 10

## The Section on the Clinical Psychology of Women (Section 4), 1980–

It is worth remembering that when clinical psychology began, women could not even vote in national elections in the United States (female suffrage was not achieved until 1920), and female schoolteachers who married had to quit their jobs. Most psychologists were male. At present, in contrast, women receive over half the doctoral degrees in psychology and if present trends continue will constitute a majority of the field (Strickland, 1987).

Boyd McCandless (1968–1969) once argued that the culture of the public schools tends to be feminine, whereas that of universities is more dominated by masculine values, setting the stage for considerable conflict between the two. Many of the persons working in all kinds of clinical field settings have been women. Thus, women have played a rather prominent role in clinical psychology right from the beginning. One of the founding officers of the American Association of Clinical Psychologists in 1917 was Leta Hollingworth, who also had done research on women's issues (for example, the effects of menstruation on women's performance). Hollingworth fought for the right to vote for women. A retrospective article on her career described it in more contemporary feminist terms as "Ms. Pilgrim's Progress" (Shields, 1975). In another sense, however, Leta Hollingworth could be considered to have played "second fiddle" to her experimental psychologist husband, H. L. Hollingworth, who was president of APA in 1927. Even within the original clinical psychology organization, Wallin took the chair, and Leta Hollingworth served as the secretary.

In 1926, Augusta Bronner became the first woman to serve as the chair of the APA Clinical Section. She was a leader in the child guidance movement, cofounder of the Judge Baker Guidance Center, and, at one time, president of the American Orthopsychiatric Association. She had done her doctoral dissertation under E. L. Thorndike at Columbia on female delinquents, showing that their problems were probably due to faulty "character" rather than low intelligence. Like Leta Hollingworth, Bronner was also overshadowed by her husband, psychiatrist William Healy.

We have already mentioned Gertrude Hildreth for her important role as one of the organizers of the American Association for Applied Psychology and as the first person to write a book on school psychology. Interestingly, she was also chair of the old APA Clinical Section in 1937, when it disbanded itself in favor of the Clinical Section of the AAAP.

During World War II, Ruth Tolman (1943) wrote concerning the wartime organizational activities of women psychologists. Tolman (who was the sister-in-law of Berkeley psychologist Edward C. Tolman) was long prominent as a psychology supervisor at the Los Angeles Veterans Administration Hospital and was a Division 12 officer.

The first woman to serve as president of APA Division 12 (in 1955–1956) was Jean W. Macfarlane. She is best known as the director of the longitudinal Berkeley Guidance Study and a longtime director of the clinical psychology training program at the University of California, Berkeley. She brought in many well-known scholars, among them Erik Erikson, to consult on her research project and to help devise new measures to be administered to her subjects.

Another woman psychologist who served as president of Division 12 (in 1957–1958) was Anne Roe. She is known for applying psychological research measures including projective tests to the study of careers, in particular the study of 64 eminent scientists (Roe, 1953). In this way she was able to take advantage of the entree to the broader scientific world provided by her marriage to the well-known evolutionary biologist George Gaylord Simpson. In fact, the two of them made a case for the argument that scientific research would be advanced if more people in different disciplines "went to bed together" or at least got to know each other well. In 1959 Anne Roe and her husband became the first married couple that Harvard named to its faculty (Wrenn, 1992).

The next woman president of Division 12 was Florence Halpern, who served in 1967–1968. She had worked at Bellevue Hospital for many years as an MA level psychologist but finally was able to complete her doctoral work and be regarded as a fully qualified clinical psychologist. She played a key role in the New York State Psychological Association in its battle to get a psychology licensing law passed. Halpern also set an example to her colleagues by traveling to Mound Bayou, Mississippi, to participate in the national civil rights movement and to deliver psychological services to the rural minority poor. She had convictions and the courage to live by them (Halpern, 1973).

Outside APA, an important event in relation to the ultimate formation of Section 4 was the emergence of the Association of Women in Psychology in 1969 (Strickland, 1987). The greatest impetus to the development within the division of an emphasis upon the clinical psychology of women may have been provided by Bonnie Strickland, who served as president of Division 12 in 1982–1983 and who was the founder of the Section on the Clinical Psychology of Women (Section 4). Strickland was concerned not only about the neglect of women by clinical psychology. (Consider, for example, the high prevalence of untreated depression among the female population.) She was also concerned about other underserved populations such as ethnic minorities and gays and lesbians and their lack of representation in the field. From 1975 to 1978, well before her presidential year, Strickland chaired the divisional Equal Opportunity and Affirmative Action (EOAA) Committee. Its members included William H. Anderson, Asuncion M. Austria, Carole Rayburn, and Julia Ramos-McKay. The EOAA Committee paved the way for both Section 4 and later Section 6, the one concerned with ethnic minority clinical psychology. Strickland's own best-known research concerned depression in women. It also may be that her research interest in internal vs. external control of rewards is related to the EOAA Committee's emphasis upon self-advocacy by various disadvantaged groups. In 1987, as APA president, Strickland initiated the Task Force on Women and Depression.

## The Founding of Section 4

Section 4, concerned with the Clinical Psychology of Women, came into existence in 1980, with Rachel T. Hare-Mustin as the first president (Sobel & Strickland, 1980). Hare-Mustin, an expert on the topic of gender, describes "alpha prejudice" as attitudes that exaggerate gender differences and "beta prejudice" as ones that ignore true differences between men and women. She has written about the challenges no doubt experienced by many women in the field, of combining work in psychology with heavy family responsibilities (Hare-Mustin, 1987). Hare-Mustin herself said that if she had her life to live over again she would still choose to have her children while she was young. At that time she worked when necessary at what she called "jobbies" (that is, jobs that were not too demanding and certainly ones with relatively low pay). She returned to fully demanding professional employment as the children were able to take care of themselves. Among other demanding positions Hare-Mustin held was one as a faculty member in Harvard University's Graduate School of Education, where its doctoral program in clinical psychology and public practice was then located. (This program was subsequently discontinued.) In discussing the clinical psychology of women, in relation to Freud's early patient, "Dora," Hare-Mustin (1983) made the following striking statement:

> It may be that the fields of clinical psychology and psychiatry could not have developed and flourished if it were not for the pervasive and chronic unhappiness of many women who somatized their pain through physical ailments and vapors or who struggled with experiences of depression and anxiety. (p. 583)

Another particular concern of Section 4 in regard to psychotherapy has been the problem of sexual intimacy between (mostly male) therapists and (mostly female) patients (e.g., Pope & Bouhoutsos, 1986).

The second president of Section 4 and the initial winner of its award for distinguished contributions was Elaine Blechman, known for her innovative research combining behavioral and family systems approaches to intervention (e.g., Blechman, Olson, & Hellman, 1976). Originally trained at UCLA, Blechman subsequently began a behavior therapy program at Albert Einstein College of Medicine involving research, training, and service delivery to a mostly disadvantaged, inner-city population of families. This is a good example of the movement of the behavioral approach into a setting traditionally dominated by psychodynamic views. Blechman also edited an innovative volume on behavioral medicine for women.

Sandra Harris was president of Section 4 in 1983 as well as having edited *The Clinical Psychologist* from 1978 to 1981. She is a faculty member at the Graduate School of Applied and Professional Psychology at Rutgers and also a prominent behavioral therapist who works with autistic children (e.g., Harris, 1976). Given her particular interests and talents, she probably could have equally well served as president for sections 1, 3, or 5. She just happens to be a woman psychologist of considerable competence, and it has been part of Section 4's role to call the division's attention to such people.

Carole A. Rayburn, who has been involved with Section 4 from its beginnings and who served two terms as its president (1984 and 1985) has a career that may be unique among the leadership of clinical psychology organizations. She is not only a PhD clinical psychologist but a Master of Divinity with a major in ministry—she received her theological training in Michigan as a member of the Seventh-day Adventist denomination. This background enabled her to carry out formal research on the psychological and social problems experienced by women clergy in various groups, including women rabbis as well as Protestant ministers (the Roman Catholic church, among others, of course, still bans women from the priesthood, and the Seventh-day Adventists, to which Rayburn belongs, do not permit women to be ordained, either).

The current president of Section 4 is Asuncion "Siony" Austria, who developed the section's newsletter in the direction of being more than "just" a newsletter. This publication is called *The Clinical Psychology of Women*.

Like many other sections of Division 12, Section 4 is also related to another APA Division. In this case, Division 35, the Psychology of Women, is of obvious relevance. Many of the presidents of Section 4 have been fellows if not officers of Division 35, and a continuing question may be whether these individuals will continue to have enough energy to keep both organizations going.

It is easy to show that clinical psychology organizations have not paid as much attention to their women members as their numbers warrant. At present, the membership of Division 12 is about 30% women, and yet fewer than one tenth of the organization's chairs or presidents over the last 75 years have been female. Psychologists Interested in the Advancement of Psychotherapy (the division's original Section 2) never had a female president during its brief existence. The Corresponding Committee of Fifty also never had a female chair, and the Section on Continuing Professional Education had only one during its 13-year existence. Only in 1993 did Section 3's Distinguished Scientist Award at last go to a woman psychologist. In other words, the Section on the Clinical Psychology of Women has its work cut out for it just making sure that the field itself does not continue to disregard its female members. Section 4 accepts male members as well as female ones and has on occasion elected at least one male to office. In 1993 it also gave a special award to David Barlow for his supportive attitude toward women in the field.

# 11

# The Society of Pediatric Psychology (Section 5), 1968/1980–

The Society of Pediatric Psychology is an interest group concerned with the delivery of psychological services to children in nonpsychiatric medical settings and research in child health psychology. It began as an organization in 1968 but did not become an official Division 12 section until 1980. Before that it was loosely affiliated with Section 1, the other child-oriented group in the division.

The collaboration of psychologists with pediatricians dates back to the very beginnings of clinical psychology. Witmer (1896) was a member of the editorial board of an early pediatrics journal and wrote about the common interests of the two fields.

In the "prehistory" of pediatric psychology, another pioneer figure is Arnold Gesell, who was a PhD psychologist and an MD specializing in work with children. Thus he could be called the first developmental pediatrician, although this term was not in use in those days. Beginning in 1915, he was employed by the state of Connecticut with the title of "school psychologist," another first. Gesell was a charter member of the American Association of Clinical Psychologists in 1917. In a talk intended for presentation to the AACP in 1918 and published the next year (Gesell, 1919), he voiced a clear awareness of the need for the skills of the clinical psychologist in dealing with children in a medical setting. He saw a role for psychiatry, too, in dealing with abnormal behavior as opposed to developmental problems. It was Gesell who represented the AACP in its negotiations to become the Clinical Section of APA in 1919. Gesell was also on occasion temporary chair of the APA Clinical Section.

Two early clinical psychologists who worked for part of their careers in childrens hospitals or university departments of pediatrics were Jean W.

Macfarlane, in 1917–1918, in San Francisco, and S. I. Franz, in Los Angeles (at the Children's Hospital), beginning in 1946. The first known use of the term *pediatric psychology* was by Brennemann (1933), but it was not used in its current sense.

In 1957, Division 12 appointed a committee consisting of Boyd McCandless, Sibylle Escalona, and Donald B. Lindsley to look into the activities of psychologists in medical school pediatrics departments around the country (Sibylle Escalona's sister is the pediatrician Barbara Korsch). They wrote an interesting report about their survey of the faculty of the Department of Pediatrics at the University of Iowa and the Albert Einstein College of Medicine at Yeshiva University in New York (McCandless, 1957). However, nothing in particular seemed to follow from this committee report. It seems to have been premature.

In 1966 the University of Iowa announced the availability of traineeships funded by the National Institute of Child Health and Human Development. (The training grant was written by psychologist Leonard Eron and pediatrician Gerald Solomons.) These funds were intended to encourage pediatricians to seek the PhD degree in child development, but there proved to be no appropriate candidates. Therefore, beginning in 1966, the funds were used instead to fund clinical psychology graduate students who took extra courses in child development and did practicum work in a pediatric clinic. This was the first doctoral training program explicitly in "pediatric psychology" (Routh, 1969).

Logan Wright (1967) wrote an influential article in the *American Psychologist* on the pediatric psychologist as a role model. At the time he was director of pediatric psychology at the Children's Memorial Hospital of the University of Oklahoma Health Sciences Center in Oklahoma City.[1]

---

[1] When I was visiting in Oklahoma City in June, 1992, I talked to Gordon Deckert, a physician who was (in 1992) the chair of the Department of Psychiatry and Behavioral Sciences there. He gave me an interesting account of how the Oklahoma Children's Memorial Hospital first came to have a pediatric psychologist. During the early 1960s, a new chair was hired by the Department of Psychiatry at Oklahoma, a physician named L. Jolyon West from the University of Minnesota. When he arrived in Oklahoma City, he was horrified to see in his department signs on the rest rooms labeling them as being for "white" or "colored" people. His response was to take down the signs immediately, inadvertently integrating the restrooms by sex as well as by race. But Gordon Deckert told me that, in addition, the head of the Pediatrics Department at Oklahoma at that time was offended by what he regarded as overly liberal racial and social attitudes on the part of psychiatrists. Therefore, in order to handle the mental health services of the Children's Hospital, he decided to hire his own psychologist instead of depending on consultation from faculty child psychiatrists.

## THE FOUNDING OF THE SOCIETY OF PEDIATRIC PSYCHOLOGY

There were three founders of what became the Society of Pediatric Psychology: Dorothea Ross, of the University of California Medical School, San Francisco; Lee Salk, of the New York Hospital, Cornell University Medical School; and Logan Wright, of the University of Oklahoma Health Sciences Center, in Oklahoma City. In 1968 these three served as a committee of Division 12 (chaired by Wright) that tried to identify psychologists working in departments of pediatrics in medical schools around the United States. To their surprise, there turned out to be about 300 such individuals, more than enough to organize a viable interest group (*The Clinical Psychologist*, 1968, 22 (1), p. 62). Of the three "founders," Dorothea Ross was the one who did most of the actual correspondence. For example, she surveyed the chairs of all medical school pediatrics departments in the United States She later served as the first secretary-treasurer of the Society of Pediatric Psychology. Ross had received her PhD from Stanford University, where she was a coauthor of some of Albert Bandura's well-known "Bobo doll" studies (e.g., Bandura, Ross, & Ross, 1961) on the effects of modeling on children's aggression. In her subsequent career, she exemplified the pediatric psychologist as a researcher and scholar. She received considerable federal grant support. Her research and writing concerned such topics as mental retardation, hyperactivity in children, and factors related to how children deal with pain. She wrote influential books on the latter two topics.

In 1968 Lee Salk organized the production of the first newsletter of the society, called *Pediatric Psychology*, with G. Gail Gardner of Cornell University Medical College as its editor. Salk was undoubtedly the pediatric psychologist who was best known to the public, through his appearances on the NBC "Today" show, his column for parents in *Redbook* magazine, and his popular book for parents, *What Every Child Would Want His Parents to Know*. In his private life, Salk participated in the highly publicized child custody battle previously mentioned. His posthumous book (Salk, 1992) was entitled *Familyhood*. The Society of Pediatric Psychology has recently decided to rename one of its awards the Lee Salk Distinguished Service Award in his memory.

Logan Wright served as the first president of the Society of Pediatric Psychology in 1968. In 1971 he announced the first NIMH-funded internship program with an emphasis on pediatric psychology (*American Psychologist*, 1971, 26, 747). He had been training such interns since 1966–1967. The administration of this internship program and its expansion to include a postdoctoral fellowship program in pediatric psychology was carried out by C. Eugene Walker. (Thomas J. Kenny, who served as president of the pediatric psychology group in 1975–1976 and later received an award, set up the second pediatric psychology internship in the country to receive NIMH support.) Of the founding committee, Logan Wright was the most active in psychological politics, serving as president of the Southwestern Psychological Association, of APA Division 31, of Division 12, and subsequently of APA. In more recent years Wright has served as the executive director of the American Association for Applied and Preventive Psychology and as the managing editor of its journal.

The Society of Pediatric Psychology adopted its official bylaws at its business meeting in Miami, Florida, on September 7, 1970, in conjunction with the APA convention that year.

After the pediatric psychology group had organized itself and had begun to publish its newsletter and to sponsor symposia at the APA conventions each year, it faced a sort of crisis as to whether it would continue as a viable organization. At that point it was not yet a section but basically an interest group attached to Section 1, without a source of income of its own. It was at this point that Arthur Wiens as president set the group on the path to stability. Wiens convinced the other officers that if the group was going to survive, its executive committee would have to meet at midyear and not just at the APA convention, and it would have to make the decision to collect its own dues and not depend on Section 1 for financial support.[2]

## THE JOURNAL OF PEDIATRIC PSYCHOLOGY

The next important development for the group was the gradual development of its newsletter into the *Journal of Pediatric Psychology* in the hands of Diane J. Willis. The author took over this journal from Willis in its first year of existence in 1976 and served for two terms but did not succeed in finding a printer as inexpensive as the one in Oklahoma had been. As a result, the society was driven almost to the point of having a "bake sale" to maintain the financial support of the journal—many members contributed out of their own pockets to keep it going. The person who then saved the day was Phyllis Magrab, who negotiated the arrangement for Plenum Publishing Corporation to take over as the publisher of the journal in 1979.

---

[2] Having been at this meeting myself, I will always think of the midyear executive committee meeting of the Society in 1972 as the point at which the organization survived its first crisis. This meeting was in Oklahoma City, beginning on December 11, and featured an ice storm. The executive committee members had paid their own way to the meeting and wondered more than once if their commitment to pediatric psychology was great enough to justify this hardship.

The journal has been in good financial shape ever since (as has the society, carefully following "Magrab rules" in its financial dealings). Magrab was also the capable administrator who organized several successful midwinter meetings for Division 12, beginning in Melbourne, Florida, in January, 1986 (where there was definitely no ice storm).

The third editor of the *Journal of Pediatric Psychology* (1983–1987) was Gerald P. Koocher, who later received a special award from the society for his scholarly contributions as editor. During his term, the journal began an explicit emphasis on the ethical conduct of research and clinical work with children and families, and expanded its subscription list to many more libraries. Koocher is presently the director of the psychology internship program at Boston Children's Hospital and Judge Baker Children's Center. (It has perhaps the best-known internship in the country in the areas of clinical child and pediatric psychology.) Koocher has served as president of both Sections 1 and 5 of Division 12 and has received awards from both sections for his research and professional contributions.

The fourth editor of the *Journal of Pediatric Psychology*, Michael C. Roberts (1988–1992), is one of the most energetic leaders in the history of Section 5. He received his PhD from Purdue University, which has emerged as the alma mater of more pediatric psychology officers than any other school. He interned at the University of Oklahoma Health Sciences Center and has been involved in the field ever since. It was Roberts who started up the pediatric psychology newsletter again, after the previous newsletter had turned into a journal. In 1990, as editor of the journal, he expanded it to a bimonthly (six issues a year). Like Koocher, Roberts later received an award from the society for scholarly contributions as editor. His research has concerned (among other topics) the prevention of accidental injuries in children, the No. 1 killer of persons age 1 to 44 years (e.g., Roberts, Fanurik, & Wilson, 1988). As the person who is currently among the most knowledgeable about current research developments in the broad field of child health behavior, Roberts has recently accepted the job of editing the revised edition of the *Handbook of Pediatric Psychology* to be published in the mid-1990s.

Taking over as editor of the *Journal of Pediatric Psychology* in 1993 is Annette M. La Greca, who had already served as president of Section 5. La Greca's research interests concern diabetes in children and adolescents—especially in relation to compliance with a complex medical regimen, and children's social skills and social anxiety (e.g., La Greca, Dandes, Wick, Shaw, & Stone, 1988). Like other Society of Pediatric Psychology presidents Walker, Roberts, and Wallander, La Greca received her PhD from Purdue. Since that time she has been a faculty member at the University of Miami, where she has done much to help develop graduate, internship, and postdoctoral programs in clinical child and pediatric psychology.

In its earlier years, the Society of Pediatric Psychology seemed to have developed some important links with service delivery to mentally retarded or other developmentally handicapped children. For example, one of its presidents and awardees, Gary B. Mesibov, was best known for his work with adolescents and adults with the severe disorder of communication and behavior known as autism. Mesibov carried out a critique of the overly rigid application of the "normalization" principle to autistic persons living in the community. However, as time has gone on, pediatric psychology has moved more in the direction of child health, and away from its previous focus on developmental disabilities.

In the beginning, the Society of Pediatric Psychology recruited most of its members from university medical schools, in other words, people working in so-called tertiary care settings. As the society developed, others were attracted, for example, from community hospitals (secondary care settings) and pediatric group practices (including those devoted to primary care). One possible advantage of "health psychology" as opposed to traditional clinical psychology is its possible universality. Although most people go through life without ever suffering from mental health problems (at least of a severe nature), 100% of the population have health problems occasionally. If psychology can be shown to relate to health in general, it could get to the point where everybody would need the services of a psychologist occasionally just as part of routine health care. The challenge of involving pediatric psychology in primary health care was met in an examplary way by Carolyn S. Schroeder. She developed her practice in conjunction with Chapel Hill Pediatrics, a private group practice serving approximately 10,000 families. Any parent whose child was being cared for in this pediatric practice could obtain at no extra charge a brief telephone consultation with a mental health professional regarding a developmental or behavioral problem of the child. (The most common ones concerned toilet training or temper tantrums.) For a fee, various parent group meetings were held in the evenings, for example, how to cope with a new baby, or pointers on dealing with teenagers. Screening for developmental and behavioral problems was routinely carried out by the nurses as part of the well-baby or well-child visits. Families could also schedule several brief visits in person with a psychologist or social worker but were referred to other community services if necessary. In other words, Schroeder and her colleagues developed and implemented an efficient and cost-effective way to prevent or handle children's mental health problems in a primary care setting. Her model has begun to be replicated with variations in other communities such as Dubuque, Iowa; Durham, North Carolina; and Ft. Worth, Texas.

Brian Stabler, another individual receiving one of the Society of Pediatric Psychology's awards, became known especially for his skills as a consultant, working on what is generally called a "consultation/liaison" team. Stabler's research interests focused particularly on children with short stature, often seen in pediatric endocrinology clinics (e.g., Stabler & Underwood, 1986). Besides his wide knowledge of medical–psychological issues, Stabler's dapper appearance and his droll British sense of humor seem to have helped him establish quick rapport with children and families in the hospital and with the pediatricians caring for them. In his subsequent work, he has found the same approach effective in consultation/liaison work with adult medical patients.

## THE SOCIETY OF PEDIATRIC PSYCHOLOGY BECOMES SECTION 5

The Society of Pediatric Psychology became a regular section (Section 5) of Divison 12 on October 1, 1980. At that time, the group considered as one alternative becoming some kind of special interest group within Division 38, the Division of Health Psychology (which does not have formal sections). Compared to Section 1 (which overlaps with it by about a third of its membership), Section 5 has always been more behaviorally oriented and perhaps more accepting of members with research/academic interests. In addition to the National Institute of Mental Health, a number of other federal health institutes support research related to Section 5's interests. Three former Society of Pediatric Psychology officers, Logan Wright, the author, and Michael Roberts, have served on the Behavioral Medicine Study Section of the National Institutes of Health. Pediatricians themselves often look to researchers in child development to provide the basic behavioral sciences research underlying their practice. It is perhaps for this reason that developmental psychologists such as Jerome Kagan (and not clinical child or pediatric psychologists) have been asked to be members of the National Advisory Committee of the NICHD.

In 1977, the Society of Pediatric Psychology began its yearly Distinguished Contribution Awards. Naturally, the first three of these went to its founders, Salk, Wright, and Ross. The pattern developed of giving these awards to persons who formerly held leadership roles in the society. As noted above, this award was recently named after Lee Salk (who had been its first recipient). A separate award was begun for significant research contributions. The first of these research awards went to John J. Spinetta, who had pioneered research on terminally ill children and their psychological isolation from their families (e.g., Spinetta, Rigler, & Karon, 1974). The second and third research awards went to two individuals who had intensively studied interventions with children undergoing aversive medical procedures, Lizette Peterson (Peterson et al., 1984) and Barbara Melamed (Melamed & Siegel, 1975). The 1993 research award went to Dennis Drotar, for his studies on nonorganic failure to thrive in infants and his influential writings on the psychological aspects of chronic illness in children (e.g., Drotar, 1981).

One of the recent presidents of Section 5, Sue White, initiated regional research conferences in pediatric psychology. The first of these and the pattern for others was the "North Coast" Conference, originally held in Cleveland in 1987. Others have now been held on the West Coast and in the southwestern United States The pattern has developed of having these regional conferences in alternate years. In the years between regionals there is a national pediatric psychology research conference. So far these national conferences have been held in Gainesville, Florida, beginning in 1988, sponsored by the Department of Clinical and Health Psychology of the University of Florida and organized by James H. Johnson and Suzanne Bennett Johnson (who, despite their similar names, are not related to each other).

One additional possible activity of a psychological organization is to sponsor the publication of books. Section 5 sponsored a *Handbook of Pediatric Psychology* (Routh, 1988), has published the first volume of a series of *Advances in Pediatric Psychology* (La Greca, Siegel, Wallander, & Walker, 1992), and has several others including a book of readings and a revised version of the handbook now in the planning stages.

It was pediatrician C. Henry Kempe of the University of Colorado Medical Center who in 1962 led the revival of medical interest in the problem of child maltreatment. During the years since Kempe's landmark paper, psychologists have been supportive of the new child abuse reporting laws and child protection teams. The identification, remediation, and prevention of child maltreatment is complicated and involves social and forensic as well as medical facets. Section 5 leaders have been deeply involved in this field. An example is Sue White's research and workshops on the use of anatomically detailed dolls in interviewing children with suspected sexual abuse (e.g., White, Strom, Santilli, & Halpin, 1986).

# The Section on Ethnic Minority Clinical Psychology (Section 6), 1986–

Up until 1920, not a single African-American received a PhD in psychology. Then, at Clark University, Francis Cecil Sumner broke this barrier (Korchin, 1980). As the widely read book by R. V. Guthrie (1976) stated, in psychology, "even the rat was white."

No African-American, Hispanic, or Asian names appear among the leadership of the AACP, the Clinical Section of the old APA, the Clinical Section of the AAAP, or of Division 12 in its early years. The leadership roster did, however, contain the names of many European emigrants. J. E. Wallace Wallin, the founder of the organization, was of Swedish ancestry, as his association with Augustana and Upsala colleges might suggest. Many others who were active in the organization, such as Thorleif G. Hegge, were first-generation emigrants.

In the years before World War II, and to a lesser extent since that time, the United States was characterized by anti-Semitism, but clinical psychology has a good record of combating this. For example, Frederick C. Thorne, the founding editor of the *Journal of Clinical Psychology*, wrote an anti-Semitic editorial in 1945. His words were as follows:

> A further practical problem of importance in the selection of students involves the avoidance of undue representation of any one racial group among those accepted to training. Perhaps because of long racial experience with suffering and personality problems, certain groups of students show an unusual interest and propensity for psychological science. (Thorne, 1945, p. 13)

Carl Rogers and several other prominent individuals resigned as consulting editors in protest. Clinical psychologists with Jewish origins have certainly been among the most honored leaders of the field (consider, for example, three famous Davids: Shakow, Wechsler, and Rapaport). And Jews, having experienced persecution themselves, have often been leaders in the civil rights movement. Florence Halpern, at 68 years of age, when she was president of Division 12, was working in Mound Bayou, Mississippi, for this "cause" (Ochroch & Kalinkowitz, 1982). R. Nevitt Sanford was honored by Division 12—he had been among the coauthors of a well-known book on the "authoritarian personality," dealing with social prejudice.

On another dimension of diversity, Harry V. McNeill (1947), who was secretary of Division 12, argued that "it is high time that Catholics and Freudians got together and swapped some of their trade secrets" (p. 350). As an historical example of the cooperation of the religion and mental health fields, McNeill cited the therapeutic effectiveness of the Catholic community at Gheel, Belgium.

Still, there was relatively little ethnic diversity among the leadership of clinical psychology before the 1980s. In an address given in response to the division's highest award, Sheldon Korchin (1980) spoke of the great need to educate qualified minority psychologists to study and serve their own ethnic groups. As he put it, the field badly needs cornbread, tortillas, and bagels, and not just Wonder Bread. Finally, in 1981, Samuel M. Turner, an African-American faculty member at the Western Psychiatric Institute and Clinic of the University of Pittsburgh, was appointed editor of *The Clinical Psychologist*. Diane J. Willis, a part-Kiowa Indian clinical psychologist, was elected as an APA council representative from Division 12 in 1984, and Samuel Turner became a council representative in 1987.

Bonnie Strickland, who was president of Division 12 in 1982–1983, had chaired an Equal Opportunity–Affirmative Action (EOAA) Committee beginning in 1975 within the division to try to do something about the lack of diversity in the division. As Diane Willis recalls the meetings of this committee, among the first individuals it heard from were two clinical psychologists who were openly gay males. As might be expected, they complained that the clinical psychology organization had disregarded people with their sexual orientation. (It might be recalled that Division 12 in 1974 had at least honored Evelyn Hooker for her research concerning the psychological normality of homosexuals—she had first received a federal grant to study this topic in 1954 through the assistance of NIMH staffer Harold Hildreth, a well-known clinical psychologist.) In any case, in the end, the EOAA Committee moved in a somewhat different direction. Willis herself suggested the possibility of a section devoted to ethnic minority concerns within clinical psychology. After all, such a section could do things that a mere committee could not do. It would have a voting representative on the Division's Board of Directors; it would have program time at the convention; it would have built-in continuity, and so forth. Therefore, a petition was circulated, and when it had the requisite 50 names, it was approved by the board on September 26, 1986.

Section 6 itself welcomed ethnic diversity. The president for its first 2 years, Gail E. Wyatt, was an African-American. The second president, Lillian Comas-Diaz, was Hispanic. And the subsequent presidents, Reiko H. True and Jean Lau Chin, are of Asian ancestry. From the division's point of view, the most visible person in Section 6 has been Russell T. Jones, an African-American, who served as its representative for the first 5 years (he was recently replaced in this role by Bernadette Gray-Little, another well-known African-American clinical psychologist).

Like other relatively small sections, Section 6 has had some difficulty in maintaining itself as a stable organization. Its elections have not always been held on a regular schedule, requiring some officers to serve longer than the usual terms. On occasion its materials for the APA convention program have had to be put together at the last minute in response to the entreaties of the division program chair. Persons of ethnic minority background are grossly underrepresented in the field of psychology as a whole, and those who are APA members find themselves in great demand to serve on various boards and committees. There is also competition for their interest from Division 45, the Society for the Psychological Study of Ethnic Minority Issues. Thus, it has only been because of the hard work and commitment of a relatively small network of individuals that Section 6 has thus far survived.

The author has only recently become a member of Section 6, and it does not publish a newsletter. Thus it is more difficult to track its history than that of the larger sections. However, from the standpoint of the division it has been a clear success. The division Board of Directors is at last guaranteed some representation of ethnic minority views in its meetings. The same thing can be said of the division's annual convention program. Section 6 may have had some "growing pains," but if it ever ceased to exist, the division would probably press someone to reinvent it.

# 13

# The Section on the Theory and Practice of Group Psychotherapy (Section 7), 1988–1991

Section 7 was perhaps the smallest section of Division 12 and certainly the most short lived. It was formed in 1988 and disbanded itself only 3 years later, in 1991. The only president it ever had was Arthur Teicher, who also served as representative to Division 12 during most of the section's existence. Jules Barron also played a prominent role in Section 7, being listed as its president-elect for 3 years but never actually serving as president. Barron of course had been president of Division 12 in 1986, and his continuing influence on the board was important in the division's approval of the new section.

In retrospect, Section 7 of Division 12 is probably best seen as an offshoot of other organizations, because some of the same personnel also formed a group psychotherapy section of Division 29 (Psychotherapy) and of Division 39 (Psychoanalysis). Of course, there is an interdisciplinary American Group Psychotherapy Association outside the APA to which many psychologists interested in group therapy belong.

The disbanding of Section 7 took place soon after the APA Council announced the formation of Division 49, Group Psychology and Group Psychotherapy. It appeared that the psychologists who formed this new division did not have enough energy to keep the group therapy sections in three other divisions going as well. Even before the new division formed, Section 7 did not seem to hold regular elections and had difficulty on occasion getting its materials in to the Division 12 program chair on time.

# The Spinoff of Other Specialty Groups Related to Division 12

In a sense, the modern subdivisions of psychology go back all the way to Wilhelm Wundt, who pointed out that what he called "physiological psychology" could be considered a scientific field in the same sense as physiology was defined as a science. What is often not recalled is that according to Wundt, another whole side of psychology existed that did not so easily lend itself to scientific methods such as formal experimentation. This Wundt labeled as *Völkerpsychologie* (perhaps translatable as "cultural psychology") and defined to include language, religion, and other historical and cultural matters obviously related to human behavior (Cahan & White, 1922). In contrast, Sigmund Freud defined his proposed science of psychoanalysis to include a broad range of phenomena ordinarily considered in American universities to be a part of the "humanities." It is interesting that in Europe and to an increasing extent in the United States, Freudian influence on the so-called humanities has been greater than on academic psychology. Among the well-known psychoanalysts of our day are Erik Erikson (who was an artist and a Montessori teacher before becoming an analyst) and Peter Gay, Freud's modern biographer (who is a professional historian).

Francis Galton, James McKeen Cattell, and other pioneers were interested in individual differences and mental testing. Perhaps they can be seen as the earliest representatives of the development of an applied branch, psychological engineering, as it were, as opposed to the pure science approach of earlier academicians.

Organizationally, the American Psychological Association, founded in 1892, attempted to encompass all of psychology as its members defined the field. Titchener's group of "experimentalists" (the present-day Society of Experimental Psychologists) was but the first U.S. attempt to divide the psychological sheep from the goats, with the "sheep" in this case being the true "scientific" psychologists and the "goats" everyone else in the field (including the mental testers). A similar though less exclusive theme of scientific elitism characterized the founding of other APA spinoff organizations over the years, including the Psychonomic Society, in 1959, and most recently, the American Psychological Society in 1988 (VandenBos, 1989).

The original American Association of Clinical Psychologists, founded in 1917, and just about every clinical psychology organization founded since then, had the additional goal of maintaining high professional standards. In other words, in order to serve the public, a professional must be experienced and competent in somewhat the same fashion as a master plumber is certified competent by a union. Even by virtue of excellent scientific training, a physicist or a chemist would not necessarily be able to install the sinks in a house properly. An early dilemma was created by the legitimate presence of certain purely scientifically oriented members in any clinical psychology group. These individuals might do competent research on abnormal behavior without having any interest in the practical evaluation and treatment of patients or clients. The pre–World War II APA tried unsuccessfully to solve this problem by creating a separate subgroup of certified "consulting psychologists" who had suitable professional qualifications.

In addition to the important difference between psychological scientists and "engineers," there emerged early some important content-area specialization within psychological practice: clinical vs. industrial psychology. Industrial and organizational psychology, as exemplified in the work of such pioneering figures as Hugo Munsterberg, Walter Dill Scott, and Walter Van Dyke Bingham, appeared just about as early as clinical psychology. The important difference here may be that the clinical psychologist tries to use the principles of psychology to help people one by one (or at most in couples, families, or small groups), whereas the I/O psychologist takes as clients private and public organizations, such as business firms or government agencies. There was discussion of having a separate industrial psychology section in the old APA, and the AAAP did have separate sections in the two areas. At the present day, the separation between clinical and organizational/industrial psychology (e.g., Division 12 and Division 14) seems to be more or less complete, and one would rarely expect the same individual to be well qualified in both areas. It is true that in most states and provinces in the United States and Canada, psychology licensing is "generic" and does not even make the distinction between clinical, industrial, or other areas such as applied experimental and the like.

Organizationally, there was also relatively early differentiation among clinical, school, and counseling psychology. Before the founding of the AAAP in 1937 there was little meaningful distinction among these three areas, but professional walls have now been built to try to separate them. There were already distinct psychological organizations beginning in 1937, that is, the clinical and educational sections of the AAAP. After 1945, there was a further proliferation of organizations. There was, of course, Division 12 for clinical psychology. For school psychology there was Division 16 and an organization outside APA known as the National Association of School Psychologists (NASP). For counseling psychology there was Division 17 and a separate organization, the Association for Counseling and Development. The American Board of Professional Psychology has for many years offered separate diplomas in clinical, counseling, and school psychology.

Division 29, Psychotherapy, was the first one to break off specifically from Division 12. Note, however, that there are no special APA-approved training programs in psychotherapy as such, which is now taught to virtually all clinical and counseling psychologists and to many school psychologists as well. Similarly, there is no separate ABPP diploma in psychotherapy. In other words, psychotherapy skills are "generic" to both clinical and counseling psychology at the very least, not to mention allied fields such as psychiatry, social work, marriage and family therapy, and so forth.

Various writers have argued that the barriers among clinical, counseling, and school psychology are artificial and perhaps counterproductive. Leon Levy (1984) has in fact described a graduate training program in what he calls "human services psychology" that encompasses elements of all three of these areas of psychology (but does not attempt to include I/O). Bonnie Strickland, in her term as Division 12 president, tried to provide a forum for discussion among the leadership of other human services areas (school and counseling) with clinical psychology. She pointed out that the APA accreditation guidelines were mostly generic to professional psychology. They required courses in statistics and research design, the biological bases of behavior, social bases of behavior, individual differences, and so forth, as well as practicum and internship training. Seymour Sarason (1983) argued for the [re]integration of clinical and school psychology. Similarly, Ronald Fox (1982) spoke of the need to reorient psychology as a health profession toward general practice including preventive services, perhaps in collaboration with primary care physicians such as family practitioners, pediatricians, and internists.

When one considers the proliferation of APA divisions in recent years, only a few of them could be considered to represent genuine specialty areas, perhaps specialties "within" human services psychology. ABPP and other such boards recognize a number of these: psychological hypnosis (Division 30), health psychology (Division 38), clinical neuropsychology (Division

40), and family psychology (Division 43). Certainly for neuropsychology, these days, postdoctoral training seems to be essential. Joseph D. Matarazzo is a Division 12 member especially associated with the area of health psychology. He is certainly an effective scientific entrepreneur. Matarazzo founded the first graduate department of psychology on the model of a "basic science" department in a medical school, at the Oregon Health Sciences University in Portland. Although psychologists affiliated with this department also administer internship and postdoctoral programs for clinical psychologists, the PhD program is concerned strictly with training researchers. Similarly, Matarazzo was the founding chair of the ad hoc Behavioral Medicine Study Section of the National Institutes of Health—at that time a subgroup of an epidemiology and disease control research review group. Matarazzo et al. (1984) thus had an unparalleled opportunity to influence the direction of behavioral health research in this country and to participate in the founding of the field of health psychology, including the APA division of that name (Division 38). (Matarazzo received the Division 12 scientific award in 1983.)

Another example of a specialized human services area is represented by APA Division 28, Psychopharmacology and Substance Abuse. There was a Center for Alcohol Studies established at Yale in 1940 that moved to Rutgers in 1962. It has been a beacon in this area (Nathan, 1987). Certain clinical psychologists such as Peter Nathan and Alan Marlatt (active in Division 12 or honored by it) have made outstanding contributions to this area as have others. On the topic of the neuropsychology of alcoholism, it would be difficult to find a more renowned expert than Oscar Parsons, another Division 12 award winner. (The newest APA division, approved shortly before these words were written, deals with the psychology of substance abuse.)

Other APA divisions appear (at least at the present time) to overlap greatly with clinical psychology and have no distinct training requirements or diplomate status. These overlapping groups include Division 13 (Consulting), Division 18 (Public Service), Division 22 (Rehabilitation), Division 27 (Community), Division 31 (State Psychological Association Affairs), Division 33 (Mental Retardation and Developmental Disabilities), Division 37 (Child, Youth, and Family Services),[1] Division 39 (Psychoanalysis), Division 42 (Independent Practice), and Division 49 (Group Psychotherapy and Group Processes). Division 20 (Adult Development and Aging) has

---

[1] I have personal knowledge as a member of Divisions 33 and 37 and have served as president of each of them.

now, in a sense, become linked with Division 12 through Division 12's newest "Section 2," clinical geropsychology, just established.

These days, Division 33 (Mental Retardation and Developmental Disabilities) seems to be dominated by two somewhat distinct subgroups. One of these is mental retardation researchers, who have a pattern of federal grant support (often from the Mental Retardation Branch of the National Institute of Child Health and Human Development) and who often attend the annual conference on theory and research in MR/DD at Gatlinburg, Tennessee. The other major group is the service providers, who are increasingly concerned with applied behavior analysis in family settings, classrooms, group homes, and inpatient settings. Neither of these groups is very strongly identified with clinical psychology. Seymour Sarason, a clinical psychologist who was highly involved in advocacy for the mentally retarded, tried to explain his motives in such personal terms as: "I am Jewish. I had polio; I was a Trotskyite in my youth" (Award Citation, *American Psychologist*, 1985, 40, p. 334). In contrast to a Yale professor like Sarason, many of the present-day providers of psychological services to the developmentally disabled have master's degrees, work in the public sector, and have generally been scorned by organized clinical psychology. Division 33's highest award is, however, named for Edgar A. Doll, the prominent early clinical psychologist.

Division 37 (Child, Youth, and Family Services) is concerned with advocacy. Its members are a mixture of developmental psychologists, clinical child and pediatric psychologists, school psychologists, and individuals who are sophisticated about the law–psychology interface. Recent Division 37 task forces have produced a notable series of books that provide scientific and scholarly perspectives on many important public policy issues such as child maltreatment, adolescent pregnancy, custody evaluation, and the like. This division does not particularly involve itself with practitioners' concerns about being reimbursed for their services or with psychological research as such except as it impacts on policy issues and advocacy. Division 37's highest award to psychologists (it also gives an annual award to child advocates who are not psychologists) is named after Nicholas Hobbs, another prominent clinical psychologist.

To return once more to Division 29, one that emerged from a Division 12 section and still overlaps heavily in its membership with Division 12, it is important to understand the linkages between this group and various state and local organizations. Clinical psychologists who are in practice as psychotherapists often form the backbone of local organizations, where they provide each other with peer support, continuing education, a base for political action activities, and so forth. A representative example might be the Los Angeles Society of Clinical Psychologists in Private Practice.

Similar groups exist in any large city, and such local organizations are often very influential in state organizations (e.g., the California State Psychological Association) and various APA divisions (in this case, Division 29). In 1976, Max Siegel as president of Division 12 formed a committee to engage in liaison with local clinical groups, beginning with those in New York, New Jersey, California, and Florida. A group of such practitioners in psychology has been particularly effective politically, linking up with like-minded psychologists around the country. As Cummings (1985) relates the story:

> Early in the 1960's I joined a group of mavericks from California, New York, and New Jersey who were determined to make the APA more responsive to professional concerns and to wrest it from the strangle-hold that academic psychology held. Affectionately termed "The Dirty Dozen," this group includes such household names as Rogers Wright, Allen Williams, Milton Theaman, Don Schultz, Theodore Blau, Herbert Dorken, Ernest Laurence, Eugene Shapiro, Marvin Metsky, Max Siegel, and Jack Wiggins. The rest is history.

It is evident that the efforts of this group and others like it were successful. In some ways, this is merely a modern version of what happened in the 1930s when the state organizations coalesced to form the Association for Consulting Psychology and eventually the AAAP, which then merged with APA in 1945. But the political success of the practitioners within APA from 1977 (when the first independent practitioner became APA president) on was probably a factor in the formation of the American Psychological Society in 1988 as a separate organization, as academic psychology fought back.

# II

# Issues and Personalities

# Research and Scholarly Activities: Basic Science and Psychopathology

Up to this point, this book has provided a chronological narrative of clinical psychology organizations. Now its emphasis shifts. The next several chapters are devoted to some areas in which the organizations had an impact and some of the officers and awardees of the organizations who made a difference, that is, "issues and personalities."

The first such issue is research. There was never a time in its brief history when clinical psychology has not been considered to be a scientific field. The original 1917 bylaws of the American Association of Clinical Psychologists (see Appendix A) included the object "to encourage research in problems related to mental hygiene and corrective education," and almost half of the members of the organization were academics (see Chapter 2). This and the following two chapters therefore discuss the same major content areas of research in clinical psychology: basic science, psychopathology, assessment, and intervention.

## BIOLOGICAL BASES OF BEHAVIOR

The premier example of a basic scientist associated with the early clinical psychology organizations was S. I. Franz. Franz obtained his PhD at Columbia, studied under Wundt, and worked as a research psychologist at such institutions as McLean Hospital, St. Elizabeth's Hospital, and later the Children's Hospital in Hollywood, California. Franz was highly respected by experimental psychologists; for example, it was he who taught Karl S. Lashley ablation techniques for studying the rodent central nervous system (e.g., Franz & Lashley, 1917). Franz once edited the *Psychological*

*Review*, then and now perhaps the most influential journal in psychology. His acceptance by physicians was such that his colleagues at George Washington University awarded him an honorary MD. He was also an honorary member of the American Psychiatric Association. His research was too broad to be classified as merely concerning psychopathology, assessment, or intervention. For example, Franz wrote a handbook of methods on mental examination (Franz, 1919) and an early monograph on what we would now term *neuropsychological and psychiatric rehabilitation* (Franz, 1923). He was a scientist–practitioner before this concept was articulated by Shakow. Franz saw the dividing line between basic and applied research to be an artificial one. He could speak of brain functions in terms of the behavior of a rat or the recovery of a human patient from aphasia. (Franz was chair pro tem of the Clinical Section of APA in 1929–1930.)

## COGNITIVE AND AFFECTIVE BASES OF BEHAVIOR

Carney Landis was a research psychologist at the New York State Psychiatric Institute and Columbia University from 1930 on (Hunt, 1962). One of Landis's best-known studies, done with William A. Hunt, was based on analyzing high-speed motion pictures of unsuspecting adults just after they heard a gunshot. Landis and Hunt were able to characterize the precise, universal movements of the startle response occurring within the first few moments following such an event (Hunt & Landis, 1935; Landis & Hunt, 1939). (Landis was on the Division 12 executive committee beginning in 1939.) William A. Hunt was later the chief clinical psychologist in the Navy and had a distinguished postwar career at Northwestern University (Matarazzo, 1987). (William A. Hunt [not to be confused with J. McV. Hunt] was Division 12 president in 1953–1954 and received a division award in 1967.) Another colleague of Landis at the New York State Psychiatric Institute was Joseph Zubin, who was also a prolific researcher in psychopathology. Zubin had a talent for presenting research in a way that was exciting to clinicians. (He gave so many successful "postdoctoral institutes" sponsored by Division 12 at APA that the division gave him a special award in 1966.)

Julian Rotter's (1954) social learning theory, including his influential concept of internal versus external locus of control, has led to a sizable body of research in psychology. Rotter attributed much of the success of his work to the fact that it was based on a coherent theoretical framework and that his early introduction of it came in the form of a monograph including a systematic series of related studies (Rotter, 1966). Too much research, according to Rotter, is conceived and carried out as unrelated studies, published piecemeal, without an overarching theory. Rotter was trained as a clinical psychologist—his mentor was C. M. Louttit at Indiana University. (He received Division 12's award in 1968 and served as president in 1970–1971.)

## Individual Differences

### Henry Murray, the Harvard Psychological Clinic, and Personology

Henry Murray was certainly an effective liaison person between clinical psychology and psychoanalysis; he however considered himself mainly as a "personologist," and is indeed among the founders of the scientific study of personality. The Harvard Psychological Clinic, mentioned earlier in connection with its founder, Morton Prince, was an important influence on the field of clinical psychology and trained many influential clinical psychologists.

Clearly, Henry Murray was an original (Robinson, 1992; Smith & Anderson, 1989). Although his role was not entirely encompassed by the term *clinical psychologist*, he had a massive influence on the development of the field. Murray came from a wealthy family, which may account for some of his independent ways. He was a Harvard undergraduate with a somewhat indifferent academic record. He completed Harvard Medical School, did a residency in surgery, and worked for a time in research at the Rockefeller Institute. Next he went to Cambridge, England, where he completed a PhD in biochemistry.

Despite these accomplishments, Murray was unsatisfied with the drift of his career. As a rebel from conventional puritanical values, he found a kindred spirit in novelist Herman Melville and wished to devote himself to some of the important human issues he found in Melville's writings. Some intimations of what direction Murray's life might take came along in the form of Carl Jung's book, *Psychological Types*. Murray found this book captivating and journeyed to visit Jung in person as soon as the opportunity arrived. Their conversations in 1925 were, it seemed, also a powerful experience for Murray.

Then, fortuitously, in 1926 it became possible for Murray to obtain a position at the new Harvard Psychological Clinic and also a faculty appointment in the psychology program at Harvard, despite his lack of any formal graduate training in the field. In fact, the more Murray found out about the details of what was studied in academic psychology, the more it seemed to him that sophisticated and quantitative methods were being applied to trivial and uninteresting problems (compared, for example, to the issues that concerned Melville and Jung). Murray was quite alienated from the usual activities of psychologists in universities. He once wrote that "academic psychology has contributed practically nothing to the knowledge of human nature" (Murray, 1935, p. 805). He dismissed conventional research in the field as consisting of a sort of "eye, ear, nose, and throat psychology" (Robinson, 1992, p. 150). As a physician, Murray had no trouble in obtaining psychoanalytic training in Boston and was one of the founders of the Boston Psychoanalytic Society. He began to carry out the intensive personological studies of Harvard undergraduates and other nonclinical research participants that formed the basis of his book, *Explorations in Personality* (Murray, 1938). The Thematic Apperception Test he and his colleague Christiana Morgan developed (Morgan & Murray, 1935) as an assessment procedure did not seem to Murray to be as important a contribution as others in the field found it to be—another example of his independent attitude in viewing his work. Another contribution made by Murray in his work for the Office of Strategic Services (predecessor to the CIA) in World War II (OSS Assessment Staff, 1948) was what became known as the Assessment Center Method. This approach is now used frequently in the selection of high-level personnel and even in some of the examinations for diplomas of the American Board of Professional Psychology.

Murray in his work trained—and influenced—a large number of students who later contributed to clinical and personality psychology: R. W. White, Nevitt Sanford, Saul Rosenzweig, Silvan Tomkins, Gardner Lindzey, and numerous others. In fact, all of Murray's students just mentioned were subsequently selected for Division 12's award, a record not likely to be equaled by any other teacher. R. W. White, for example, himself went on to become a Harvard professor. He wrote a famous article introducing the concept of "competence" to psychology (White, 1959). His influential book, *Lives in Progress* (White, 1952), was based on a longitudinal study of undergraduates originally seen at the Harvard Psychological Clinic. Besides being beautifully written, this book truly represents Murray's kind of personology.

Murray's attitude toward psychoanalysis was that it was a valuable method for dealing with human problems—he found Freud's approach more suitable in clinical work than Jung's—but, like Morton Prince, Murray was not about to swallow Freud's teachings whole (Murray, 1940). He noted the "night school" character of much of psychoanalytic training and its unfortunate tendency to produce "unskeptical religionists" (Murray, 1940, p. 155) but found this more likely to happen to physicians than to psychologists in psychoanalytic training. The psychologists generally had, he thought, a more critical and skeptical attitude. Murray did not receive tenure at Harvard until he was over 50 years old, but there is no doubt that his ultimate impact on psychology has far exceeded that of persons who traveled the more conventional route. We might well describe Murray as he once described Morton Prince—he "had no taint of limited professionalism and was always, in a sense, even in his best scientific work, a spendid amateur with a fresh and robust outlook" (Murray, 1956, p. 294). (Murray received Division 12's award in 1961.)

## Lindzey

Gardner Lindzey was coauthor of Hall and Lindzey's (1957) *Theories of Personality*, read by many generations of future clinicians. Lindzey (1954) also served as the original editor of the influential *Handbook of Social Psychology*. He was also once head of the Harvard Psychologal Clinic, was a department chair and dean, and was director of the Center for Advanced Study in the Behavioral Sciences in Palo Alto. (Lindzey received Division 12's award in 1975.)

## Mischel

Walter Mischel (1968) in his influential book on personality, served as a gadfly to clinical psychology by pointing out the rather low (approximately .30) correlations between measures of the "same" behavior in different situations. Such findings seemed to bring into question the reality of personality traits as traditionally conceived (but see Epstein's [1979, 1980] rebuttal). On the positive side, Mischel has generated ingenious studies, including experimental and longitudinal research on children's resistance to temptation (e.g., Mischel, 1958). (Mischel won Section 3's award in 1978.)

## Development

Arnold Gesell carried out meticulous descriptive research (some of it using motion picture records) on the development of infants and preschool children, conceived mostly as a biologically governed process of unfolding. Subsequent developmental psychologists have often disagreed with Gesell's interpretations, but many developmental facts he catalogued have provided a foundation for later research. (Gesell was temporary chair of the Clinical Section of APA in 1924–1925.)

Mary D. S. Ainsworth is another developmental researcher who came out of a clinical psychology background. One hardly thinks of Ainsworth's name without also recalling that of John Bowlby. In this instance, Bowlby, a psychoanalyst influenced by animal behavior researchers ("ethologists"), served as the theorist of attachment, separation, and loss while Ainsworth served as the instigator of a large body of empirical research supportive of that theory. Bowby and Ainsworth led the field to reconceptualize the previous concept of dependency, an individual personality characteristic— into attachment, a dyadic phenomenon. Attachment refers to a complex array of behaviors that function to maintain the physical proximity of the partners. Ainsworth's most notable early study was her longitudinal observations of mother–infant relationships in Uganda (Ainsworth, 1967). She later carried out similar observations of a cohort of mother–infant pairs in Baltimore. In these studies, she was able to correlate maternal sensitivity at home (as indexed by how soon a mother answered her infant's cry) to security of attachment as observed in the "strange situation" in the laboratory (e.g., Ainsworth, Blehar, Waters, & Wall, 1978). Secure infants tended to have sensitive mothers. Bowlby's theories and Ainsworth's findings have been followed up by studies done by a whole generation of researchers in developmental psychology. This research has turned out to have some direct clinical implications in that infant–mother dyads' attachment characteristics are somewhat stable over time and are to some extent predictive of later child psychopathology. Also, interesting links have been found between child abuse and neglect and certain variants in the child's attachment behavior. (Ainsworth received Division 12's award in 1984 and is slated to receive Section 1's award in 1994.)

Norman Garmezy was originally trained in the psychopathology of schizophrenia by such mentors and colleagues as David Shakow and Eliot Rodnick, with whom he developed a theory of schizophrenic cognitive dysfunction as it was affected by social censure. Garmezy later moved from this emphasis to become the principal scholar keeping track of the many NIMH-supported longitudinal studies of children at high risk for psychopathology. Most recently, Garmezy identified important individual differences among children in sensitivity to stress—or resilience in the face of adverse life experiences. Thus, Garmezy joined with other influential figures in the field such as Michael Rutter to herald a new field of developmental psychopathology, specifically the identification and longitudinal study of risk and protective factors related to the onset of psychopathology (Garmezy & Rutter, 1983). (Garmezy was president of Division 12 in 1977–1978 and received its award in 1988. He also received awards from Section 3 in 1974 and Section 1 in 1992.)

Leonard D. Eron is known for his longitudinal research following a cohort of children living in upstate New York well into adulthood.

The most recent published follow-up data span 22 years from the age of 8 up to 30 (Huesmann, Eron, Lefkowitz, & Walder, 1984). Peer-rated aggressive behavior showed impressive stability not only from year to year but also over this entire period of time, even after controlling for cognitive factors. Childhood aggression predicted adult behaviors such as traffic violations, alcoholism, and spouse abuse. There were also intergenerational findings in which children who were strongly punished not only were more aggressive at that time but also grew up to be parents who punished their own children harshly. (Eron was president of Section 3 in 1981–1982.)

## SOCIAL BASES OF BEHAVIOR

Urie Bronfenbrenner is known for his research and his conceptualization of the importance of the environmental context in influencing children's behavior (Bronfenbrenner, 1979). Bronfenbrenner's writings dealt not only with parent-child and peer dyads but also with the family, classroom, and larger systems. Bronfenbrenner's (1970) book, *Two Worlds of Childhood, USA and USSR,* also showed how peer influence could be wielded by teachers and other school officials as a force for conformity to social rules. Academic departments of the type in which Bronfenbrenner taught at Cornell University are proving to be more important to clinical psychology lately. These departments, formerly labeled as being devoted to "home economics"—in the public's image, shopping, cooking, sewing, and the like—are now being relabeled "human ecology," "social ecology," or "child and family studies," in line with the emphasis of Bronfenbrenner's research and theory. Not a few of them are now training family therapists or child and family therapists as well. The field of clinical psychology as a profession would do well to understand what is happening in these settings, which have now become a part of its ecology as well. (Bronfenbrenner received Section 1's award in 1988.)

## MENTAL RETARDATION AND DEVELOPMENTAL DISABILITIES

Edgar A. Doll was responsible for documenting the relationship between birth injuries and mental retardation (Doll, Phelps, & Melcher, 1932). (Doll was chair of the APA Clinical Section in 1932–1933.) Doll's contributions to the area of the assessment of the retarded are detailed in the next chapter.

SCHIZOPHRENIA

David Shakow, in his doctoral dissertation and related reaction-time studies, clearly demonstrated the attentional problems that keep individuals with schizophrenia from maintaining an adequate "preparatory set." (Shakow was president of Division 12 in 1947–1948 and won its award in 1959. He was the first to win Section 3's Distinguished Scientist award in 1971.) As previously noted, Shakow's name is attached to Division 12's new early career award.

In his APA presidential address on schizophrenia and schizotypy, Meehl (1962) did much to persuade his fellow psychologists of the importance of genetic factors in schizophrenia. Other contributions by him are mentioned in subsequent chapters. (Meehl won Division 12's award in 1967 and that of Section 3 in 1976.)

Sarnoff A. Mednick and his colleagues have been working in Denmark over the last two decades, using large-scale epidemiological methods. There, government recordkeeping tends to be very thorough. This makes the task of researchers who want longitudinal data from the community much easier. It is thus possible to detail the pedigrees of people with schizophrenia, alcoholism, and other such disorders, using data from both hospitals and the community (e.g., Mednick, Parnas, & Schulsinger, 1987). (Mednick received Section 3's award in 1983.)

Robert E. Drake found important practical differences in living preferences among mental patients (Drake & Wallach, 1979). Some indeed said that they preferred their freedom even though this meant the harsh conditions of the street. Others understandably stated a preference for the regular meals, warm bed, and activities provided by a mental hospital. These preferences were significant predictors of prognosis in the sense of likelihood of rehospitalization. (Drake won Section 3's dissertation award in 1980.)


AFFECTIVE DISORDERS

Martin E. P. Seligman at the University of Pennsylvania is one of the few who have been able to draw convincing links between animal models and human psychopathology. Seligman originally carried out research with R. L. Solomon on dogs' reactions to shuttle-box avoidance training, that is, learned helplessness. Analogies were then made both on a hormonal and behavioral level between this and mental depression in humans. A theory of depressogenic attributional style was developed (and revised) to predict which people would be most likely to respond to stress by depressive episodes (e.g., Seligman, 1975). (Seligman will be president of Division 12 in 1994. He won Section 3's award in 1986.)

Original research in suicide prevention was carried out by Edwin S. Shneidman and Norman Farberow, who served as codirectors of the NIMH-funded Los Angeles Suicide Prevention Center (e.g., Shneidman, 1985). Shneidman had done an innovative study based on a large collection of suicide notes. Farberow actually served as a deputy coroner in Los Angeles. Shneidman in 1968 began the journal, *Suicide and Life Threatening Behavior*. (Farberow was president of Division 12 in 1971–1972 and Shneidman was president in 1972–1973. They both won Division 12's award in 1977.)

Another clinical psychologist whose work dealt with the confrontation of death was Herman Feifel (1969; Feifel & Branscomb, 1973). He remarked that dealing with death is a major (perhaps the major) theme of religion and philosophy and of the whole social fabric. He reminded us that fears of death are also a major part of coping with pain, stress, and disease and thus cannot be neglected by any clinician. (Feifel won Division 12's scientific award in 1990.)

## CHILDREN'S AGGRESSIVE BEHAVIOR

Gerald R. Patterson is a pioneer in the direct observation of family interaction. He developed "coercion" theory to conceptualize the role of the family in the development of children's aggressive behavior and did controlled research on behavioral interventions with these children and their families (e.g., Patterson, 1974). (Patterson won Section 1's award in 1987.)

## ATTENTION DEFICIT HYPERACTIVITY DISORDER (ADHD)

Virginia Douglas (1972) made an influential address to the Canadian Psychological Association, entitled "Stop, Look, and Listen." Her research was largely responsible for changing mental health professionals' concept of "hyperactivity" in children to one of "attention deficit disorder." (Douglas received Section 1's award in 1990.)

Russell A. Barkley is also an authority on the topic of ADHD. He and his colleagues carried out research using the drug Ritalin to disentangle the direction of effect in parent–child social interaction. As Ritalin began to normalize the child's behavior, the mother tended to back off in her attempts at control, suggesting that it was abnormal child behavior rather than family discipline that caused the problem originally. Barkley also studied family interventions with ADHD children and adolescents. He wrote several influential professional books on ADHD (e.g., Barkley, 1990) as well as giving hundreds of workshops on the topic. Recently he was elected president of an interdisciplinary, international organization called the Society for Research in Child and Adolescent Psychopathology. (Barkley was president of Section 1 in 1988.)

## DISSENTING VOICES REGARDING RESEARCH

Skeptics of the value of clinical research such as Raush (1974) argued that the usual scientific paradigms were not helpful to practitioners. Raush, who at one time directed the clinical psychology training program at the University of Michigan, believed the solution to this impasse between the profession and the science of clinical psychology required new approaches that broke out of the usual mold. Thus, he voiced more admiration for the writings of Erich Fromm, Abraham Maslow, and Rollo May (1950) than for the work of researchers usually considered to be rigorous scientists. Raush believed that in clinical research, practitioners should be regarded as the producers of ideas and scientists as the consumers, rather than the other way around. Raush (1974) went so far as to state, paraphrasing Eysenck, "there is simply no evidence that traditional research works better than an untreated control group" (p. 681). (Raush received a Division 12 professional award in 1985.) Probably an example of the kind of researcher favored by Raush would be Silvan S. Tomkins, who originally majored in play writing as an undergraduate and got his PhD in philosophy, but was attracted by Henry Murray into psychology, where he contributed greatly to our understanding of human emotional expression, using the TAT and other imaginative methods (Tomkins, 1982). (Tomkins received a Division 12 award in 1971.)

## RESEARCH SUPERVISION

A further, sometimes unsung role is that of research supervisor. By several reports, one of the best of these was E. Lowell Kelly (Fiske, Conley, & Goldberg, 1987). Kelly once said:

> Agree to advise a thesis on any topic you think you are, or can become competent in.... If you have agreed to advise, see the student as often as he or she asks and be prepared for your appointments by reading and thinking about what the student assigns you. (Fiske et al., p. 511)

Among Lowell Kelly's students were Roger Brown, Donald Fiske, and Lewis Goldberg. (Kelly was president of Division 12 in 1959–1960 and received a Division 12 award in 1972.)

# Research and Scholarly Activities: Assessment

F. L. Wells could serve as the prototype of the pre–World War II clinical psychologists whose role was that of expert psychological examiner. He seems to have been the only person who was both certified as a consulting psychologist by APA and later became a diplomate of the American Board of Professional Psychology. Like S. I. Franz, Wells worked for a time at the McLean Hospital. He was later affiliated with the Boston Psychopathic Hospital and then with the Department of Hygiene of Harvard University. Wells was more of a scholar than a researcher. For example, one of his claims to fame was as an interpreter of psychoanalysis to his psychologist colleagues. He was not a psychoanalyst and was careful to maintain a sense of objectivity and nonpartisanship in the many such articles he wrote, beginning in 1912 (Shaffer, 1964). Wells had spent some time in Germany as a child and was fluent in German, which helped in this interpretive task. Wells's handbook of informal mental examination procedures (Wells & Ruesch, 1945) was of great value to clinical psychologists and to those who had to learn hurriedly to become clinicians during World War II. He was not a man of narrow interests, either. One of the items on his curriculum vitae was a letter to the editor of *Science* commenting on the nocturnal habits of spiders (Wells, 1944). (In 1922–1923, Wells was chair of the APA Clinical Section and later served as chair of the APA committee that certified consulting psychologists. He received one of the first Division 12 awards for scientific and professional contributions in 1958.)

## INTELLECTUAL ASSESSMENT

The well-known Porteus Maze Tests came out of the research of Stanley D. Porteus in Australia beginning in 1913. These tests proved to be valuable not only in evaluating a person's "planning ability" and intellectual status but also neuropsychological functioning, and the tests provided a "qualitative score" sensitive to psychopathy as well (Porteus, 1965). Porteus was the director of research at the Vineland Training School following Goddard and preceding Doll. He became known for his cross-cultural research involving Australian aborigines as well as different groups living in Hawaii and in sub-Saharan Africa. (Porteus received Division 12's award in 1962.)

Edgar A. Doll developed the Vineland Social Maturity Scale (Doll, 1935), a measure that was based on an interview with the parent or someone else who knew the patient well. Partly because of the influence of Doll's research, mental retardation is still officially defined as a combination of low intellectual functioning and impaired "adaptive behavior." (Doll was a leader of the APA Clinical Section and its successors for many years, first serving as chair of the Section in 1932–1933.)

One of the early triumphs of applied psychology was the success of its mass testing program for screening military recruits for World War I. Robert Yerkes, partly as a result of his position as president of APA at the beginning of the U.S. involvement in the war in 1917, led the committee that planned and carried out this evaluation. The Army Alpha, the test used for recruits who could read and write, resembled the Binet Scale in terms of its verbal emphasis. The Army Beta, used for illiterate recruits, was more innovative in its use of nonverbal materials. Although the Army Alpha and Beta were group tests, their principles were soon applied to individual testing as well, and verbal tests like the Binet began to be supplemented by various "performance" tests. One psychologist who was ingenious in devising such nonverbal tests materials was Rudolf Pintner. Pintner developed, for example, tests to be used with deaf and hearing- impaired persons. These also lent themselves for use with others who could not easily communicate verbally with a psychological examiner: non-English speakers, aphasics, etc. (Pintner was an elected member of the executive committee of the Clinical Section of APA in 1921–1922.)

David Wechsler published his first intelligence test, the Wechsler-Bellevue, in 1939, the Wechsler-Bellevue II in 1942, the Wechsler Intelligence Scale for Children in 1949, the Wechsler Memory Scale in 1945, and the Wechsler Preschool and Primary Scale of Intelligence in 1967. Among the well-known early innovations introduced by Wechsler was the use of standard scores normed on particular adult and child age groups rather than the ratio IQ used by the early Binet tests. He also provided a varied battery of "performance" tests to supplement the mostly verbal items characterizing the Binet. His practical approach plus the provision of carefully designed norming procedures have kept the Wechsler tests in constant use for an impressive number of years in the absence of any fundamental change in the nature of the tests or the concept of intelligence. The same facts support the view that the field of clinical psychology, like other professions, can be very conservative in terms of its rate of change. (Wechsler was president of Division 12 in 1948–1949.)

## THE WOODWORTH PERSONAL DATA SHEET

The first example of what is now categorized as the self-report personality questionnaire would be the Personal Data Sheet, devised by Robert S. Woodworth in 1917 as a way of screening military recruits in World War I for "neurotic tendency." Woodworth devised these questions rationally on the basis of reading textbooks of psychopathology and did not attempt to validate the test empirically. As previously indicated, Woodworth was a well-known experimental psychologist and was not generally considered to be a clinician. However, he did play a quiet but effective role in founding the the the Society for Research in Child Development (at that time the psychology of child development was considered to be part of applied or clinical psychology). Finally, Woodworth was the faculty member at Columbia University who supervised the doctoral dissertation of Samuel J. Beck on the Rorschach Test. Woodworth was at one point a member of the Clinical Section of APA, but evidently the closest he got to a leadership role in a clinical organization was his membership on the executive committee of the New York State Association of Consulting Psychologists in 1921 (already mentioned in a previous chapter).

## THE RORSCHACH TEST

As is well known, the Rorschach Test, the one in which the examinee responds to 10 cards with ink blots, was developed by psychiatrist Herman Rorschach in Switzerland (Rorschach, 1921). Most of the conventional interpretive hypotheses still used today came directly from Rorschach's original research with these ink blots: the identification of the accurate use of form with good reality testing, of the use of color with affective response, of human movement with fantasy, and the like. Unfortunately, Rorschach died in 1922, well before the full development of the use of his test had occurred.

The first person to use the Rorschach Test in the United States was evidently child psychiatrist David Levy, in New York City, in 1924 (Beck, 1972). Levy taught the use of the test to the psychology trainee Samuel J. Beck, and as already noted Beck did his doctoral dissertation in 1930 at Columbia University on the test. In line with his research training, Beck

(1944, 1945) championed a rigorous scientific approach to the Rorschach. For example, he identified the different "locations" selected on the blots as major or minor details in terms of their statistical frequency of use rather than upon subjective estimates of their size. Similarly, he published statistical tables of responses to the different locations for use in determining "good form" responses. Beck continued research using the Rorschach throughout his career. He was especially interested, for example, in using different types of test responses to characterize different groups of schizophrenic patients. However, at least for many years it appeared that Beck's rigorous scientific approach represented only one of several available alternative approaches in the development of the Rorschach Test, as many practitioners adopted a more informal and intuitive strategy in interpreting projective tests. The Society of Personality Assessment and the University of Chicago have established an award for young investigators named after Samuel Beck. (Beck was president of Division 12 in 1950–1951 and received an award from the division in 1961.)

Another clinical psychologist who was identified with the development of the Rorschach Test was Bruno Klopfer. Klopfer received his PhD from the University of Munich and in 1933 went to Zurich to work with Carl Jung (Klopfer became a Jungian analyst and carried on in this role throughout his career). While he was in Switzerland, Klopfer found employment administering and scoring the Rorschach inkblots, which he had known nothing of before. In fact, it was said that Klopfer did not particularly like this job (Exner et al., 1989). In 1934, when he moved to the United States, Klopfer repeatedly found himself being asked to conduct informal workshops on the Rorschach. At one point he tried to offer an official course on the test in the Department of Psychology at Columbia University but was rebuffed by Robert S. Woodworth there. Teachers College of Columbia and the City University of New York were more receptive, however.

Klopfer coauthored a very influential book on the Rorschach (Klopfer & Kelley, 1942). In contrast to that of Beck, his approach to the test was more intuitive and less quantitative. For example, the rating of individual responses as plus or minus in terms of form quality was a matter of judgment for the examiner rather than referring to some table of norms. Whether the location of a response on the blot was classified as a major or minor detail was also based on the examiner's impression. For many years, Klopfer served as the editor of a journal published by the organization now known as the Society for Personality Assessment. One of the society's awards is now known as the Bruno Klopfer Award. (Klopfer received Division 12's award in 1965.) The journal went through a series of name changes that accurately reflect the changing conceptions of this field: first it was called the *Rorschach Research Exchange*, then the *Journal of Projective Techniques*, then the *Journal of Projective Techniques and Personality Assessment,* and finally the *Journal of Personality Assessment.*

More than clinical psychology itself, Bruno Klopfer, his journal, and the Society for Personality Assessment have seemed to maintain an ambivalent and at times even a hostile relationship with academic psychology. Klopfer never had much use for statistics and quantitative approaches. The papers accepted in his journal were at times the subject of criticisms from such well-known scholars as Lee Cronbach (1949) and Joseph Zubin (1954) for methodological and statistical limitations and frank errors. An experimental paper by Richard Lazarus (a leader in Section 3 of Division 12) showed that what had been called "color shock" by Rorschach workers was not in fact caused by the color of the blots (Lazarus, 1949). The editorial board of the *Journal of Personality Assessment* and its predecessors was, at least at one time, notable for the absence of reviewers associated with universities. For many years there was considerable diversity in the approaches used even in administering and scoring the Rorschach, with some clinicians favoring the Beck method and others the Klopfer approach. The principal writer concerning the psychoanalytic interpretation of the Rorschach, Roy Schafer (1954), seemed if anything to encourage an even more intuitive approach to interpreting test protocols than Klopfer did. (Schafer was a Division 12 Member-at-Large in 1954–1955.)

The Society for Personality Assessment remained an independent group and resisted suggestions that it become either a section of Division 12 or a division of APA. According to a personal communication from George Stricker, a former president of the society, this was perhaps for fear of being somewhat overwhelmed by these larger organizations.

The Rorschach Test in a more standardized form developed by John Exner continues in widespread use by clinical psychologists and in clinical training programs but seems to have all but disappeared from the clinical research literature. Behavioral clinicians in particular have tended to reject the test outright.[1]

## OTHER PROJECTIVE TECHNIQUES

Murray's Thematic Apperception Test (TAT) was and is widely used and has led to many spinoffs and imitations. It was developed by Christiana

---

[1] Perhaps my own experience in graduate school at the University of Pittsburgh was not unusual. We basically had one graduate course in how to use projective techniques, and in another required course they taught us why these procedures were "no good."

Morgan and Henry Murray (1935) (Murray's work was discussed in Chapter 15). No single scoring or interpretive system for the TAT has ever achieved dominance, however. It is thus usually used only as an informal procedure in clinical assessment. Researchers who use TAT-related methods, for example in "psychological anthropology," generally use ad hoc scoring systems developed for the particular study. One well-known Murray student and TAT researcher who has done influential research on affective expression was Sylvan S. Tomkins (1962–63), already mentioned in the previous chapter. (Tomkins won Division 12's award in 1971.)

David Rapaport, a refugee psychologist from Budapest (and a poet) solved the problem of what to do in his career by becoming an expert in projective testing, integrating psychoanalytic theory with psychometric procedures. When Karl Menninger said of David Rapaport that he was probably the best clinical psychologist in the United States, he seemed to be referring mainly to Rapaport's status as a sort of Talmudic scholar of Freud and his skills in psychodiagnosis (Friedman, 1990). In their books on psychological testing published in 1945 and 1946, Rapaport, Gill, and Shafer set the pattern for what is still meant by a "full battery" of psychological tests: the Wechsler Adult Intelligence Test, the Rorschach Inkblot Test, and the Thematic Apperception Test, integrated with a psychoanalytic account of the patient's psychodynamics. Rapaport (1951) went on to write a well-received book, *Organization and Pathology of Thought*. As a therapist, Rapaport worked with some borderline patients primarily in order to study their thought processes and never gained full self-confidence in this role (Gill, 1961). However, it was said not entirely humorously in a Division 12 award citation that Rapaport was able to read more into Freud than Freud would have realized he had written. (Rapaport was secretary of Division 12 beginning in 1946–1947 and received its award in 1960.)

Roy Schafer was Rapaport's colleague at Menninger and later at the Austen Riggs Center in Stockbridge, Massachusetts, and was another of the elected leaders of Division 12 in the immediate postwar years. Unlike Rapaport, Schafer did manage to make it all the way to the "promised land" by becoming a full-fledged psychoanalyst. He is now well known to psychoanalysts (who may or may not be psychologists) for some of his later writings, for example, on the language of psychoanalysis. Schafer once served as the Freud Memorial Lecturer at the University of London. However, as noted above, within clinical psychology, Schafer is perhaps best known for his 1954 book on the psychoanalytic approach to projective testing. His approach was to treat the Rorschach protocol much like a patient's free associations in a psychoanalytic session. He did not, however, carry out formal psychological research on the validity of this procedure, and it continues to appeal mainly to Freudian psychologists. (Schafer was a Division 12 Member-at-Large in 1954–1955.)

Another individual with a widely recognized name in the area of projective testing who was honored by a Division 12 award (in 1980) is Karen Machover, the author of a book on the clinical use of human figure drawings (Machover, 1949). Partly because of Machover's influence, such drawings are among the most commonly used psychological assessment procedures. In 1934, Machover had been one of the organizers of the Psychologists' League, an organization that tried to deal with the problems of unemployed psychologists during the Great Depression. (The league was accused by New York newspapers at the time of trying to "Bolshevize" Bellevue Hospital!) Another psychologist who was a leader and award winner of Division 12's Section 3, Loren Chapman, published with his wife Jean a series of studies on the phenomenon of "illusory correlation," using erroneous interpretations of human figure drawings as a prime example (Chapman & Chapman, 1967). In the Chapmans' research, both clinicians and university undergraduates erroneously believed in the association of aspects of drawings with traits (such as large head size with overconcern with one's intelligence). They persisted in these beliefs even when the data they were shown indicated the lack of valididty of such cues. In honoring both Karen Machover and Loren Chapman, Division 12 and its section acknowledged the diversity in viewpoints within the Division regarding acceptable scientific methodology.

## THE MINNESOTA MULTIPHASIC PERSONALITY INVENTORY

The history of the development of so-called objective personality questionnaires has been more generally considered successful than is the case with the Rorschach and other projective tests. The Minnesota Multiphasic Personality Inventory (recently updated as the MMPI-2 for adults and the MMPI-A for adolescents) is probably the most widely used test of its kind in the world. Its original developers were a clinical psychologist, Starke Hathaway, and physician J. C. McKinley (Hathaway & McKinley, 1940, 1942). They exemplified a degree of interdisciplinary cooperation that is too rare in the mental health field. As Dahlstrom, Meehl, and Schofield (1986) aptly stated:

> With the possible exceptions of Binet and Simon, or Terman and Merrill, it is difficult to name a pair of collaborators in the mental health field who have had as pervasive an impact on the lives of people around the world as that generated by Hathaway and McKinley in their

development of the Minnesota Multiphasic Personality Inventory (MMPI). (p. 835)

Hathaway received a Division 12 award in 1959 and was president of the division in 1963–1964. One thing that was innovative about the MMPI is that its scales were empirically generated and cross-validated. For example, every item on the MMPI Depression Scale (Scale 2) discriminated between a group of psychiatrically identified depressed patients and a "normal" control group consisting of hospital visitors and other conveniently available nonpsychiatric patients. In fact, the original developers of the MMPI manifested what came to be called "dustbowl empiricism" in their statements that they did not really care about the explicit content of a test item as long as it discriminated the criterion group from controls. Surely few test developers would proceed in this way today; like Jane Loevenger, they would now demand that items justify themselves on theoretical grounds as well as empirical ones. In any case, the MMPI was a big success, as shown by how little those who did the MMPI-2 revision were willing to tamper with the original scales. This seems to be another example of the conservative nature of practice in clinical psychology.

Another noteworthy feature of the MMPI was its use of "validity" scales. The L scale was intended to pick up crude or naive attempts to dissimulate but also turned out to be sensitive to highly moralistic attitudes (i.e., the person who claims never to have laughed at a dirty joke is either lying or is highly prudish). The F scale highlighted a pattern of picking statistically infrequent responses, as seen, for example, in persons who were highly confused, psychotic, or who had difficulty in reading the items. The K scale was originally devised simply to improve the discrimination provided by the clinical scales by detecting defensive attitudes, but it turned out to be sensitive to socioeconomic status and, to some extent, genuine psychosocial competence. Again, the success of these validity scales can be judged by the fact that the MMPI-2 has even more of them.

Another eminent clinical psychologist whose name is associated with the MMPI is Paul E. Meehl (he won Division 12's award in 1967). Although contributing greatly to the development of the MMPI, Meehl's work was less test-bound than that of his mentor Hathaway. Like many other psychologists, Meehl had personal reasons in addition to scientific curiosity for being interested in the field. Meehl's father killed himself when Paul was 11 years old, and his mother suffered from many psychosomatic "heart attacks" (Award Citation, *American Psychologist*, 1990, 45, p. 656). Cronbach and Meehl's (1955) classic article on construct validity in psychological tests is still required reading for graduate students and is still being reread by faculty members.

Meehl (1954) became widely known for his writings on clinical versus statistical prediction, that is, for the view that it is difficult to beat a linear regression equation in prediction. Other prominent clinical writers such as Robert R. Holt (associated with the original Menninger group including Rapaport, Schafer, and others) still do not appear convinced. (Holt served as Division 12 president in 1961–1962.) Once more, by honoring persons with such opposite views, Division 12 reveals its own diversity.

## OTHER SELF-REPORT PERSONALITY MEASURES

Janet T. Spence is known as a person trained in clinical psychology who went on to a rigorous scientific career. Early in her work, she developed the manifest Anxiety Scale (MAS) based upon a rational combination of MMPI items. Then she used this as a novel way to define "drive" within Kenneth Spence's theoretical system (Spence & Taylor, 1953). This may have been a radical combination of clinical and experimental psychology, but many of the theoretical hypotheses derived were confirmed by research findings. Studies using the MAS and paradigms from experimental psychology for a time became a major fad in the literature. Even after 20 years, this theory still "refused to die" (Spence, 1971).

Janet Spence herself in the meantime moved on to several other theory-based, productive areas of research involving new assessment procedures, including sex roles and achievement motivation. Professionally, she long served as an effective liaison between clinical and experimental psychology, for example, between APA and such organizations as the Psychonomic Society. She was one of the founders of the American Psychological Society in 1988. (Janet Spence received Division 12's award in 1982.)

Charles Spielberger made his reputation as a researcher by capitalizing on the distinction between "trait" and "state" in the domain of personality assessment. By changing the time period referred to by the items on a questionnaire, one can have an item deal with what is happening at the moment (state), what happens usually (trait), or in between the two extremes. Spielberger devised and validated the well-known State Trait Anxiety Inventory (STAI; Spielberger, Gorsuch, & Lushene, 1970) and more recently a state–trait anger inventory. State anxiety measures usefully tap people's reactions (for example) to brief stressful events such as medical procedures, whereas trait anxiety measures are more sensitive to enduring psychopathology including anxiety. Spielberger is also strong in leadership ability; his work as APA treasurer helped put the organization on a sound financial footing after the *Psychology Today* disaster. Under his leadership as its president, the Society for Personality Assessment multiplied its membership dramatically (Spielberger, 1989). (Spielberger was president of Division 12 in 1989 and won its award in the same year.)

James H. Johnson is known as the coauthor of one of the most widely used "life events" measures of stress in children and adolescents. He also wrote a book on psychological stress in children that has been influential (Johnson, 1986). (Johnson was president of Section 1 in 1986.)

## BEHAVIORAL ASSESSMENT

As part of the behavior therapy movement (discussed in the next chapter), there also was a rise in behavioral approaches to assessment. This was not labeled as personality assessment because of objections to the idea of personality traits. As Rosemery Nelson (1983) commented, behavioral assessment underwent a boom, especially in the 1970s, when some people thought it might replace traditional psychological assessment entirely. Then some disillusion set in as it became apparent that "standard" behavioral measures were difficult to develop, and perhaps not a desirable goal. (Nelson was president of Section 3 in 1979–1980.)

# *Research and Scholarly Activities: Intervention*

As noted in previous chapters, after World War II, clinical psychologists went beyond individual psychological assessment to engage in intervention. Research on clinical interventions, in contrast to that on mental testing, more often obeys the canons of experimental work. The emergence of controlled treatment research therefore conferred greater scientific respectability on the field of clinical psychology at the same time that it expanded its professional scope.

## PSYCHOTHERAPY

Many clinical psychologists after World War II wished to become psychotherapists, but to repeat David Rapaport's (1944) statement, "there [was] still no paved way for a psychologist to become a psychotherapist" (p. 300). Actually, up until World War II, even psychiatrists were often not psychotherapists either (Whitehorn, 1944) but the administrators of mental hospitals, physicians who carried out mental status exams, and so forth. As Shaffer (1947) stated:

> Psychiatry is experiencing the same revolution [as psychology]. We tend to think of all psychiatrists as therapists, but this has not always been so. Until quite recently, most psychiatrists were skilled primarily in diagnosis and institutional care, but now the dominant group in psychiatry has psychotherapy as its main interest. (p. 459)

The arrival of European refugees caused a markedly greater impact of all strands of psychoanalysis upon psychiatry as well as psychology. Thus in the postwar period psychiatrists who wished to be at the forefront of their profession often sought psychoanalytic training during their residency or fellowship training or afterwards. Many of the leading medical school departments of psychiatry sought persons with psychoanalytic training as their chairs.

Paul Meehl is another example of a research clinical psychologist who contributed to the psychotherapy literature as well as to that on psychopathology and assessment. Despite what some might view as its incompatibility with his empirical orientation, Meehl maintained an active practice as a psychoanalytically oriented therapist. Meehl's other writings ranging from law to philosophy of science to religion proved what a genuine polymath he was. Clinical psychologists can regard themselves as lucky that their profession was able to attract such a capable individual. (As already noted, Meehl received Division 12's award in 1967.)

Carl Rogers was the principal pioneer in doing empirical research on psychotherapy. Rogers developed a new type of psychotherapy called at first "nondirective," then "client-centered," and finally "person-centered" therapy. Rogers was the first to do actual electronic recording of psychotherapy sessions so that the details of the therapist–client interaction could be studied. He did psychotherapy outcome and process research at a time when many therapists did not believe that this would ever be possible (Gendlin, 1988). The career of Carl Rogers was important to the field of clinical psychology in two ways. First, he served as a major role model for the clinical psychologist as psychotherapist (Rogers, 1942, 1951). Second, he showed that the roles of therapist and researcher could be integrated. (Rogers headed the Clinical Section of the AAAP in 1941–1942 and received Division 12's award in 1962.)

Hans Strupp was a pioneer in carrying out rigorous psychological research on psychodynamic psychotherapy. He also developed a new form of brief therapy and subjected it to controlled research. (Strupp was president of Division 12 in 1974–1975 and received its award in 1981.)

## BEHAVIOR THERAPY

The developers of behavior therapy included many psychologists. An early clinical study in the behavioral tradition was Mowrer and Mowrer's (1938) development of the "bell and pad" device for treating bedwetting in children. The use of a bell to signal that a child had wet the bed had come from previous work by the pediatrician Pfaundler. The therapeutic efficacy of the device was a serendipitous discovery, which the Mowrers replicated and explained in terms of Pavlovian conditioning principles. In fact, Hobart Mowrer, a psychologist who was respected by nonclinical as well as clinical researchers, found it somewhat deflating to think that he might be remembered in connection with this bedwetting treatment. Parenthetically,

Mowrer will no doubt also be remembered as a psychologist who endured several severe depressions, some requiring hospitalization. His life ended in suicide, but he was an outstanding scientist, clinician, and teacher (Hunt, 1984). (Hobart Mowrer was president of Division 12 in 1952–1953.)

In the heyday of the behavioral revolution within clinical psychology, schizophrenia was one major focus (Bellack, 1986). Token economies were developed by behavioral researchers. Unfortunately, this emphasis has lessened. Nevertheless, the technology of applied behavior analysis has clear applicability to ward management, problems of compliance with psychotropic medication regimens, and day treatment in the community. (Bellack is a coeditor of the *Clinical Psychology Review*, for 5 years an official publication of Division 12.)

## COGNITIVE BEHAVIOR THERAPY

One of the most original scientists ever produced by clinical psychology was George A. Kelly. As is the case for many persons with highly original ideas, it is a little difficult to say where Kelly got them. He was only a graduate student for a single year at the University of Iowa (where he got his PhD), so in effect he may have to be regarded as his own mentor. He went off to teach at the Fort Hayes Kansas State College and set up his own psychological clinic there, so he certainly had no opportunity to be indoctrinated into psychoanalysis or any other existing system. When his most famous book, *The Psychology of Personal Constructs* (Kelly, 1955), was published, this was readily recognized as an important event. Carl Rogers, for example, was asked by *Contemporary Psychology* to serve as a reviewer and recognized the originality of the book, although of course he did not agree with its viewpoint—too cognitive. This review reminded the author somewhat of Ralph Waldo Emerson's comments upon reading Walt Whitman's (1855) *Leaves of Grass*, where he said that this book must have had a "long foreground somewhere" (Emerson, 1855, quoted in Perlman, Folsom, & Campion, 1981, p. 1).

Credit can be given to Kelly for inventing a new psychotherapy and doing research on it (somewhat like Rogers), but his work was more than just a new psychotherapy. He also invented a new assessment device, the Repertory Grid (see Fransella & Bannister, 1977). In addition, it could be said that he pioneered the cognitive approach to therapy before its time, but this may not do Kelly justice. His work may have the potential of outliving present cognitive approaches (this is said with all due respect for Aaron Beck, Donald Meichenbaum, Philip Kendall, Albert Ellis, and others like them).

Kelly placed an emphasis upon how his clients construed the world, and the influence of their thinking upon their psychopathology, defined as unduly limited ability to predict what was going to happen in the world. Besides this, he developed a new approach to conceptualizing human beings as "scientists." Kelly attempted to deal in a rigorous fashion with the ideographic, the "ideoverse" of each person in understanding that person's actions. Naturally, such a theory is appealing to the historian.

Kelly died essentially in midcareer in 1967. He influenced many graduate students. One of these was Lee Sechrest, an expert on research methodology and on the dissemination of scientific knowledge, who served as president of Division 12 in 1985. Not only has Kelly's work not faded away in the quarter of a century since his death. It seems to have inspired the development of a whole new variety of psychology, centered in London and represented by such researchers as Donald Bannister and Fay Fransella. Conferences on personal construct theory have been held all over the world since 1975. Various edited volumes keep emerging in this area. There is also a *Journal of Personal Construct Psychology*, founded in 1988. An article, "Whatever Became of George Kelly?" (Jankowicz, 1987), had to conclude that his influence is still very much alive. (Kelly was president of Division 12 in 1956–1957 and received its award in 1965.)

Peter Lang and A. David Lazovik at the University of Pittsburgh carried out controlled research on Wolpe's (1958) systematic desensitization procedure, using college students with snake phobias as subjects (Lang & Lazovik, 1963). (Lang received Section 3's award in 1980 and the APA Distinguished Scientific Award in 1993.) Another influential experimental study of desensitization as compared with a more traditional "insight" therapy was carried out by Gordon Paul (1966). (Paul won Section 3's award in 1977.)

Albert Bandura's reputation as a researcher began with studies demonstrating the efficacy of modeling as a method of learning (and hence of treating disordered behavior). The modeling principle was demonstrated to be an effective way of helping children to overcome fears, as when a child who is afraid of dogs observes a fearless model interact with a dog. According to this line of research, better yet would be a "coping" model who is initially afraid but then is observed to overcome this fear. Bandura later expanded his "social learning theory" to a "cognitive social learning" one, demonstrating the importance of processes such as attending to the model and mentally rehearsing the behaviors observed. Most recently, Bandura has continued his leadership role in his theory and research on self-efficacy, demonstrating again the clinical relevance of cognitive processes. Bandura is thus a good example of a behaviorist who has profited by joining the so-called cognitive revolution in human experimental psychology (e.g., Bandura, 1977). (Bandura was a member of the original organizing committee of Section 3 and won the section's award in 1977.)

Another influential clinical research psychologist within the cognitive-behavioral area is Richard Lazarus. Lazarus has written influential books on stress, appraisal, and coping (Lazarus, 1966; Lazarus & Folkman, 1984). Some of Lazarus's classic experiments showed that subjects could attenuate even their physiological responses to "horror" pictures by the attitude they took toward them. For example, a detached "scientific" attitude caused pictures of penile subincision rites to produce less fear in observers. (Lazarus was president of Section 3 in 1968–1969.)

## MARITAL AND FAMILY THERAPY

John Elderkin Bell was among the first to carry out conjoint family therapy—working with teenagers and their parents in simultaneous sessions—and to write about his experiences. His monograph on this topic circulated privately for 6 years before finally being published (Bell, 1961). He was among the group in Palo Alto that started the interdisciplinary family therapy movement and its principal journal, *Family Process*.

Neil Jacobson's research has focused on behavioral marital therapy and has involved both controlled experimental studies of treatment outcome (e.g., Jacobson, 1989) and the development of new, higher standards of clinical significance in such research (Jacobson & Revenstorf, 1988). His dialogue with persons such as Alan Gurman has begun to build some lasting bridges between behavioral and more traditional approaches to marital and family therapy. (Jacobson was president of Section 3 in 1987–1988.)

# 18

# *Education and Training: The Boulder Model*

David Shakow lead the way in establishing modern clinical psychology training. In 1945 the Veterans Administration came to the APA, asking for a list of university training programs whose doctoral graduates would make acceptable clinical psychologists. At about the same time, the National Institute of Mental Health announced its plan of supporting graduate training in mental health fields, including clinical psychology. The postwar situation was described by clinical psychologist Jerry W. Carter, Jr. (1950), an NIMH official:

> Mental disorders among veterans accounted for as much as a third of all pensionable disabilities and over one half of hospitalizations in the Veterans Administration. (p. 112)

According to Carter, only about a third of the psychologists in the community services field at that time held the doctoral degree, whereas about 60% of the APA membership did. The requests from the VA and NIMH provided an impetus for the American Psychological Association to set up its apparatus for accrediting doctoral training programs in clinical psychology. (Carter received Division 12's award in 1968.)

Carl Rogers, who was the president of APA at the time, appointed David Shakow as chair of its Committee on Training in Clinical Psychology. The committee issued what became known as the Shakow Report (Report of the Committee, 1947), which the Boulder Conference subsequently endorsed (Hodges & Weatherley, 1990; Raimy, 1950). In other words, Shakow was responsible, more than any other person, for the Boulder model of the clinical psychologist as a scientist–practitioner.

The Conference on Graduate Education in Clinical Psychology was held at the University of Colorado, Boulder, in August, 1949. It was sponsored by the National Institute of Mental Health and was attended by approximately 70 participants (Raimy, 1950). Perhaps a third of these were

123

(at one time or another) among the leadership of Division 12, and many others were leaders in psychology-at-large. The model of clinical psychology training agreed upon at the Boulder Conference aimed at training scientist-practitioners. The didactic and scientific part of the training was already well understood by graduate schools; that is what they had been doing all along. What was less familiar was the attempt to include "experiential" training as well—practica and internships, and to allow students to do research on clinical as well as traditional topics. The Boulder model may also be seen as a historic synthesis between the goals of academicians and clinicians. It let universities accept VA and NIMH training funds to support clinical students, but at the same time permitted them to continue with the research training they preferred to do. This kept the laboratories running but also supported the students while they began to acquire clinically relevant knowledge and skills. Naturally, some friction was inherent in the process, as many students felt themselves being pulled in two directions by their academic and clinical mentors. (Victor Raimy, who chaired the Boulder Conference, was president of Division 12 in 1962–1963.)

Shakow's own training at Harvard, followed by an extensive period working at Worcester State Hospital, culminating in a PhD based on experimental studies of mental patients, became the paradigm for clinical psychology doctoral programs: 2 years of basic academic training, a third year internship in a psychiatric setting, and finally, a dissertation on real clinical problems. (Shakow was president of Division 12 in 1947–1948 and received its award in 1959. He was the first to receive Section 3's award in 1971.)

In 1946 the APA published it first highly tentative list of graduate training facilities in clinical psychology (Sears, 1946), noting which universities offered specialized clinical staff, graduate training in tests and measurement, in therapy and counseling, and supervised practicum facilities. The next published list of training facilities (Sears, 1947) was based on a questionnaire survey. The minimum practicum facilities for a university were then: (a) a "psychiatric facility"—typically connected with a Veterans Administration hospital, (b) a child clinic, and (c) at least one other site. Only 18 universities met all of the APA committee's criteria. The first list of internship facilities was published by APA the next year (Wolfle, 1948).

## PSYCHOLOGY INTERNSHIPS

As noted earlier, psychology internships have been around for a long time, the earliest one at Vineland having been established in 1908 by Henry Goddard. William Healy trained psychology interns at the Juvenile Psychopathic Institute in Chicago, as did Robert M. Yerkes at the Boston Psychopathic Hospital, all before 1915 (Laughlin & Worley, 1991). In 1920, Edgar Doll stated that no one could be regarded as a qualified clinical psychologist without an internship. He considered it just as important as the doctoral degree in psychology. The basic format of such an internship has always been similar—spending a year in full-time clinical work under the direction of experienced supervisors. A persistent minority view in the field has been that internships should be settings where active research is underway as well as the delivery of clinical services.

Before World War II, although there were some schools such as the University of Pennsylvania that offered explicit training programs in clinical psychology, most graduate training was strictly academic, requiring only classwork and supervised research leading to the completion of a doctoral dissertation. Graduate students had to find field training experiences on their own, and it was up to them to decide whether to do an internship. The APA-accreditation procedures set up after World War II began to require an internship. Shakow's model put the internship in the third year so that students could get a deep exposure to clinical issues while they were still in graduate school. Presumably they would go back to their university in the fourth year and ask to be allowed to do research testing some clinical hypothesis (as Shakow himself had done for his PhD at Harvard), rather than doing traditional experimental psychology.

The decision to require students in APA-approved clinical psychology programs to do internships meant that some procedures had to be developed to evaluate the quality of the internships. If the field training site was near the university setting, presumably the psychology faculty could be responsible for monitoring its quality. But for distant internship sites, this often proved impractical. So a separate system for evaluating internships was devised. It included self-study, site visits, and accreditation committee review. The biggest barrier to completing this process was the VA. Because of the high expense of paying site visitors' airfare and hotel expenses, it was only in 1958 that the VA was persuaded to budget such funds and to allow its various facilities to be examined one by one. At present, VA facilities participate in the APA internship accreditation program just like any other hospital or clinic.

After World War II there was considerable demand from psychology training programs for psychiatrists, for example, in the VA system, to supervise psychology interns. This fit the traditional mental health "team" concept and also presumably provided psychologists a way to get psychotherapy supervision when many staff psychologists were not themselves therapists. Subsequently, the pattern of psychologists supervising psy-

chologists has reasserted itself on the theory that, as Samuel Kutash reportedly said, "only cats give birth to kittens" (*Newsletter, Division of Clinical
Psychology*, 1957, 11(2), p. 5). (Kutash was a Division 12 member-at-large in
1955–1956.)

There are now over 150 APA-approved doctoral programs in clinical
psychology and over 400 APA-approved internship programs (see Table
18–1). In the 1950s, the directors of doctoral programs began to meet at the
time of the APA conventions in a group called the Council of University
Directors of Clinical Psychology. Also, in 1968 the internship directors
formed an organization known as the Association of Psychology Internship
Centers (APIC; now changed to the Association of Psychology Postdoctoral
and Internship Centers, or APPIC). The founder of this organization was
clinical psychologist Ronald Fox (who was recognized for this and other
professional contributions by a Division 12 award and, as these words are
written, was elected president of APA).

APPIC publishes an annual directory to serve as a guide to prospective interns, and by the early 1970s worked out a standardized date on
which internship offers are supposed to be made and accepted—the infamous second Monday in February. Despite the addition of "Postdoctoral"
to APPIC's title, there is as yet no formal accreditation of postdoctoral
training. A national conference in Gainesville, Florida, in 1987 proposed
that the internship be made a 2-year process, with the second year being
postdoctoral. However, it is too soon to see whether the proposal will be
fully implemented.

TABLE 18-1. *Growth in Number of APA-Approved
Doctoral and Internship Programs in Clinical
Psychology*

| Year | Doctoral programs | Internships |
|------|-------------------|-------------|
| 1946 | 22 | — |
| 1956 | 45 | 27 |
| 1966 | 71 | 99 |
| 1976 | 107 | 121 |
| 1986 | 147 | 306 |
| 1991 | 173 | 411 |

*Source: American Psychologist.*

Thus, the national system of internships has made considerable progress. But it is not agreed that all is well with internships. Rotter (1973) for one complained about internships' lack of commitment to research. He recommended that psychologists should only do their internships in settings where serious research occurs evaluating what is being done. Certainly, the early internship settings discussed in this book, such as Vineland, the Juvenile Psychopathic Institute in Chicago, the Boston Psychopathic Hospital, and Worcester State Hospital, were all places that were notable for their research and scholarly output as well as for the clinical services they provided. A graduate director of clinical training looks through a fresh group of internship brochures from all over the country every year. In many of them, one cannot recognize a single name of a psychology staff member as having contributed to the research literature, and there is often not a single citation of local research activity. There are exceptions to this generalization. Internship programs such as those at Brown, Duke, Judge Baker Guidance Center, the University of Mississippi, the University of Pittsburgh, UCLA, and the University of Washington, Seattle, come to mind as having psychology staff who are highly visible in producing research. Graduate students who read internship brochures recognize this fact, but some of them may feel that they have had quite enough exposure to research already at their university. These students prefer to escape into what they regard as the "real world" where clinical services are provided but not formally evaluated. The modern university medical center in a large city contains an incredible wealth of scientific as well as professional resources, if they can only be harnessed for the benefit of the psychology trainee. For example, Ivan Mensh (who was president of Division 12 in 1965–1966) mentioned to the author that when he was chief psychologist at the UCLA Neuropsychiatric Institute, the adjunct faculty there amounted to about 1,000 individuals.

## FURTHER COMMENTS ON THE BOULDER MODEL

It is evident from the material already discussed in this chapter that beginning shortly after World War II, clinical psychology went from being a field with extremely fluid boundaries to one that was better defined. Then (at least in theory) a clinical psychologist could be described as a person who had a doctoral degree from an APA-approved graduate program in clinical psychology, including a 1-year predoctoral internship, and was licensed to practice in a particular state or province. Such licensure laws typically required 2 years of supervised professional experience, and the predoctoral internship was allowed to count for one of these. Having a doctoral degree, such an individual was trained in the basic content of psychology and had demonstrated the ability to carry out independent research. Having an internship and supervised postdoctoral experience, the clinical psychologist would presumably be competent to do intellectual evaluations and personality assessment as well as to do psychotherapy or other interventions. Five years after receiving the doctoral degree (the scenario continues), the competent clinical psychologist would be expected to attain, and deserve, an ABPP diploma in clinical psychology.

Obviously, the above idealized portrait was not the reality. The Boulder-model (scientist–practitioner) clinical psychologist was described in 1949 as the kind of person the profession wished to train. However, it was obviously going to be quite a number of years before many such graduates were available. In the meantime, where were the universities supposed to go for faculty to teach clinical courses and to supervise practicum work? Where were the internship agencies supposed to find clinical psychologists capable of high-level supervision of therapy as well as assessment? How were licensing boards (as they came "on line" beginning in 1945) supposed to decide who was competent to practice? As Molly Harrower (1948) remarked at the time, "there are no uniformly trained clinical psychologists in the sense that we have doctors, lawyers, dentists, or educators" (p. 23). (Harrower received an award from Division 12 in 1980.)

True, there were a few thoroughly competent individuals such as F. L. Wells and David Shakow around, but for many years most who were available would have patched together their own academic and clinical training programs the best way they could. It had to be a sort of bootstrap operation in which training institutions used what people they had and tried gradually to improve what they offered.

Disillusion with the Boulder model began to set in quite early. Seymour Sarason, who was one of the psychologists at the Boulder conference, argued at the time that the conference was taking the wrong tack. He subsequently wrote about this extensively (Sarason, 1988), saying that it was a mistake for clinical psychology to separate itself artificially from its work with children and in community settings such as schools, and a mistake to use psychiatry as its role model. Sarason had spent some formative professional years working with the mentally retarded, and during his time at Yale was the founder of the Yale Psychoeducational Clinic, which had a strong community orientation.

It rapidly became apparent that many clinical psychologists despite their training in "Boulder model" programs did not go on to do research beyond the dissertation. In fact, their modal number of publications was zero (Levy, 1962). This was especially likely to be true of those who worked in strictly clinical settings, where there were no demands for research from either their employers or their clients. In retrospect, it is not clear why this should have been a surprise. After all, many individuals trained as experimental psychologists have ended up at small colleges with heavy teaching loads and no support for research, and they tend not to publish, either (Routh, 1982).

A second complaint about Boulder-model training, coming from the practitioner side of the field, was that some of the universities did not take clinical practicum training sufficiently seriously. This may have been a problem especially in the case of universities located in small, semirural communities without easy access to clinical facilities.

E. Lowell Kelly, a Division 12 president, did extensive longitudinal research on a postwar cohort of clinical psychologists who were VA trainees and found that after a number of years many of them were not very pleased with their career choice. Most of them said they would go into some other field besides clinical psychology if they had it to do over again (Kelly & Goldberg, 1951, 1959).

Some major private universities, Cornell, Dartmouth, and Princeton, for example, were never interested in doctoral programs in clinical psychology. They wished to train only academic/research psychologists. Other such private universities (often the ones located in large cities rather than in semirural settings) were involved in clinical training for a time but later decided that the training funds available were not worth the distortion of their preferred academic emphasis. The Department of Psychology at Columbia University is a case in point. Robert S. Woodworth, as an influential faculty member at Columbia, probably had a role in steering that department away from further involvement in training clinical psychologists (Thorne, 1976). When APA-accredited training programs became possible after World War II, this department did not seek to develop one, and an APA-accredited clinical program at Teacher's College, Columbia developed instead. In any case, Columbia University was the leading institutional origin of fellows in clinical psychology right up into the 1980s (Robyak & Goodyear, 1984). A similar story could be told of Harvard, the University of Chicago, and Stanford. Their psychology departments seem quite willing to train what might be called experimental psychopathologists or clinical scientists but without providing the more standardized curriculum, practicum training, and internships necessary for an APA-approved program. Their graduates have still been able to find positions in universities and research institutes. They have often won grant support for their research. Thus, many of them have been ultimately accepted into Division 12 and similar organizations on the basis of their research contributions to the field.

Those graduates who later decided that they needed clinical training after all were often able to get it informally by some "back-door" route, that is, a postdoctoral internship, even though they did not have all of the previous relevant coursework and practicum training. However, in 1976, the APA Council tried to close the door on such attempts. The new APA rules specified that people who wished to change their professional specialty (for example, from experimental to clinical psychology) could do so only by going back to graduate school, taking all the required coursework and practicum experiences, and then obtaining a regular internship. Division 12's membership rules soon followed suit. Persons trained in academic psychology after 1976 were expected to undergo formal graduate retraining in clinical psychology before they could be accepted into the division. (Exceptions were still made, however, for persons regarded as having made significant research contributions to clinical psychology.)

One can, of course, find examples of clinical psychologists who appear to be strongly committed to both practice and research and thus exemplify the Boulder model. One such is Norman Abeles. Though Abeles graduated from a counseling psychology program and is an ABPP diplomate in counseling psychology, he is also a Fellow of Division 12. He runs a psychology clinic in the Department of Psychology at Michigan State University, a position requiring continuing clinical involvement. In addition, Abeles maintains a research program concerned both with psychotherapy and neuropsychological assessment. He served as editor of *Professional Psychology: Research and Practice* beginning in 1983. (Abeles was president of Division 12 in 1990.)

Also, it could be argued that the government got its money's worth when it supported the training of clinical psychologists. Nicholas Hobbs made this argument convincingly when he testified before Congress (*American Psychologist*, 1963, *18*, 295–299), presenting data that during 1947–1959, over 90% of the approximately 1,000 NIMH trainees had gone either into public sector service or university faculty positions.

Many psychology departments that became involved in formal clinical psychology training after the Boulder Conference must have been satisfied with the compromise between academic and clinical values involved. The evidence for this is that they have continued their scientist–practitioner clinical training up to the present even after government training grants became much more difficult to obtain. Probably this statement is true of most of the psychology departments in state universities.[1]

---

[1] At least I judge this to be true from my experiences at both the University of Iowa and the University of North Carolina.

# Education and Training: The Practitioner Model

Physicians and lawyers existed long before medical schools and law schools developed. The traditional method of training in these professions was through apprenticeship to a practitioner. Even when formal education began in these fields, most students aimed to go into practice rather than to be scientists, scholars, or professors. Psychology reversed this sequence in that the academic field came first and the practice later. The explicit training of practitioners in psychology occurred only after a struggle, one in which several Divison 12 leaders were involved.

## The Idea of a Doctor of Psychology Degree

As early as 1938, A. T. Poffenberger suggested the possibility of a new type of professional degree for clinical psychologists, which he labeled as a PsD. After World War II, Harvard University appointed a commission, headed by physician Alan Gregg (1947) of the Rockefeller Foundation and a number of other prominent persons (only a few of whom were psychologists) to try to resolve the issue of the place of psychology in an ideal university. Over the objections of all its psychologist members, the commission's recommendation was that there should be two types of training in psychology, one the traditional scientist, a PhD, and the other a new type of professional with a new degree, the PsyD or doctor of psychology. Both degrees were recommended to be given by the Department of Psychology in the Faculty of Arts and Sciences. However, Harvard rejected the commission's plan. The Harvard Department of Psychology had existed separately from the Department of Philosophy only since 1934. After World War II, it divided into two units, one still called the Department of Psychology but consisting only of biologically oriented faculty such as Karl Lashley. The other unit was called the Department of Social Relations and included such areas as personality and social psychology and the faculty associated with the Harvard Psychological Clinic, for example, Henry Murray. Both departments offered the PhD degree.

In Canada, at least one university, the University of Montreal (a French-language institution), began a professionally oriented PsyD program rather early on, and it seemed to work satisfactorily, but this was done without much fanfare and had little effect on the field at large.

## THE PROGRAM AT ADELPHI

In the United States, a pioneer in developing a practitioner-oriented doctoral program in psychology was Gordon Derner (Stricker, 1985). Derner was a graduate of Teachers College, Columbia University, and had undergone advanced training in psychoanalysis at the William Alanson White Institute in New York. When Derner became a faculty member at Adelphi College, it had only an undergraduate program in psychology. Before he was through with his work there, there was a PhD program in clinical psychology and also a postdoctoral program in psychotherapy and psychoanalysis involving many different part-time faculty who lived and practiced in the New York area. Even though Derner developed a program offering a PhD, it aimed mainly to train practitioners rather than researchers (the program also had a separate research training track). Derner labeled his clinical program as one designed to train "scholar–practitioners," in other words, persons capable of understanding the scientific literature and making use of it in their practice but not expected to do research themselves. Doctoral dissertations could therefore be theoretical formulations or psychohistories and did not have to be projects based on data collection and statistical analysis. This program began in 1951, and Derner worked to try to get it approved by the APA. He was told by various people that he was 20 years ahead of his time and would not be able to do so.

To make a long story short, Derner finally did get his program approved in 1957—on appeal, and after a battle. The response from people in Division 12 to this event ranged from enthusiastic to hostile; but enough clinical psychologists liked Derner's ideas that he served as president of the division in 1975–1976. Derner was also the founding president of the National Council of Schools of Professional Psychology (NCSPP). Despite disclaiming the goal of training scientist practitioners, Derner produced at least one student who became an eminent clinical scientist, Paul Ekman, who helped to bring the study of facial expression back into scientific fashion (e.g., Ekman & Friesen, 1978). After Derner's death, his program at Adelphi was named in his honor. George Stricker, a subsequent president of Division 12, later served for a time as the dean of the Derner Institute at Adelphi. Following Derner's lead, Stricker (1973) has also endorsed—and implemented—the argument that doctoral dissertations in psychology might consist of theoretical formulations or psychohistories and not only traditional empirical studies.

In 1968, Donald Peterson, the director of Clinical Training at the University of Illinois (not, however, a person who was ever in a leadership role in Division 12), and Lloyd Humphries, the Department Chairman there, introduced a new PsyD program, the only one of its kind in the United States at that time. The PsyD students were to have classwork as rigorous as that of their fellow students who were working for a PhD, but instead of doing research-based dissertations, they spent more time in practicum work and submitted a final document focusing more on a clinical demonstration project instead. Peterson wrote widely about this new venture and produced data showing that these PsyD graduates were well accepted by employers and by clients. Nevertheless, this approach appeared to be incompatible with the academic values of most Illinois psychology faculty and was soon discontinued.

## THE CALIFORNIA SCHOOL OF PROFESSIONAL PSYCHOLOGY

Next the story shifts to California, where the existing APA-approved clinical psychology programs (for example, at Berkeley and UCLA) produced only a small number of PhD clinical psychology graduates each year, albeit persons with excellent research training who were generally well prepared to compete for academic/clinical jobs. The California Psychological Association (CPA) became aware of a large number of individuals, many of them with master's degrees and extensive clinical experience, who could not get into such a research-oriented PhD program in clinical psychology. The CPA lobbied the state government to get the University of California to increase its production of clinical psychologists. As reported by observers within the CPA, there was instead an actual decrease in such graduates!

Next, several theological seminaries in California, for example, Fuller and Rosemead, began professional psychology training programs. Then the CPA took action on its own. In 1969, under the leadership of Nicholas Cummings and with the cooperation of many CPA members, some of whom served as faculty members for a time without pay, the California School of Professional Psychology (CSPP) was founded, with campuses in Los Angeles, Berkeley/Alameda, San Diego, and elsewhere (Dorken, 1975). The influence of Adelphi as a model for this activity was evident in that

Cummings was an Adelphi PhD. However, the CSPP campuses ultimately offered the PsyD as well as the PhD degree. Once more, there was a battle for APA accreditation, again a successful one. The CSPP even received an NIMH training grant, further evidence of its respectability. Also, as the number of professional programs began to grow, they banded together into the new organization mentioned above, the NCSPP. The California School of Professional Psychology set certain other precedents as well. At least at first, all of its faculty were part-time, hired on contracts. In other words, there was no full-time or tenured faculty.

## PROFESSIONAL SCHOOLS IN STATE UNIVERSITIES AND TRADITIONAL PRIVATE UNIVERSITIES

Many other states have followed suit. The state psychological association in New Jersey considered sponsoring a free-standing (non-university-affiliated) school of professional psychology (independent of any university). Instead, it was able to persuade Rutgers, the State University of New Jersey, to sponsor what is perhaps the most influential of the professional schools yet—the Graduate School of Applied and Professional Psychology (GSAPP) at Piscataway (offering PsyD degrees in clinical and school psychology).

Bernard N. Kalinkowitz tried unsuccessfully to start a PsyD program at New York University, perhaps the largest producer of clinical psychologists in the United States. In 1961, Kalinkowitz had founded the NYU Postdoctoral Program in Psychotherapy and Psychoanalysis, which he directed until his death in 1992. This was the first program to give comprehensive training in each of the different psychoanalytic orientations. Kalinkowitz, himself a graduate of NYU and of the William Alanson White Institute, urged training programs to supplement their emphasis on research and scholarship by also seeking excellent practitioners as faculty. He asked, "Is it fantasy to expect a major university to award a psychologist with ten years of superior professional experience an Associate Professorship with tenure in a clinical training program—even if the professional is part-time?" (Kalinkowitz, 1978, p. 4). (Kalinkowitz won Division 12's award in 1978.)

Similarly, the Ohio Psychological Association under the leadership of Ronald Fox successfully lobbied the state legislature to create a school of professional psychology at Wright State University. In discussing how this was carried out, Fox stressed the importance of political savvy (Fox, 1986). Members of the network set up by the Ohio Psychological Association spoke informally with many different legislators, supported their campaigns, and successfully elicited their help. Officials at Wright State University supported the professional school because it would permit their university to offer a doctoral degree, which up to that time it had not been allowed to do. At legislative hearings, Fox said he found it amusing to listen to academic psychologists from other universities in the state presenting "only" rational arguments in their testimony—at a time when the state psychological association forces already had their support firmly lined up and were at the point of "counting heads." The reader of Fox's words is made to realize that practitioner psychologists have a grass-roots political network that is beyond any force that could be mounted by academicians, at least at the state level.

Robert Weitz, a New Jersey clinical psychology practitioner for many years, helped found the Graduate School of Applied and Professional Psychology at Rutgers. He was also the leader of a group that founded a school of professional psychology in Miami in 1977. This program was later taken over by a private university—Nova—in Ft. Lauderdale. Thus, there are many examples of recognition provided by Division 12 for advocates of practitioner-oriented training. (Weitz won Division 12's professional award in 1987.)

## THE VAIL CONFERENCE

It is therefore easy to see in retrospect why the national conference held in Vail, Colorado in 1973 succeeded in legitimizing practitioner-oriented training programs in psychology (Korman, 1974, 1976), despite the vigorous objections of academics. In fact, since that time these professional schools have begun to turn out almost as many graduates as the Boulder-model programs. A recent sign of the times may be seen in the appointment of the former dean of one of the campuses of the California School of Professional Psychology—Joann Callan—as the head of the new Education Directorate of the APA. In the view of the academic/research community, this might be seen as a case of the fox guarding the chicken house.

At present there are two separate organizations of educators of clinical psychologists. One is called the Council of University Directors of Clinical Psychology and is dominated by faculty associated with traditional Boulder-model programs. The other is the NCSPP mentioned above and is more oriented toward training practitioners.

# Credentials for Practitioners
## ABPP, Licensing, and the National Register

From their beginnings in 1917, clinical psychology organizations wanted some means by which competent professionals in their field could be identified by the public, some way they could be easily distinguished from quacks and charlatans. As previously described, the plan of having APA certify "consulting psychologists" had to be abandoned in 1927. After World War II, one important event in this domain was the development of the American Board of Examiners in Professional Psychology (ABEPP— later simply ABPP, the word "examiners" being dropped from the board's title). Other such events included the development of state licensing, of the *National Register of Health Service Providers in Psychology*, and the continuing discussions of "the master's issue."

## THE AMERICAN BOARD OF PROFESSIONAL PSYCHOLOGY

The first postwar attempt by psychology to set professional standards was to develop specialty certification by an independent board conceived as analogous to the boards of various medical specialties. It is of some interest in this respect that the American Board of Psychiatry and Neurology had been first set up in 1934 to provide board certification to psychiatrists. When the independent American Board of Examiners in Professional Psychology (ABEPP) was developed by APA in 1947, there was cheering from Division 12. As might be expected, the first group of ABEPP Diplomates in clinical psychology included a number of names of Divison 12 leaders: Stark R. Hathaway, George A. Kelly, Jean W. Macfarlane, Carl R. Rogers, David Shakow, F. L. Wells, David Wechsler, and Joseph Zubin (*American Psychologist*, 1948, 3, p. 184). When Division 12 first began to give out its awards for contributions to the science and profession of clinical psychology, in 1958, one of the first ones went to John G. Darley (even though he was a counseling psychologist rather than a clinical one). The reason was simply that Darley had served as one of the first officers of ABEPP. Another such award later went to clinical psychologist Noble H. Kelly, who for over 20 years headed the board and who was known as "Mr. ABEPP."

When it first began its work, ABEPP allowed well-established professionals to receive its diploma in clinical psychology through a "grandfather" clause, whereas less experienced ones could do so only by examination. Although these "grandfather" board diplomas were still available only up until 1949, several hundred clinical psychologists received them. Then the number of new diplomates per year of ABEPP (ABPP) went down. (Perhaps this should not be considered surprising.) Moreover, the total number of living ABPP diplomates in clinical psychology never quite reached 2,000 and has been decreasing slightly from year to year during the past decade. It is not entirely clear why the initial wave of enthusiasm for ABPP leveled off, but many clinical psychologists of acknowledged competence have not sought such a diploma. As noted previously in this book, others at Division 12 and section board meetings have called for more serious research on the validity of the ABPP examination as an index of clinical competence.

## STATE AND PROVINCIAL LICENSING

A more conventional way of indicating to the public that a person who offers a service is competent to do so is the mechanism of certification or licensing by a state or provincial government. Physicians and lawyers are licensed for this reason, and so are barbers and plumbers. The usual distinction between certification and licensing—not always maintained consistently—is that certification protects the "title" of an occupation, whereas licensing covers the actual duties of the occupation. Thus, a certification law might specify which individuals could call themselves psychologists, whereas a licensing law would specify which persons were qualified to offer specific types of psychological services to the public.

The first psychology licensing law in the United States was passed in Connecticut in 1945 (Heiser, 1945), and the next one soon afterwards, in 1946, in Virginia—the Virginia law actually applied to "clinical" psychologists (Buck, Finley, Spelt, Rymarkiewiczowa, & Finger, 1946), but most such laws are generic, referring to many kinds of psychology and a variety of psychological services. In 1947 the first meeting of the Conference of State Psychological Societies was held in Detroit. Obviously, an important item on its agenda must have been licensing laws. By 1977, with the passage of a psychology licensing law in Missouri, all states in the United States were covered by such laws. Occasionally one of these state laws is at least temporarily nullified due to the use of "sunset" procedures by legislatures, but so far every time this has happened, the psychology licensing law has eventually been put back into force.

Probably the fiercest battle that was fought in passing a state psychology licensing law was that in New York. Getting such a law passed required a coalition to be formed among the many competing psychology organizations in New York and overcoming the opposition of the psychiatric community. In 1951 the New York legislature passed a licensing bill only to have the legislation vetoed by Governor Dewey because it was opposed by the psychiatrists. But even in New York a psychology licensing law was ultimately passed. Molly Harrower (who received Division 12's award in 1980) chaired the New York State Joint Council of Psychologists, which coordinated efforts leading to this licensing law. Florence Halpern also played an important role in the New York battle.

The state psychology licensing laws are generally enforced by a board consisting of psychologists and public members appointed for this purpose. In 1961 a national organization of these psychology boards was formed (Carlson, 1978), and this was later enlarged to include Canadian provinces. The current name of the umbrella organization is the Association of State and Provincial Psychology Boards (ASPPB). The group meets annually, usually in connection with the APA convention, and publishes its own journal, *The Professional Practice of Psychology*. Arthur Wiens has been influential in the development of ASPPB and in establishing its journal. (Wiens was president of the Society of Pediatric Psychology—later Section 5 of Division 12—in 1972–1973 and received its award in 1980.)

Although Division 12 was naturally in favor of the licensing of psychologists, it was not in a favorable position to do very much about it directly. The political action and lobbying activity involved in getting such legislation through naturally had to go on at the state and provincial level, and a national group like Division 12 could only provide consultation or just stand on the sidelines and cheer.

## THE NATIONAL REGISTER

A related development was the emergence of the *National Register of Health Services Providers in Psychology* in 1975 under the leadership of Carl Zimet. Zimet also directed the *Register* board for 12 years. The *Register* met a need of insurance companies and other third-party payers. It furnished a list of psychologists who were trained to provide "health services" including individual psychologicial assessment and psychotherapy. This was necessary precisely because state and provincial licensing laws were generic, including industrial psychologists and others who did not usually deal with individuals as clients. To be listed in the *Register*, a psychologist had to have a doctoral degree in psychology, an internship, and at least 2 years supervised experience in a "health setting." (Zimet received Division 12's award in 1981.)

## THE "MASTER'S ISSUE"

One policy issue frequently addressed by the Division was the level of professional required for licensing, for example the master's degree or the doctorate. Clinical psychologists, at least partly because of their awareness that an important part of their "competition" consisted of psychiatrists (who are MDs), have almost universally favored the licensing only of psychologists with doctoral degrees. The only notable Division 12 leader who seems to have favored master's-level licensing was Nicholas Hobbs, and the rationale for his views reveals much about him as well as about the issues involved.

Nicholas Hobbs together with Lloyd Dunn set up an unusual program in psychology, special education, and mental retardation research at George Peabody College for Teachers (Peabody is now part of Vanderbilt University) in the 1950s and obtained support for it from the National Institute of Mental Health. Hobbs thus had the wisdom and the good fortune to become involved in this area before its boom years under President John F. Kennedy. After that time, Peabody probably trained more behavioral scientists (including clinical psychologists) to do research on mental retardation than any other program in the world. Hobbs went on to become the provost of Vanderbilt, the president of APA, and received many awards from his colleagues. The Peabody campus today has both a John F. Kennedy Center and a Nicholas Hobbs Laboratory of Human Development.

Hobbs was also what we would today call a clinical child psychologist who developed innovative programs for dealing with the problems of children with emotional and behavioral problems, called "Re-Ed" (Hobbs, 1966). He set up Re-Ed schools in Tennessee and North Carolina that still operate and with Laura Weinstein engaged in NIMH-supported controlled outcome research (regrettably, still unpublished) on the efficacy of this approach.

The versatility of Hobbs's involvement in policy issues can be illustrated by various other examples. He set up assessment procedures for selecting and placing Peace Corps volunteers. He was also the person who chaired the committee that devised the Ethical Standards of the American Psychological Association, adopted in 1952 by the council. His idea was that a statement of ethical principles should be based on real-life experience rather than merely a set of theoretical principles. Using Flanagan's (1954) critical incident technique, Hobbs therefore sought out survey data on actual ethical dilemmas that psychologists confronted and how they dealt with these (Hobbs, 1948).

To return to Nicholas Hobbs's views on the "master's issue," he was most aware that especially in the public sector most human services workers do not have doctoral degrees and perhaps given the limitations in taxpayer support could never be expected to achieve such a level of training. In addition to master's-level "psychologists," they include teachers, case workers, nurses, probation officers, rehabilitation counselors, psychometricians, and many others. Many such workers indeed have master's degrees either in psychology or some related area of the behavioral and social sciences or education. Such persons do important work and indeed probably provide most of the human services delivered by the government. Should all of them then be excluded from professional status as psychologists? Hobbs thought not. (Hobbs was president of Division 12 in 1960–1961 and received its award in 1966.)

Perhaps the most important constituency in psychology to oppose the requirement of a doctoral degree for licensure has been the school psychologists, for whom the master's or specialist's degree has become the main entry level for employment (mostly in the public sector). It is sometimes said that school psychology "stayed home" in the professional territory first staked out by clinical psychology, that is, work with children, concern with mental retardation, and academic problems, whereas clinical psychology "left home" in order to cohabit with psychiatry. It is no accident that (as previously mentioned) it is now Division 16, the Division of School Psychology, not Division 12, that offers a "Lightner Witmer Award" as a form of early career recognition.

Another psychologist besides Hobbs who lamented the separation of school and clinical psychology was Seymour Sarason, who has written at length criticizing the "asocial" and "misdirected" path he considered clinical psychology to have taken. Sarason also contributed in major ways to the psychology of mental retardation, for example, the book by Sarason, Gladwin, and Masland that set the stage for a renaissance of research in this area in the 1960s. (Sarason received Division 12's award in 1969 and was president of the Division in 1979–1980.)

A marked contrast to the situation in school psychology is provided by another public sector activity, the Veterans Administration (VA; now the cabinet-level Department of Veterans Affairs). Under the leadership of its chief psychologist Harold Hildreth from 1948 to 1956 (not to be confused with Gertrude Hildreth, no relation), the VA from very early on required individuals to have the doctoral degree in order to take positions as staff clinical psychologists. This was certainly the direction in which most of Division 12 wanted to see the government go. Division 18—Psychologists in Public Service—has named its principal award after Harold Hildreth. (Besides his work for the VA, Hildreth went on to become a research administrator for the National Institute of Mental Health. There his work played a critical role in supporting the clinical research of such psychologists as Evelyn Hooker, who pioneered a demonstration of the psychological "normality" of gay men; and Edwin Shneidman, who studied suicide and its prevention.) (Hildreth was president of Division 12 in 1954–1955 and received its award posthumously in 1966.)

In conclusion, most of Division 12 has always thought that the doctoral degree should be required to obtain professional credentials in clinical psychology. But there were some dissenters from the majority view.

# 21

# The Economics of Psychological Services: The Public Sector

In the earliest years of their profession, most clinical psychologists worked for universities, for public school systems, or perhaps for state or private institutions for the retarded or mentally ill. Economic issues were more the problems of these employing institutions than those of their employees, professional or not. These psychologists working in the nonprofit or public sector of the economy felt (perhaps naively) that they did not have to be preoccupied with where the money for their work came from. Also, because they were generally not administrators or policymakers, they were not the ones who determined whether mental health services were delivered comprehensively to people in need of them.

Universities have continued to obtain their income mostly from tuition, from state appropriations, and from endowment funds. The clinical psychologist who is a liberal arts faculty member is still not very directly involved with any of these funding sources. This statement would presumably apply to Lightner Witmer, the founder of clinical psychology. At least there has been little discussion of the fees charged by his clinic. To provide a more recent example, Carl Rogers (1974), the most prominent leader of the field of clinical psychology after World War II, once remarked that though he had done psychotherapy much of his life, he never had to support himself from fees for his services. When he worked for Ohio State or the University of Chicago, the counseling services were offered free to undergraduates as part of general student services. Of course, the schizophrenic patients Rogers studied at the University of Wisconsin were in a state hospital and were generally indigent and not required to pay for therapy. Rogers therefore earned extra income mostly from his books, not his psychotherapy.

## STATE INSTITUTIONS FOR THE MENTALLY ILL AND
## MENTALLY RETARDED

Aside from those in hospitals for military veterans, the severely mentally ill probably have never had much access to the services of psychologists. Jules Holzberg (1952) wrote about the practice of psychology in one state mental hospital. For 79 years after the founding of that particular institution (Connecticut State Hospital), there had been no psychologists there. Psychometric testing of a routine nature had been carried out by nonpsychologists. Even after 1946 (when the first psychologist was appointed), the psychology staff was miniscule in relation to the size of the patient population. (Jules Holzberg was president-elect of Division 12 in 1972–1973, though he did not live to serve as president.)

The development of neuroleptic drugs beginning with Thorazine in the 1950s initiated a process in which there was a vast decline in the census of state mental hospitals. The new community mental health centers that came along in the 1960s were supposed to take care of the chronically mentally ill but were not given the funds to do so effectively. Thus, many people with severe or chronic mental health problems simply ended up on the street—as homeless persons—or in nursing homes where they were rarely seen by professionals knowledgeable about mental health issues. The most effective advocacy for this group came, not from psychology or any mental health discipline, but from the families of the patients. The National Alliance for the Mentally Ill (NAMI) organized itself and effectively lobbied the NIMH and other government agencies to act in behalf of their family members. Indeed, the NIMH training grants that remain available are targeted to certain priority populations of underserved persons, for example, people with severe and persistent mental health problems.

Like mental hospitals, institutions for the mentally retarded have over the last several decades discharged the majority of their residents. Now the emphasis is on "normalization," community care, and attention to family issues. It cannot be said that APA or (Division 12) has been effective in advocacy for these people, at least not lately. As noted already, psychologists did much better at this in Nicholas Hobbs's generation (e.g., the 1960s). The most effective advocacy for the mentally retarded in more recent years has come from parents' groups such as the Association for Retarded Children (later called the Association for Retarded Citizens, and still more recently, simply the ARC), and The Association for the Severely Handicapped (TASH). Part of the problem is that most of the psychologists who provide services to the mentally retarded are persons with master's degrees rather than doctoral degrees—these days they are often involved in either assessment or in applied behavior analysis—"behavior modification."

Most are not eligible to become members of Division 12, if indeed they wished to join it. Actually, there is another APA division (Division 33) devoted to mental retardation and developmental disabilities, and there are organizations outside APA such as the Association for Behavior Analysis (ABA) that are much more receptive to the needs of these service providers than is Division 12.

## SEVERELY EMOTIONALLY DISTURBED (SED) CHILDREN

Still another neglected public sector group is children in the category of "severely emotionally disturbed" (SED). This category has been hard to define precisely. It includes many children who are involved with the special education system (in classes for the emotionally disturbed), the child welfare system (physically abused, sexually abused, neglected, or in foster care because of family dysfunction or breakdown), or the juvenile justice system (emotionally disturbed or dependent offenders). This heterogeneous group is also a priority in terms of NIMH training grants, but at least the two Division 12 "child" sections seem to be involved in advocacy for them.

## ETHNIC AND RACIAL MINORITY CLIENTS

An additional NIMH priority (for training funds) at present is ethnic and racial minorities. There has been much recent discussion in the media about the problems of minorities, especially in the inner city. For example, the Rodney King disturbances in Los Angeles in 1992 highlighted the problems of poverty, racism, violence, and the destruction of property. Newspaper readers have learned that young African-American males are more likely to go to prison than to college and that this group's most severe public health problem is the threat of violence. According to those concerned with the public sector, this is exactly the sort of problem to which psychologists need to pay attention.

## VETERANS AFFAIRS TRAINING FUNDS

A previous chapter described the massive amount of federal funding that went into the training clinical psychologists after World War II. In providing these funds, the U.S. Congress naturally had the expectation that the individuals trained would benefit the public mental health, in this case by serving in Veterans Administration Hospitals.

However, the most receptive APA "home" for psychologists currently employed by the Department of Veterans' Affairs may be Division 18 (Psychologists in Public Service) rather than Division 12.


## THE PREVENTION MOVEMENT

George Albee has long been an advocate for the involvement of clinical psychologists primarily in the public sector. Relatively early in his career, he carried out a study of mental health manpower (as it was then called) and wrote at length on the subject (Albee, 1968). At that time he came to believe that psychotherapy was relatively ineffective and very expensive. He thought there were *never* going to be enough therapists to treat all the individuals who might be considered to need such treatment. Under these circumstances, the only possible answer, Albee argued, was to emphasize prevention rather than treatment. Also, he felt that social problems such as poverty, racism, sexism, and ineffective educational approaches were more important than biological variables as causes of psychopathology (Albee did not believe that neuroscience research was going to be very practically useful in this area).

In 1970, Albee gave an address in Miami Beach that may have been received more negatively than any other such speech in the division's history—it was on "The Uncertain Future of Clinical Psychology." In words reminiscent of those of J. E. Wallace Wallin, Albee stated that clinical psychologists were still treated as second-class citizens both by medical colleagues and by experimental psychologists in their own departments. He thought that clinical psychologists needed a separate home of their own in which to train students and deliver services. As the title of Albee's speech suggests, he predicted the demise of the field, at least as one providing diagnosis and treatment of mental health problems. In this speech Albee made at least one prediction that was, arguably, on target. He suggested that within 10 or 20 years the field of psychology would split, and there would be an "American Professional Psychological Association" and an "American Scientific Psychological Association" (Albee, 1970, p. 1078). The current APA and the American Psychological Society (originating in 1988) at least in some respects fit his prophecy. Similarly, Albee was asked to contribute an article to the journal *Psychotherapy* for the 1992 centennial year, on "the future of psychotherapy." Albee's article consisted of two pages that were blank except for his name and university affiliation. In other words, according to his view, psychotherapy had no future. Perhaps his goal was for prevention to make psychotherapy unnecessary.

On the more positive side, Albee, since he moved to the University of Vermont, participated in the annual production of the series of Vermont conferences on the primary prevention of psychopathology. The conferences have generated an impressive series of books, which have no doubt encouraged the National Institute of Mental Health to continue its funding of prevention research. With Logan Wright and other colleagues, Albee founded an organization called the American Association of Applied and Preventive Psychology (AAAPP) in 1991. This group in 1992 began a journal, *Applied and Preventive Psychology*, with Wright as managing editor, publishing solicited review articles only.

Albee is an effective public speaker (often with provocative or even irritating messages, in the opinion of many members of his audiences). On the other hand he makes a highly positive impression on other members of the same audiences and had received many honors in the field. (Albee was president of Division 12 in 1966–1967.)

## FEDERAL HEALTH CARE PROGRAMS

Instead of seeking employment in a government institution or agency, other clinical psychologists have tried to get public sector support for activities such as psychotherapy that had previously not been available to the poor. The participation of psychologists in such government health care programs has required active legal advocacy on both federal and state levels. For example, in 1989, legislation for the first time included psychologists as providers under the Medicare program for elderly and disabled individuals. Half the states also now reimburse psychologists under their Medicaid programs for the economically disadvantaged. Psychologists had previously obtained access to provider status in another federally sponsored system known as CHAMPUS (Civilian Health and Medical Program of the Uniformed Services), which provides health care insurance to members of the armed services and their families. They are also included within another system called Federal Employees Health Benefits Program (FEHBP), which provides similar health insurance coverage to nonmilitary federal employees and their families. Clinical psychologists such as Patrick DeLeon have played an important role in getting coverage by clinical and other professional psychologists written into such federal legislation. DeLeon became a lawyer as well as a psychologist and serves on the legislative staff of U.S. Senator Daniel Inouye of Hawaii. DeLeon has thus been in an insider position and has both exerted influence and helped to guide the efforts of APA public interest staffers. What could Division 12 do to facilitate this process? Well, it could certainly give some recognition to the accomplishments of the people involved; thus it is no accident that DeLeon served as the president of the division in 1987 and received its award in 1989. DeLeon has also recently been appointed editor of the APA journal, *Professional Psychology: Research and Practice*.

It is obvious that the problem of providing health care services, including mental health services, to the entire population at a reasonable cost is far from solved. As these words are written in 1993, there is a sizable part of the American public that has no health insurance at all. In the area of physical health, infant mortality rates and the prevalence of premature births are high, and (despite the Clinton administration's good intentions) child vaccination rates are still scandalously low in this country. One reads in the newspaper that our country spends more money on health care than other nations and excels in high-technology medicine, yet the health of the people who live here is actually poorer than in many countries where less is spent per capita. And the provision of mental health services lags far behind routine medical care.

## CONCLUDING COMMENT

Psychologists in Division 12 who focus on public interest issues have been impressed by the effectiveness of both national and state-by-state lobbying and court battles for "guild" issues by clinical psychologists in the private sector. These advocates believe the same forces could be harnessed in support of various public policy issues such as those discussed above. In other words, the economics of psychological services must include the poor and underserved as well as the affluent.

# The Economics of Psychological Services: The Private Sector

In a well-known address on applied psychology, James McKeen Cattell (1937) mentioned that in about 1885 he had had the idea of opening a kind of clinic at Columbia University, following the example of Frances Galton at the International Exposition in London, who had offered to test people and report their scores to them. Those who could pay would be charged a small fee for these services (this is how Galton had financed his testing), and this income would be used to defray the cost of testing the indigent. According to Cattell, this idea was quashed by President Low of Columbia, who did not think it proper for the university to sponsor a profit-making venture. In the late nineteenth century, when clinical psychology began, the notion of insurance covering mental health services would have seemed utopian indeed.

## The Economics of Psychoanalysis

Sigmund Freud has served as a role model for psychology in financial respects as in many others. One feature of the success of psychoanalysis as an outpatient psychotherapy was that patients sought it out, and would pay for it. In retrospect, it has been realized that Freud's practice consisted almost entirely of wealthy, upper-class patients. Psychoanalysis of the classic variety remains almost prohibitively expensive. Imagine what it takes to pay for 5 or 6 hours per week of any professional's time. This is why George Albee (1977) once asked the question, not facetiously, whether the public provision of psychotherapy as a health benefit might not be "a subsidy of the rich from the poor" (p. 719). Freud was, however, supportive of the provision of subsidized treatment by the Berlin Psychoanalytic Institute and other organizations for persons who could not pay such high fees.

As psychoanalysis developed, it turned out that many of the patients were themselves aspiring mental health professionals. Although not justified in economic terms, this was one effect of requiring that anyone who wanted to be a psychoanalyst should receive a personal psychoanalysis.

As long as they did not engage in psychotherapy or enter independent practice, psychologists were not required to confront the issue of how patients/clients were going to pay for a clinical psychologist's services. Psychologists working as mental testers of private patients referred by psychiatrists (the role played with such excellence by David Rapaport, for example) could participate in the fees paid by the patient or by some third party to the psychiatrist. But when psychologists wished to serve as psychotherapists or as providers of other mental health services on their own, they had to develop a concern about who was going to pay their fees.

## EARLY ATTITUDES OF CLINICAL PSYCHOLOGY TOWARD PRIVATE PRACTICE

After World War II, when the VA and the NIMH were funding most graduate trainees in clinical psychology, it was considered a major policy failure when an individual took government training grant funds and then went into independent practice. In fact, prominent psychologists of that era such as David Shakow felt that private practice for psychologists should be discouraged altogether. He considered the high incomes of psychiatrists in private practice at that time to be rationally indefensible. Naturally, other clinical psychologists, as adherents of the free enterprise system, simply considered such incomes to be worth seeking for themselves. This was no doubt even more true among students who did not receive grant or fellowship funds but instead had to support themselves, pay high tuition, or go into debt to complete graduate school or a school of professional psychology. The general attitudes within the field have gone in this direction to the point where the Division of Independent Practice of APA is now its largest division.

## CHANGES IN THE U.S. HEALTH CARE SYSTEM

At the same time that psychologists began confronting the economic issues of private practice, the health care system of the United States was undergoing various changes. In the 1930s the American medical community stood united against any change in a fee-for-service system of health care. The Blue Cross and Blue Shield plans later worked out by medical societies aimed to cover physician and hospital costs to private individuals who could afford the insurance premiums.

The main way psychologists (and others such as optometrists and podiatrists) have tried to get their own services covered in such plans was through "freedom-of-choice" legislation at the state level. Thus, the state psychological association would lobby for a law requiring that if an insurer covered reimbursement for the costs of psychotherapy from a psychiatrist, it would be required to reimburse similar services from a psychologist. In other words, the company was required to provide freedom to the consumer in the choice of service provider. State psychological associations were often effective in getting their legislatures to pass such laws. Beginning in the 1960s, California, Michigan, New Jersey, New York, and Utah were the first to enact such legislation. More than 40 states presently have freedom-of-choice laws on the books. Division 12 did not participate directly in this lobbying, but it provided praise and recognition in the form of awards or election to division office to some of the persons who had been successful in making this happen.

After a freedom-of-choice law was passed, it was then necessary to monitor how seriously the state enforced it. Another route that could be taken in a particular state was to sue health insurance providers if they did not reimburse psychologists as providers. Suits were brought by the consumers or the practitioners themselves (as the injured parties), but national organizations were free to enter the cases as "friends of the court" (i.e., in amicus curiae briefs) to support their point of view. The well-known "Virginia Blues" case (Kiesler & Pallak, 1980) arose out of this type of situation. Blue Shield of Virginia refused to reimburse licensed psychologists without both physician supervision and referral and was therefore sued by the Virginia Academy of Clinical Psychologists. Blue Shield won the case in U.S. District Court in 1979, but with the benefit of an amicus brief from APA, the ruling was reversed upon appeal. Psychologists thus won a skirmish in the battle to win third-party payments. Once more, Division 12 provided some recognition to individuals who played important roles in this process. Robert Resnick, the psychologist who was the plaintiff in the "Virginia Blues" case, was given Division 12's Distinguished Professional Contributions Award in 1993 and was also recently elected president of APA.

In response to freedom-of-choice legislation and litigation, insurance companies complained that they did not know which psychologists could legitimately claim reimbursement. Because state and provincial licensing was often generic, an applied experimentalist or an industrial psychologist might be licensed but be an inappropriate choice as a psychotherapist. As noted previously, Carl Zimet headed up efforts to establish a *National Register of Health Service Providers in Psychology* and headed this program for 12 years. Partly in recognition of this work, Zimet was honored by a Division 12 award (Zimet, 1981).

In 1978, California passed legislation fostering hospital practice by psychologists, so that, for example, if an individual being seen by a therapist was hospitalized, the same therapist could continue to be involved in the plan of care. A lawsuit, known as *CAPP v. Rank*, was subsequently initiated that invalidated regulations the state issued in violation of this law. At present, six states have passed laws allowing psychologists to practice independently in hospitals: California, Florida, Maryland, North Carolina, Ohio, and Wisconsin.

## THE HEALTH MAINTENANCE ORGANIZATION

During World War II, the Kaiser Steel Company pioneered the offering of a new kind of health care program to its employees, both union and nonunion. This was the first Health Maintenance Organization in which each member was assigned to a primary care physician, responsible for prevention, screening, and the care of minor ailments. The primary physician then served as the gatekeeper who could refer the patient for specialized services (including psychotherapy or inpatient care for mental health problems). In the 1930s the American Medical Association and other such traditional groups vigorously opposed the HMO idea as threatening the doctor–patient relationship. But eventually, this was the way in which the national health care system moved. After all, it seemed much more cost-effective to prevent health problems altogether or to identify them early than to wait and treat them when they had become severe. Also, the gatekeeper system kept patients from approaching expensive specialists before really knowing what specialist care was necessary.

Now some psychologists realized how they could fit into an HMO model. Jack Wiggins is a clinical psychologist who is extremely knowledgeable in this area—he won a Division 12 award (and was elected APA president) partly on the basis of such contributions. In a representative article, Wiggins (1976) discussed the implications of Public Law 93–222, the Health Maintenance Organization Act of 1973, for psychologists as health care providers. Nicholas Cummings, who was mentioned before, also played an important role. He carried out research (Cummings & Follette, 1967) suggesting that if frequent utilizers of HMO services were provided timely access to brief psychotherapy or crisis intervention, this decreased their subsequent inappropriate utilization of physicians. It has long been known that a sizable proportion of the patients in the medical system have emotional rather than physical problems. Cummings and Follette (1967) documented the fact that it was more cost-effective to recognize these psychological problems as such and to try to do something to help. Naturally, Cummings's findings were welcome news to psychologists (and other mental health service providers) who were trying to break into the HMO system. Cummings was also the first chair of the APA Committee on Health Insurance, which concerned itself with these matters. (He was Division 12 president in 1978–1979.)

## Newer Approaches

New approaches are constantly being tried. For example, besides the HMO, there are "preferred provider organizations" or PPOs. Another new system called "managed care" is now in vogue in which utilization reviewers (who have not themselves seen the patient) decide what services are justifiable (DeLeon, VandenBos, & Bulatao, 1991). It seems that each time some new scheme such as this comes along, psychology practitioners have to begin all over again the fight to be included. Legislative advocacy at the state level—perhaps the main battleground—takes continuing effort and political organization. In some ways the model for this kind of activity seems to be that of other groups who are also on the fringes of legal status as "physicians"—namely optometrists, podiatrists, and, let's admit it, naturopaths and chiropractors. Compared to psychology practitioners, the optometrists and other such groups seem to be more politically committed and experienced—and the dues of their state and local organizations are far higher. As a result, they may be somewhat more effective in fighting battles similar to the ones being engaged in by professional psychology. One name that naturally comes to mind in this connection is that of Rogers H. Wright. He is in practice in California but spends many hours per week of his own time as a political advocate and organizer of professional psychologists. He is especially knowledgeable about health insurance issues, is indefatigable, and is known as a fierce opponent of those who disagree with his views. (Rogers Wright was president of Division 12 in 1988 and received its professional award in 1990.) He has served as the executive director of the Association for the Advancement of Psychology, an organization involved in such political advocacy.

Another recent attempt to control runaway health care costs is the concept of the diagnostic related group (DRG). If health care providers are allowed to charge for each procedure they perform, for example, X-rays, laboratory tests, and the like, and by the number of days a patient stays in the hospital, they seem to conform to capitalist expectations of human nature by finding that each patient needs a lot of procedures done, needs to stay in the hospital longer, and so forth. The DRG scheme for reducing costs tells the physician, in effect, if the patient has appendicitis, the insurance will pay only a fixed fee for that diagnosis regardless of how many tests are run or how many days the patient stays in the hospital. This system made it to the provider's advantage to economize on procedures and hospital time and indeed has led to many economies such as the efficient use of history and physical examinations and short hospital stays or even outpatient surgery. However, in the area of mental health disorders, the DRG approach may have backfired. Proprietary mental hospitals have become remarkable producers for their investors, at least in the short run. Many such hospitals advertise to attract customers with heath insurance, seem to be biased toward the use of diagnostic categories (e.g., major depressive episode) that justify inpatient treatment, and often find that the patient needs to stay in the hospital until the insurance runs out.

## THE ATTITUDES OF ACADEMIC PSYCHOLOGISTS

Not everyone in the field has been sympathetic with the efforts of clinical psychologists to be covered by private health insurance. For example, academic psychologists with no interest in the applied areas of the field may resent paying high dues to psychological organizations to hire expensive lobbyists and related costs. (Well, perhaps they do not mind paying for lobbyists who are seeking to increase federal research funds for the behavioral sciences.) In response to these divided constituencies, APA instituted a special dues assessment to be paid only by practitioners, to be spent in advocating their guild-related interests. So far, Division 12 has not found it necessary to put such a differential dues structure into place.

## CONCLUDING REMARKS

The involvement of clinical psychologists in the private sector has increased to an extent never foreseen by Galton and Cattell, or even by Rogers or Shakow. The attitude of psychology organizations toward the independent practice of psychology has also undergone approximately a 180-degree turn. Instead of discouraging private practice, Division 12 and many other groups are doing what they can to be supportive of the private practitioner.

# III

# Summing Up

# 23

# *Conclusion*

## THE SCIENCE OF CLINICAL PSYCHOLOGY

One proven way to earn the respect of colleagues in other sciences and professions, of academics in our own field, and of the public as well is to be responsible for scientific breakthroughs.

Unfortunately, no clinical psychologist has yet won a Nobel prize or its equivalent. In fact, psychology, as one of the "softer" sciences, has visibly trailed behind physics, chemistry, and the biological sciences in its rate of advance. So far, psychology has no Einstein, Darwin, or Watson and Crick. There have been several Nobel prizes to individuals whose work borders on the behavioral sciences: Ivan Pavlov, the discoverer of conditioning; Roger Sperry, the neurologist who demonstrated psychological differences between the functioning of the left and right hemispheres of the brain; Konrad Lorenz and Niko Tinbergen, "ethologists" who have illuminated the evolutionary nature of animal behavior; and Herbert A. Simon, the pioneer in the field of artificial intelligence.

> In response to the above paragraph, historian John M. Reisman reminded the author (in his letter of August 11, 1992) that: Nobel Prizes are awarded only in the areas of Medicine & Physiology, Physics, Chemistry, Economics, Peace, and Literature... [W]hen Freud abandoned hope of getting a Nobel Prize in medicine, his boosters tried to see if they could get him one in Peace or Literature ... without much luck.

In any case, we need not hang our heads in shame as scientists. Two individuals closely associated with clinical psychology were elected to the U.S. National Academy of Sciences by peers representing the whole scientific spectrum. One of these was Lewis M. Terman, the developer of the Stanford-Binet intelligence test and author of a life-span study of gifted individuals. The other was Paul E. Meehl, who did research on the Minnesota Multiphasic Personality Inventory, actuarial vs. clinical assessment, and the genetic basis of schizophrenia. In terms of theoretical contributions, Meehl also wrote on construct validation and the philosophy of science, among other topics.

Many other clinical psychologists have been recognized for their scientific accomplishments by fellow psychologists. For example, the APA Distinguished Scientific Contribution Award list includes Carl Rogers, Paul Meehl, Henry A. Murray, David Shakow, Albert Bandura, Walter Mischel, Julian B. Rotter, Hans Eysenck, Richard Lazarus, and Peter Lang. Their research spans topics from social learning theory to schizophrenia and from personology to psychotherapy.

The science of clinical psychology is a very young one. Yet at least two of its deceased leaders, George Kelly and Carl Rogers, already have proved to have significant posthumous influence. There are scientific journals, international conferences, and a multitude of books concerned with both personal construct theory and person-centered therapy.

In the author's opinion, all of the above distinguished researchers in clinical psychology have influenced practice, directly or indirectly.

The pages of this book are filled with a large number of additional examples of productive research careers and interesting research findings of clinical psychologists. As a legacy of the Boulder model, almost all of the over 6,000 members of the Division of Clinical Psychology have carried out at least some research, if only as a part of their graduate training. Even if they do not personally continue to do research, many feel an obligation to justify their professional practices in terms of the research database.

## THE PRACTICE OF CLINICAL PSYCHOLOGY

An even surer way to earn the respect of clients or patients, and ultimately of physicians, social workers, and other practitioners as well, is to devise accurate methods of prognostication, and interventions that clearly make a difference in individual lives.

It was said earlier in this book that unlike other forms of practice, clinical psychology was an academic and scientific field first, and a profession later. Perhaps this was a naive statement. Although they did not go by the name of "clinical psychology," the roles of oracle and healer are ancient. They continue to be played among us in the old ways as well as modern ones.

The reader will perhaps forgive a personal example. In 1988 the saddest event of my life occurred. Our 24-year-old daughter, Rebecca (Becky), was killed in an automobile accident. This event was devastating to all of her family (husband, parents, sister, and in-laws). Up to that time, she seemed to have everything going for her. She had graduated from college, had married her high-school sweetheart, was working as an obstetrical nurse and planning training as a midwife, and was pregnant with what would have been her first child. At a gathering of the bereaved family in rural Virginia, some relatives took Richard (Becky's husband, the young widower) out to the hills to see a "medium," who communicated a simple message supposedly from the spirit world, that Becky said she was "OK." I don't know if Richard believes in mediums or spirits—I certainly don't— yet in our acute distress several of us found these words to be really comforting. The thought that Becky, regardless of all the physical trauma she had experienced, was now not in any pain, was a helpful one. I must say that in my sheltered existence I did not realize before this that such people as mediums still existed, and yet they seem to be common, right here in high-tech America. I can see in retrospect that the medium was acting as an effective mental health worker, without the benefit—indeed, even in defiance of—a scientific base.

My wife and I have gotten to know Ellen Coon (Becky's sister-in-law) well since the fatal accident. She is a graduate student in anthropology and has done fieldwork in Nepal. As part of her work, Ellen has sat for hours in the modest dwellings of many a poor, uneducated Nepalese woman who has been selected (as they interpret it) as the medium of a "goddess," that is, the woman often goes into a trance and the goddess, taking possession of her, speaks to the assembled visitors. Such mediums are showered with gifts by visitors, who value the chance to communicate with the divine through them. The Nepalese priests (all males), who are educated and have custody of the sacred writings, are offended by these direct manifestations of the goddess and try to discredit them (am I wrong to be reminded somewhat, by this story, of academic clinical psychologists vs. practitioners?). Ellen Coon, as a student of anthropology, takes no position as to whether the medium or the priest is correct in this dispute. She merely observes that an amazing transfer of social power is taking place in favor of a group of impoverished women who were previously rather oppressed.

I lack any technical knowledge of Nepal or of anthropology. Still, I entertain the hypothesis that both the priests and the mediums may be performing in this exotic culture some of the functions of a mental health professional. Thus, they try to predict the future, to comfort the bereaved, or to deal with some human problems that arise. So do clinical psychologists in America.

For the sake of simplicity, let us divide the practice of clinical psychology into two phases: assessment and therapy. Considered in the broadest terms, both of these activities existed long before any explicit scientific field was developed to provide a rationale for them.

## Assessment

Psychological assessment did not begin in 1905 with introduction of the Binet-Simon scale or in 1941 with the publication of the MMPI. Astrologers from ancient times to the one consulted by Nancy Reagan have tried to foretell the future on the basis of the position of the planets and a person's date of birth. Their activities are commercially viable and support the sales of books and the many columns in daily newspapers. The oracle of Apollo at Delphi was sought out by the Greeks. The ancient Romans used augury, examining the internal organs of birds or animals seeking signs of how a battle would go. Many centuries ago, the Chinese set up examinations for the civil service positions of the Empire, for example, requiring a knowledge of the literary classics. These examinations were quite sophisticated in a sense, although they were not formally validated in a way we would now find acceptable. In the early nineteenth century, the art of phrenology flourished, and customers would certainly pay to learn what the bumps on their heads signified concerning their mental faculties. Even today the art of graphology—personality interpretation on the basis of handwriting analysis—is practiced in the absence of a convincing scientific base. "Psychics" are found in every city and are able to support themselves and pay their rent or long-distance phone bills on the basis of advice they offer. They may use "ESP," palmistry, tea leaves, Tarot cards, or other ancient arts to carry out their activities. Modern polygraph operators are paid fees by corporations and government departments to conduct lie detector tests even in the absence of solid evidence for the validity of their methods (e.g., Patrick & Iacono, 1989).

Undoubtedly, making a living in these ways requires one to be good at establishing rapport with clients and in making intuitive interpretations. We have even made some progress in understanding the factors that make for credibility in personality interpretation. According to studies of the "Barnum effect" (e.g., Snyder, Shenkel, & Lowey, 1977), the use of high-base-rate statements, mostly favorable to the respondent, will tend to induce belief in the accuracy of bogus (universal) personality interpretations.

Professional success in psychological assessment probably requires many of the same interpersonal skills as fortune telling. But surely, science can increase the effectiveness of the transaction. The procedures used in evaluating the client, to the extent that they have been empirically validated, can add something to the practitioner's intuitive ability to make predictions. It is clearly true from our previous discussion in this book that measures like the Binet, Wechsler, MMPI, and the like, do have some incremental validity. There is difficulty, however, in the transition of a society from "fortune telling" to scientifically based assessment. Practitioners who are already making an adequate living in the "old" ways must learn to look dispassionately at their own information-processing strategies to maximize the "signal" and minimize the "noise." This includes licensed psychologists who use primarily an intuitive approach to assessment. Scientific findings have to be strong enough to convince them of this need.

## Therapy

The use of psychological interventions did not begin with the publication of Freud and Breuer's *Studies in Hysteria* (1885) or of Mary Cover Jones's (1924a,b) behavioral treatment of Peter's fear. The Bible is replete with dramatic incidents of healing based upon religious faith: Lazarus was said to be brought back from the dead. A crippled man responded to the command to rise, pick up his bed, and walk. The shrine at Lourdes is littered with the crutches of worshipers who regained the use of their limbs.

In the eighteenth century, the physician Anton Mesmer went around Europe producing impressive cures (Purtscher, 1947). He was discredited by a committee including Benjamin Franklin, but only because he was foolish enough to explain his activities on the basis of a testable hypothesis—animal magnetism, considered to be actual currents of electricity passing from the therapist into the patient. When this simplistic explanation was disproved, the whole approach was unmasked as being based only on imagination. At the time, no one seemed to stop and realize that even if "imagination" was responsible, many of the cures represented genuine behavioral and experiential changes in the sufferers. Hypnosis, as it was later called, got a "bad rap," and to some extent has kept receiving one up to the present.

At the time when psychoanalysis was beginning to be developed, various other types of therapies that were also booming. In Boston there was the work of Christian Scientist Mary Baker Eddy, based on faith in the unreality of physical illness and the usefulness of reading and consultation with religious practitioners. There was also the Emmanual movement, involving an attempt to synthesize the work of medical therapists and the clergy.

Many cultures sanction folk healers. In Mexico, for example, there is a group of such healers called Curanderos. In Puerto Rico, Espiritistas serve both as folk healers and as mediums. They are points of contact with the spirit world, which in the view of the culture is involved in the occurrence of illness. The United States has, apart from its Spanish-speaking population, many religious groups that practice healing. A well-known example is the work of television evangelist Oral Roberts, who was able to finance a conventional medical school and hospital on the basis of contributions of his "prayer partners."

Therapy is thus not necessarily based on developments within scientific psychology. A good starting point in a discussion of the role of science in therapy is Jerome Frank's (1973) volume, *Persuasion and Healing*. As Frank says, a large proportion of the patients in any physician's waiting room have psychological ailments rather than, or in addition to, physical ones. "Healers" of any type (physicians, priests, shamans, and, of course, psychologists) are, more than they often like to believe, effective because of their "placebo" value. They establish rapport, listen respectfully to the patient's story, and provide reassurance and hope. Perhaps they elaborate a plausible rationale for activities expected to be of curative value. The nonspecific benefits inherent in establishing such a relationship with a patient, in combination with the natural restorative powers of the patient, are highly influential. This makes it difficult for researchers to disentangle the specific value of some particular drug or technique from nonspecific influences.

In retrospect, it is therefore easier to understand how so many different types of psychological interventions have grown up. The practitioners of each approach, whether psychoanalysis, person-centered therapy, or behavior therapy, experience the fact that their patients or clients improve. They therefore conclude that their particular treatment rationale must have been correct and derogate the approaches of other therapists who have incompatible treatment rationales.

As with assessment, many of the skills of the therapist are shared with the shaman and the faith healer: obtaining rapport, listening with respect, providing a rationale, and so on. Scientifically based therapies are helpful because they add specifically beneficial elements to the placebo factors. The scientific challenge is thus to do controlled studies varying one factor at a time to winnow out the nature of these specific elements. Until that effort succeeds, we will have only the type of contest described by Lewis Carroll's (1907/1886) Dodo in which *"Everybody* has won, and *all* must have prizes" (p. 28).

In actually carrying out therapy, in contrast to studying it, the last thing one would want to do would be to get rid of all those nonspecific factors. After all, to the therapist (and to the patient or client), the important thing is to get better, and to live. Knowing precisely why one got better is of decidedly secondary importance.

## THE ROLE OF ORGANIZATIONS

There are at least three kinds of organizations of psychologists: the learned society, the guild, and organizations that are a mixture of both. A learned society holds meetings where scholars can present their work to each other, publishes journals in which these studies can be reported, and honors by election to office those who have succeeded best in this enterprise. Such a group might also lobby the federal government for more funds to support research. That is about it. The APA before 1917 was a classic example of such a learned society. (Another example, proving the point that learned societies need not be "scientific," is the Modern Language Association.) The original AACP was founded specifically in order to break out of that mold. The pre-1945 APA, as a learned society, would not act to set professional standards for practitioners.

The second type of organization is the guild. Its meetings provide workshops and round tables where practitioners can share their experiences and learn new skills. It enforces professional standards by restricting membership to those with appropriate training. It supports external credentials of various kinds with the same purpose, enforced by state and provincial governments, boards, and registers. It honors members who work hard on behalf of their profession and further its goals. Within the APA, divisions such as 29 (Psychotherapy), 42 (Independent Practice), and 43 (Family Psychology) seem to function in this way to a greater extent than does Division 12. Their joint midwinter meeting shows how compatible their interests are. It has no papers, just workshops and symposia.

The third type of organization is a mixture of the other two, and Division 12 as it currently exists obviously fits this model. It has a heterogeneous membership, and members with different backgrounds and interests may not understand their colleagues' concepts or even their motives. It is unquestionably frustrating to many people to be in such a group. Imagine Titchener and Freud trying to talk to each other at that meeting at Clark University in 1909. They did not understand each other, and it was not because of a language barrier (they were both quite fluent in German). In more contemporary, Division 12 terms, imagine Albert Bandura and Rogers Wright trying to have a productive conversation (this is not easy to do). If that picture is not incongruous enough, imagine the ghost of Nicholas Hobbs there, too, trying to bring in his public interest concerns.

In 1986, when Jules Barron, a prominent New Jersey psychotherapist, served as president of Division 12, he hoped that he could make some changes so that the division would begin to live up to its name of "clinical psychology," by which he undoubtedly meant commitment to the profession. Many of his friends discouraged him. They conveyed the message to him that the division was "hopelessly arteriosclerotic and stuck in its own history" (Barron, 1986, pp. 13–14). Barron and his friends thus considered a diagnosis of an "organic" or a "neurotic" basis for the division's difficulties. I think they should have gone one step further and considered a social explanation. The division is full of people who are marching to at least two different drummers. The answer is not to make Division 12 an organization like Division 29, that is, a sort of guild for practitioners. Nor is it to make the division some kind of clone of the Society of Experimental Psychologists. Instead, the leadership somehow needs to stop the bands from playing from time to time and get the different marchers to talk to the persons next to them.

Some people find Division 12's appeal to lie precisely in its mixed nature. Division 12 expresses David Shakow's Boulder model in that it is one of the few places left where a real dialogue between the scientist and the practitioner can occur. It may be that this dialogue goes on most usefully within small groups, focused on some special interest. Of course, one example of this is within the sections. In Sections 1 and 5, the ones the author knows best, it seems that the researchers and the practitioners tend to like each other, to be able to talk, and to work well together.

Supporters of Division 12 may believe that not just clinical psychology, but psychology as a whole, would be the poorer if communication between scientists and practitioners breaks down. The scientists have findings that practitioners need to know about. Conversely, the practitioners have strong support from the public who make up their clientele. And they are dealing with important human problems with which scientists need to stay in touch. As Jane Loevinger (1963) said, "As in the battle of the sexes, so in the clinical research dialog[ue], if either side wins, the cause is lost" (p. 251).

In the mid-1980s, the academic/research psychologists within APA were becoming more and more dissatisfied with the direction the organization was taking and with their increasing lack of influence on it. A reorganization proposal was drafted that would have permitted more autonomy to this group. This move was resisted by the practitioner group and defeated. Thus, in 1988 the American Psychological Society was created as a separate organization from APA and achieved the desired autonomy in this more drastic way.

Having the APA and APS as separate groups has made it more difficult for those who wish to see Division 12 retain its traditional nature as what has been called here a mixed organization. Numerically, the practitioners are so dominant that they could easily turn Division 12 into a pure guild organization if they wished. The relatively new American Association of Applied and Professional Psychology was founded in part as an alternative for academic/research clinicians threatened by the practitioner dominance of Division 12 and other such APA divisions. However, the AAAPP may be equally lopsided in the opposite direction, and not the best forum in which to maintain the scientist–practitioner dialogue.

While writing this book, the author has often had the thought that in clinical psychology—in fact in the whole field of psychology—there is a need for someone like Abraham Lincoln to preserve the "union" in the face of serious threats of secession. This may seem odd, because the author's family favored Robert E. Lee, the reluctant leader of the rebel forces. In any case, this dream does not seem impossible, since Robert M. Yerkes performed the feat of unifying psychology twice before. He brought the AACP back into the old APA in 1919. And in 1945 he brought the APA and the AAAP back together.

In conclusion, clinical psychology needs to work toward the day, however far off it may be, when science and practice are but two sides of the same coin. In the words of an ancient spring carol, it might then be that "reason learns the heart's decrees, hearts are led by reason" (*Oxford Book of Carols*, 1928).

# Appendixes

# A

# Selected Examples of the Bylaws of Clinical Psychology Organizations

## AMERICAN ASSOCIATION OF CLINICAL PSYCHOLOGISTS (1917)

"The American Association of Clinical Psychologists was organized at Pittsburgh, on December 28, 1917. The membership includes men and women holding the doctorate in psychology, who are engaged in the clinical practice of psychology in the United States. The forty-five charter members are chiefly directors of clinics, of bureaus of child welfare, of institutional laboratories; in army service, as mental examiners of officers and recruits; or connected with courts, hospitals and schools.

"The objects of the Association are to promote an *espirit de corps* among psychologists who have entered the practical field, to provide media for the communication of ideas, to aid in establishing definite standards of professional fitness for the practice of psychology, and to encourage research in problems relating to mental hygiene and corrective education."

Source: *Journal of Applied Psychology*, 1918, 2, p. 194.

*Author's note*: The notable feature of the original bylaws of the AACP as compared to those of the APA was that they included the establishment of standards of professional practice as an object.

## REPORT OF THE CONFERENCE COMMITTEES OF APA AND AAACP (DECEMBER, 1919)

"1. It is proposed that the organization at present designated the American Association of Clinical Psychologists, shall be constituted a

Section of the A.P.A., to be known as *The Section of Clinical Psychology*. (The membership of the Association of Clinical Psychologists consists at present of forty-seven psychologists, all but three of whom are also members of A.P.A.)

2. The Special objects of the Section of Clinical Psychology would be:

(a) To promote a mutual understanding and an *espirit de corps* among those working in the field of clinical psychology, and a cooperative relationship with those engaged in allied fields.

(b) To encourage and advance professional standards in this field in cooperation with such committees on certification as may be appointed by the A.P.A. as a whole.

(c) To encourage research and the suitable publication of scientific results in the field of clinical psychology.

3. The Section should be constituted with a chairman, a secretary, and an executive committee. Such other committees as may be specially required from time to time may be named by the Section.

4. In order to facilitate joint action by the Section and the A.P.A. as a whole, certain actions of the Section should be submitted to the council of the A.P.A. for formal adoption, e.g., place of meeting, program.

5. The Section of Clinical Psychology should have no established dues other than those paid to the A.P.A. as a whole. Such funds as may be necessary for carrying out special projects of the Section should be raised by assessments, in a manner to be determined by the Section.

6. *Membership*. To be eligible for membership in the Section of Clinical Psychology, a psychologist must:

(a) be a member of the A.P.A.

(b) have such further qualification as may be determined by the Section.

7. The Section of Clinical Psychology shall adopt for its guidance such rules and regulations as may be deemed by the membership to be expedient for carrying on the specific work of the Section. Such rules and regulations shall now, however, be incompatible with the Constitution of the A.P.A.

For the A.P.A.                                    For the A.A.A.C.P.
Bird T. Baldwin                                  Arnold Gesell
Chairman                                          Chairman"

Source: Manuscript Division, U.S. Library of Congress.

*Author's note*: The main feature of the compromise that established the Clinical Section of the APA was that the APA agreed to appoint a committee to certify professionally competent "consulting psychologists." This is alluded to in item 2 (b).

## BYLAWS OF THE CLINICAL SECTION OF THE AMERICAN PSYCHOLOGICAL ASSOCIATION (DECEMBER 28, 1927)

"Article 1. NAME. The name of this section shall be "The Clinical Section of the American Psychological Association."

Article 2. OBJECT. The objects of this Section shall be:

1. To encourage and advance professional standards in the field of clinical psychology.

2. To encourage research and the suitable publication of scientific results in the field of clinical psychology.

Article 3. MEMBERSHIP. To be eligible for membership in this Section a psychologist, in addition to being a member or Associate of the American Psychological Association, must be actively engaged in the field of clinical psychology.

Nominations for membership shall be presented in writing to the Executive Committee and shall be signed by at least two members of the section.

Nominations which are unanimously approved by the Executive Committee shall be presented to the Section at its next subsequent regular meeting. Three fourths of the votes cast shall be necessary to election.

Article 4. OFFICERS. The officers of the Section shall include a Chairman, a Secretary, and an executive committee.

The Chairman and Secretary shall be elected at the regular annual meeting of the Section. The Chairman shall serve for one year and the Secretary for three years, or until their respective successors are elected and installed.

Article 5. EXECUTIVE COMMITTEE. The Executive Committee shall consist of three members elected by the Section, and the Chairman and Secretary as members ex officio. These members shall be elected for a term of three years, one being elected at each annual meeting.

The duties of the Executive Committee shall be:

1. To fill for the unexpired terms any vacancies that may occur in any office of the Section.

2. To arrange for the holding of the regular annual meeting, including the arrangement of the program, and to call and arrange for special meetings.

3. To perform such other functions as may from time to time be assigned to it by the Section.

Article 6. MEETINGS. The Section shall hold an annual meeting at the same time and place as the annual meeting of the American Psychological Association.

Article 7. DUES AND ASSESSMENTS. There shall be no regular dues. To defray the necessary expenses of the section, the secretary shall by direction of the Executive Committee make assessments from time to time, the amount per member not to exceed one dollar in any calendar year. Non-payment of assessments by any member for two successive years will constitute the equivalent of resignation from the Section.

Article 8. NOMINATION OF OFFICERS AND EXECUTIVE COMMITTEE. The nomination of officers and members of the Executive Committee shall be made at the annual meeting by a Nominating Committee of three (3), who shall be appointed by the retiring chairman at the previous annual meeting.

Article 9. AMENDMENTS. The by-laws of this section may be amended at any annual meeting by a vote of two thirds of the members present."

Source: Manuscript Division, U.S. Library of Congress.

*Author's note*: These bylaws were approved by the Clinical Section but not shown to APA at the time. Article 2.1 ("to encourage and advance professional standards") was the part APA later found to be objectionable.

## BYLAWS OF THE CLINICAL SECTION OF THE AMERICAN PSYCHOLOGICAL ASSOCIATION (AS ADOPTED, 1927 AND AMENDED SEPTEMBER 5, 1935)

### "Article I—Name

The name of this Section shall be "The Clinical Section of the American Psychological Association."

### Article II—Objects

The objects of this Section shall be:

1. To advance clinical psychology as a science.

2. To encourage research and the suitable publication of scientific results in the field of clinical psychology.

3. To prepare and recommend to the Program Committee of the American Psychological Association programs in the clinical field for the Annual Meeting.

### Article III—Membership

To be eligible for membership in this Section a psychologist in addition to being a Member or Associate of the American Psychological Association, must be actively engaged in the field of clinical psychology.

Applications for membership shall be presented in writing to the Executive Committee and shall be signed by at least two members of the Section.

Nominations which are unanimously approved by the Executive Committee shall be presented to the Section at its next subsequent regular meeting. Three-fourths of the votes cast shall be necessary to election.

## Article IV—Officers

The officers of the Section shall include a Chairman, a Secretary-Treasurer and an Executive Committee.

The Chairman and Secretary shall be elected at the regular annual meeting of the Section. The Chairman shall serve for one year and the Secretary for three years, or until their respective successors are elected and installed.

## Article V—Executive Committee

The Executive Committee shall consist of three members elected by the Section, and the Chairman and Secretary as members *ex-officio*. These members shall be elected for a term of three years, one being elected at each annual meeting. The duties of the Executive Committee shall be:

1. To fill for the unexpired term any vacancies that may occur in any office of the Section.

2. To arrange for the holding of the regular annual meeting, including the arrangement of the program, and to call and arrange for special meetings.

3. To perform such other functions as may from time to time be assigned to it by the Section.

## Article VI—Meetings

The Section shall hold an annual meeting at the same time and place as the annual meeting of the American Psychological Association.

## Article VII—Dues and Assessments

There shall be no regular dues. To defray the necessary expenses of the Section, the Secretary shall be directed by the Executive Committee to make assessments from time to time, the amount per member not to exceed one dollar in any calendar year. Non-payment of assessments by any member for two successive years will constitute the equivalent of resignation from the Section.

*Article VIII—Nomination of Officers and Executive Committee*

The nomination of officers and members of the Executive Committee shall be made at the annual meeting by a Nominating Committee of three (3) who shall be appointed by the retiring chairman at the previous annual meeting.

*Article IX—Amendments*

The By-Laws of this Section may be amended at any annual meeting by a vote of two-thirds of the members present."

Source: Manuscript Division, U.S. Library of Congress.

*Author's note*: These amended bylaws in effect allowed the Clinical Section only the object of advancing clinical psychology "as a science." It was no longer permitted to "encourage and advance professional standards" as an object. Thus, the section was limited to functioning as a paper-reading group, a source of dissatisfaction to its members that proved fatal to the section within 2 years.

BYLAWS OF THE CLINICAL SECTION, AMERICAN ASSOCIATION FOR APPLIED PSYCHOLOGY (NOVEMBER, 1939)

"Article I. Name. The name of this Section shall be: The Clinical Section of the American Association for Applied Psychology.
Article II. Purposes. Purposes of this Section shall be:
　　1. the association for mutual benefit of clinical psychologists;
　　2. the formation and maintenance of high standards of practice and teaching among clinical psychologists;
　　3. the education of the public in regard to the service rendered by clinical psychologists;
　　4. the stimulation of research in clinical psychology.
Article III. Membership. The Clinical Section shall consist of Fellows and Associates.
　　Fellows. To be eligible a Fellow shall (a) be a Fellow of the Association, and (b) shall have the Ph.D. or an equivalent degree in psychology from a recognized university, and shall have devoted his time for the equivalent of four full years to practice in the field of clinical psychology, or shall have an M.A. degree in psychology from a recognized university and shall have devoted the equivalent of seven full years to practice in the field of clinical psychology and have gained recognized standing in the field.

In addition, a Fellow in this Section must be devoting not less than twelve hours a week to the practice of clinical psychology. The term practice in this article shall include diagnosis and treatment in the broad sense and/or their supervision in a directive or administrative capacity.

Associates. Members at large of the American Association for Applied Psychology and members of others sections of the American Association for Applied Psychology who have done work or are doing work in clinical psychology, may, on approval of not less than six members of the Council, join the Clinical Section as Associates without further requirements. Associates shall have all the rights and duties of Fellows, except the right to vote or to hold office.

Nominations for Fellowship and Associateship shall be presented in writing to the Council and acted upon in a manner similar to that determining election to the Section.

Article IV. Officers. The officers of this Section shall consist of a chairman (who shall also be Vice-President of the American Association for Applied Psychology), a Secretary-Treasurer, one Representative on the Board of Governors, one Representative on the Board of Affiliates, and four Representatives on the Board of Editors of the Association.

The term of office and the duties of each officer shall be as provided for in the Constitution of the Association, and as further defined.

It shall be the duty of the Chairman to preside at all business meetings of the Section, to act ex officio as Chairman of the Council with the right to vote, to exercise general supervision over the affairs of the Section and to perform all such duties as are incident to his office, or as may properly be required of him by vote of the members of the Council at any duly constituted meeting. He shall set the time and place, for the meeting or meetings of the council during each annual meeting of the Section, and for such other meetings of the Council as may be agreed on by any six of its members.

It shall be the duty of the Secretary-Treasurer to keep the records of all meetings of the Section and of the Council, to act ex officio as secretary of the Council, to bring to the attention of the Council such matters as he deems necessary to conduct the official correspondence of the Section and of the Council, to function as provided for in Articles VII, VIII, and X, to have custody of all funds and properties of the Section, to collect and keep a full and complete record of all moneys received from special assessments made on members of the Section, and all moneys paid out, and shall perform such other duties as may be reasonably required of him by vote of the Council or of the Section at any duly constituted meeting.

Article V. The Council. The Council of the Section shall consist of five officers of the Section and three members at large. The officers shall be: the

Chairman; the Secretary-Treasurer; the representative on the Board of Governors; the representative on the Board of Affiliates; and the representative of the Board of Editors whose term is expiring. The members at large shall be elected for a three-year term, one member at large to be elected each year.

The duties of the Council shall be:

1. to fill for the unexpired term any vacancy that may occur in any office of the Section;

2. to arrange for the holding of meetings of the Section, as provided for in Article V, section 5, or the Constitution of the Association, and to appoint the representative of the Section to the Program Committee of the Association;

3. to solicit and receive papers and suggestions for the program of the Section at the annual meeting, for transmittal to the representative of the Section on the Program Committee;

4. to accept or reject nominations for Fellows or Associates and to determine changes in the status of members as provided for in Article III;

5. to conduct the nomination and election of officers;

6. to perform such other functions as may be assigned to it by the Section or the Association.

Article VI. Meetings. The Section shall hold an annual meeting at the same time and place as the annual meeting of the Association. Special meetings may be held on recommendation of the Council and authorization by a majority vote of members present at any regular meeting.

Article VII. Dues and Assessments. There shall be no regular dues for membership in this Section. Necessary expenditures in the conduct of the business of the Section as authorized by the By-laws or by a two-thirds vote of members present at any authorized meeting of the Section shall be paid out of special assessments made equally on all members of the Section. Such assessments shall be pro-rated by the Secretary-Treasurer and collected as provided for in Article IV.

Article VIII. Nomination and Election of Officers. Not less than five months before the regular annual meeting of the Section the Council shall issue a call for a nominating ballot for all officers of the Section, which ballot the Council shall count not less than one hundred days before the annual meeting. Immediately after completing the count it shall report to all Fellows of the Section the names receiving the larger number of votes, including not less than three candidates for each office whenever three or more have received votes. With this report, it shall call for the election ballot, which shall be counted not less than sixty days before the annual meeting and reported at the annual meeting. The call for the nominating ballot and report on its count, and the election ballot shall be sent by letter mail to each Fellow at his last known address. Election shall be by means of a preferential voting system.

Article IX. Quorums. Any five members of the Council shall constitute a quorum. Ten Fellows of the Section shall constitute a quorum for any authorized meeting of the Section.

Article X. Amendments. The By-laws of this Section may be amended at any annual meeting by a majority of the votes cast, provided that a copy of the proposed amendment has been sent by the Secretary to each Fellow at his last known address at least three months before the meeting. Voting shall be by ballot, which shall be returned to the Secretary and counted by the Council. The Council shall report the results of the vote at the first business session of the annual meeting."

Source: Manuscript Division, U.S. Library of Congress.

*Author's note*: In the light of the previous conflict between the Clinical Section of APA and its parent organization, the most important phrase of these bylaws of the Clinical Section of the AAAP was probably Article II.1, "the formation and maintenance of high standards of practice" as a purpose of the Section. It is also possible to see from these bylaws how the organization of the AAAP in the 1930s became the model for the postwar APA.

## BYLAWS OF THE DIVISION OF CLINICAL AND ABNORMAL PSYCHOLOGY, AMERICAN PSYCHOLOGICAL ASSOCIATION (SEPTEMBER, 1947)

*"Article I*

*Name and Purpose*

1. The name of this organization shall be the Division of Clinical and Abnormal Psychology of the American Psychological Association.

2. The purposes of this Division shall be to advance scientific inquiry and professional practice in clinical and abnormal psychology as a means of furthering human knowledge and welfare.

*Article II*

*Membership*

1. The Division shall consist of three classes of members: Fellows, Associates, and Life Members. All members of the Division shall be members of the American Psychological Association, and shall be persons who

are, at the time of their application, actively engaged in practice, research, teaching, or study in the fields of clinical or abnormal psychology. All classes of members shall be entitled to all the rights and privileges of the Division, except as otherwise specified in these By-Laws.

2. The minimum qualifications of a Fellow are:

(a) the requirements of a Fellow of the American Psychological Association,

(b) for designation as "Fellow in Clinical Psychology," satisfactory evidence of not less than four years of successful full-time clinical practice, or its accumulated equivalent, yielding the presumption of professional competence in clinical psychology.

(c) for designation as "Fellow in Abnormal Psychology," either acceptable published research in abnormal psychology beyond the doctoral degree, or four years of acceptable professional experience in abnormal psychology subsequent to the granting of the doctoral degree.

3. The minimum qualifications of an Associate are:

(a) the requirements of an Associate of the American Psychological Association, and

(b) satisfactory evidence of not less than two years of successful full-time clinical experience, or its accumulated equivalent, such as to yield a presumption of reasonable competence in clinical psychology, or

(c) satisfactory evidence of two years of experience in professional work that is psychological in character in the field of abnormal psychology.

4. Life Members shall be members of the Division who qualify as Life Members of the American Psychological Association.

5. Election to membership and transfer from one class of membership to another shall be accomplished as follows:

(a) Applications shall be made to the Secretary-Treasurer's Office of the Division on a form and by such a date as shall be prescribed by the Executive Committee in coordination with the Association. Each applicant shall submit formal endorsements made by two members of the Division.

(b) The Committee on Membership shall examine all applications and endorsements and shall submit recommendations to the Executive Committee.

(c) Members shall be elected by a majority vote of the members present and voting at the annual business meeting, on nomination of the Executive Committee. The election of members shall not be final until they have been elected to a like class of membership in the American Psychological Association.

(d) In accordance with the By-Laws of the American Psychological Association, persons elected as Fellows by the Division shall be recommended to the Association for designation as Fellow in Clinical Psychology, or Fellow in Abnormal Psychology, or both.

(e) The Secretary-Treasurer of the Division, directly or through the Central Office of the American Psychological Association, shall notify new members of their election immediately after the annual meeting. Such election shall not be effective unless initial dues are paid within two months after notification.

(f) The qualifications for election as Fellow or Associate may be waived in exceptional instances upon recommendation by the Executive Committee which shall state the reasons, and upon election by a two-thirds vote of the members present and voting at an annual meeting, provided that the requirements in no case shall be lower than those of the American Psychological Association.

(g) Change in the occupational status of a member shall not constitute cause for revocation of membership or reduction in class of membership except by recommendation of the Executive Committee for extraordinary reasons, after the affected member has been given an opportunity to resign or to defend his case in writing and in person before the Executive Committee as he may choose, and upon approval by a two-thirds vote by secret ballot of the members present and voting at an annual meeting.

6. There shall be a class of Affiliates of the Division who are not members of the Division and who may not vote or hold office. Affiliates may participate in the scientific and professional meetings of the Division, and may receive the printed matter and publications to which they may be entitled by the payment of subscriptions. Affiliates may have any of the following qualifications:

(a) Student Affiliates of the American Psychological Association who have completed not less than one year of graduate study in clinical psychology, or

(b) Other persons who have had not less than one year of graduate study in clinical psychology and who are engaged in further study, internship or experience in preparation for fulfilling the qualifications of membership, or

(c) Members of other Divisions of the American Psychological Association who do not fulfill the requirements for election to the Division of Clinical and Abnormal Psychology, who are interested in clinical or abnormal psychology, or

(d) Persons having appropriate training and experience in fields allied to clinical and abnormal psychology, and who desire such affiliation.

7. Affiliates shall be designated by majority vote of the Executive Committee, upon recommendation of the Committee on Membership, following application to the Secretary-Treasurer and endorsements by one

member of the Division. An affiliation may be terminated by a majority vote of the Executive Committee if the Affiliate no longer qualifies under the provisions of Section 6 of this Article.

8. Any Member or Affiliate who is in arrears in the payment of dues for a period of two years shall be presumed to have resigned from the Division.

9. Any Member or Affiliate may be expelled from the Division for cause by a two-thirds vote, taken by secret ballot, of the members present and voting at an annual meeting. Such vote shall be taken only upon the recommendation of a special committee of three members appointed by the Executive Committee to investigate the particular case, or upon recommendations of the Committee on Scientific and Professional Ethics of the American Psychological Association, only (a) after the committee has accumulated the relevant facts and has given the accused an opportunity to answer the charges against him both in writing and by appearing in person before the committee, and (b) after the committee's recommendations have been reviewed and approved by a majority vote of the Executive Committee, taken by secret ballot.

## Article III

### Officers

1. The officers of the Division shall be a Divisional President, a Divisional President-Elect, a Secretary-Treasurer, and two or more Divisional Representatives to the Council of Representatives, as provided by Article IV of the By-Laws of the American Psychological Association. All officers, except the Divisional President, shall take office at the close of the annual meeting next following their election, and shall serve until their successors are elected and qualify.

2. The Divisional President shall be the Fellow who has just completed his term as Divisional President-Elect. He shall succeed to office by declaration at the close of the annual meeting one year after the announcement of his election as President-Elect, and shall serve for one year. The Divisional President shall preside at all meetings, shall be Chairman of the Executive Committee with right to vote, and shall perform all other usual duties of a presiding officer. He shall exercise initiative in promoting the best interests of the Division, and in cooperation with the Secretary-Treasurer shall prepare the agenda for the business meetings of the Division and of the Executive Committee.

3. The Divisional President-Elect shall be a Fellow of the Division elected for a term of one year. During his term he shall be a member of the Executive Committee with right to vote, shall serve as Chairman of the

Program Committee, and shall perform the usual duties of a vice-president. In the event that the Divisional President shall not serve his full term for any reason, the Divisional President-Elect shall succeed to the unexpired remainder thereof and continue through his own term. In the event that the Divisional President-Elect shall not serve his full term, both a Divisional President and a Divisional President-Elect shall be nominated and elected at the next annual election.

4. The Secretary-Treasurer shall be a member of the Division elected for a term of three years, and shall not succeed himself more than once in this office. During his term he shall be a member and Secretary of the Executive Committee with right to vote, shall safeguard all records of the Division, shall keep minutes of the meetings of the Division and of the Executive Committee, shall maintain coordination with the Central Office of the American Psychological Association, shall issue calls and notices of meetings directly or through the Central Office, and shall perform all usual duties of a secretary. The Secretary-Treasurer shall have custody of all funds and property of the Division, shall receive all money due the Division, shall make disbursements as provided by Article VIII of these By-Laws, shall keep adequate accounts, shall make an annual financial report to the business meeting of the Division, and in general shall perform the usual duties of a treasurer.

5. The Divisional Representatives shall perform the duties specified by Article III of the By-Laws of the American Psychological Association, and shall serve as members of the Executive Committee of the Division.

6. In the case of the death, incapacity, or resignation of any officer, except the Divisional President, the Executive Committee shall by majority vote elect a successor to serve until the next annual election.

## Article IV

### Executive Committee

1. There shall be an Executive Committee of the Division consisting of the Divisional President, the Divisional President-Elect, and the Secretary-Treasurer, ex officio; the Divisional Representatives; and two members-at-large.

2. The members-at-large shall be members of the Division and shall be elected for a term of two years, one being elected each year. Members-at-large may serve no more than two consecutive terms. (At the first election following the adoption of these By-Laws, one member-at-large shall be elected for one year and one for two years.)

3. The Executive Committee shall:

(a) Exercise general supervision over the affairs of the Division, and transact the necessary business of the Division in the interval between the annual meetings of the members, provided, however, that the actions of the Executive Committee shall not conflict with these By-Laws or with the recorded votes of the membership, and shall be subject to the review of the members in annual meeting.

(b) Report its activities to the annual meeting of the members, and recommend matters for the consideration of the membership.

(c) Fill vacancies in any office of the Division, except that of Divisional President, until the next election.

(d) Appoint committees of the Division in accordance with these By-Laws.

(e) Advise the officers of the Division in the performance of their duties.

(f) Advise the Divisional Representatives in matters concerning the relationships between the Division and the American Psychological Association.

(g) Nominate new members for election by the members in annual meeting, and designate Affiliates on recommendation of the Committee on Membership.

(h) Prepare a budget for presentation to the annual meeting of the Division.

(i) Recommend or approve the disbursement of funds of the Division in accordance with Article VIII of these By-Laws.

4. The Executive Committee shall meet at least once each year immediately preceding the annual meeting of the Division, and may meet at other times on the call of the Divisional President or the Secretary-Treasurer. The Divisional President shall preside over meetings of the Executive Committee, and the Secretary-Treasurer shall act as secretary. A majority of the members of the Executive Committee shall constitute a quorum, following due notice of the meeting. Each member present shall have one vote, and no member may vote by proxy. During the intervals between meetings, actions of the Executive Committee may be taken by mail ballot which shall be mailed, counted, recorded, and reported by the Secretary-Treasurer.

## Article V

### Nominations and Elections

1. *General.* The Committee on Nominations and Elections shall be responsible for the procedures required for the nomination and election of officers, representatives, and members-at-large of the Executive Commit-

tee, of the Division. In discharging its responsibilities, the Committee may distribute ballots directly, through the Secretary-Treasurer, or through the Central Office or the Election Committee of the American Psychological Association. All aspects of nomination and election shall conform to the provisions of the By-Laws of the Association, and shall be completed by the dates specified by the Association.

2. *Nominations.*

(a) The Committee on Nominations and Elections shall nominate 2 persons for Divisional President-elect, and for Divisional President when that office is to be filled. It shall nominate 1 or 2 persons for each other office as there are positions to be filled.

(b) It shall distribute a preferential nominating ballot to all members. This ballot shall provide spaces for 3 names to be written in order of preference for each position to be filled. After counting the ballots it shall designate the 2 highest nominees for President-elect, and for President when the office is to be filled. Nominees for Divisional Representative shall also be eligible for nomination as Divisional President, Divisional President-elect, or Secretary-Treasurer, but in no other instance shall a person be nominated for more than one office. The Committee shall ascertain the willingness of each nominee to serve if elected.

3. *Elections.* The officers and representatives of the Division, and the member-at-large of the Executive Committee shall be elcted by a preferential vote of the members, on a mail ballot. The Committee on Nominations and Elections shall be responsible for seeing that the following steps are accomplished: the mailing of ballots, the preferential count of votes, the notification of the Executive Committee of the results of the election, the notification of the members who are elected, and the reporting of the election to the annual business meeting of the Division.

*Article VI*

*Meetings*

1. The Division shall hold an annual scientific and professional meeting at the time and place of the annual convention of the American Psychological Association, for the presentation of scientific papers and the discussion of professional matters in the field of the Division's interests. The Division shall hold an annual scientific and professional meeting at the time and place of the annual convention of the American Psychological Association, for the presentation of scientific papers and the discussion of professional matters in the field of the Division's interests. The Division shall coordinate its programs with, and shall participate in, the program of the Association.

2. The annual business meeting of the Division shall be held during the time and in the locality of the annual convention of the American Psychological Association. A quorum shall consist of 5% of the qualified members of the Division. Each member shall have one vote, and no member shall vote by proxy.

*Article VII*

*Committees*

1. The Committees of the Division shall consist of such standing committees as are provided by these By-Laws and of such special committees as may be established by the Executive Committee. In accordance with Article XIII, Section 2, of the By-Laws of the American Psychological Association, the formation of new committees by the Division shall be subject to the approval of the Committee on Committees of the Association.

2. All committees shall be appointed annually by the Executive Committee on recommendation of the Divisional President, except as otherwise provided in these By-Laws, and shall serve until their successors are appointed and qualify.

3. The Committee on Membership shall consist of three members: a member of the Executive Committee who shall serve as chairman, and two other members one of whom shall be appointed each year to serve for a term of two years. The Secretary-Treasurer shall be a member *ex-officio* without vote. The Committee shall receive applications and endorsements for membership or affiliation, and shall render a report to the Executive Committee as provided by Article II, Sections 5 and 7, of these By-Laws.

4. The Program Committee shall consist of three members: the Divisional President-Elect who shall serve as chairman, and two other members one of whom shall be appointed each year to serve for a term of two years. The Secretary-Treasurer shall be a member *ex-officio* without vote. It shall be the duty of the Program Committee to solicit, evaluate, and select scientific and professional contributions to the annual meeting program, in coordination with the Convention Program Committee of the Association.

5. The Committee on Nominations and Elections shall consist of five members, the most recently retired Divisional President who shall serve as chairmen, two members of the Executive Committee, and two other members. This Committee shall perform the duties with respect to nominations and elections as provided in Article V of these By-Laws.

6. The Auditing Committee shall consist of two members, one of whom shall be designated as chairman, and neither of whom shall be a member of the Executive Committee. It shall be the duty of this committee

to examine the financial records of the Secretary-Treasurer, and to make a report of its audit to the annual meeting.

## Article VIII

### Finances

1. The minimum membership dues are one dollar a year for each member, paid to the Division by the American Psychological Association out of the member's annual subscription to the Association.

2. The assessment of any additional or special dues shall be decided by a majority vote of those present and voting at the annual meeting, or by a mail ballot of the members taken upon recommendation of the Executive Committee.

3. The annual subscription of Affiliates, except Student Affiliates, shall be one dollar over and above the subscription required of such Affiliates by the American Psychological Association. No additional assessment of Affiliates shall be made, except by amendment to this By-Law.

4. The Executive Committee, on recommendation of the Secretary-Treasurer, shall prepare an annual budget of anticipated income and expenditures which shall be presented for the approval of the members at the annual meeting.

5. Disbursements of the funds of the Division shall be made as follows:

(a) Disbursements of any amount and for any purpose harmonious with the objects of the Division may be authorized by a majority vote of the members present and voting at an annual meeting, or by a mail ballot of the members taken on recommendation of the Executive Committee.

(b) The Executive Committee may authorize disbursements within the amount of the approved budget, that are not inconsistent with the By-Laws of the Division of the Association or with the recorded actions of the membership. This shall include the disbursement of unexpended balances.

(c) Routine items of expense specifically included in the budget shall be paid by the Secretary-Treasurer upon the approval of the voucher by the Divisional President.

6. The Secretary-Treasurer is hereby authorized to sign checks on behalf of the Division for the disbursement of funds duly approved under the provisions of Section 5 of this Article. In the event of the incapacity of the Secretary-Treasurer, the Divisional President-Elect is hereby authorized to sign checks on behalf of the Division under the same conditions. All financial documents, other than checks, approved by the members or by the Executive Committee in accordance with

these By-Laws, shall be signed by the Divisional President and the Secretary-Treasurer.

## Article IX

### Amendments

1. An amendment to these By-Laws may be proposed by the Executive Committee, or by a petition of fifty members presented to the Executive Committee, or by a motion passed by a majority of those present and voting at an annual meeting.

2. After an amendment has been proposed, it shall be mailed to the last known post office address of each member, or shall be published in the official journal of the American Psychological Association.

3. An amendment may be adopted by either of the following procedures:

(a) By a two-thirds vote of the members present and voting at an annual meeting held not less than one month after the mailing or publication of the proposed amendment, or

(b) By a majority vote of the members on a mail ballot which shall close not less than one month after the mailing or publication of the proposed amendment."

Source: *Newsletter, Division of Clinical and Abnormal Psychology*, 1947, 1(2), 1–8.

*Author's note*: These bylaws were unusual in comparison to the others in that Article II has separate categories of membership for those identified with "abnormal psychology" and "clinical psychology," that is, academics vs. practitioners. This was a carryover from the idea of having separate divisions for each of these groups (they would have been called Divisions 11 and 12), which was not implemented at the time APA reorganized in 1945.

The Division of Clinical Psychology established sections beginning in 1962, and the bylaws were modified to permit this. The most recent (1992) Division 12 bylaws also reflect an important decision of the division to limit its membership to persons "with training appropriate to the conduct of such clinical activities as defined by the Council of Representatives of the American Psychological Association." In this way, Division 12 reaffirmed its intention to be not merely an interest group but to restrict its membership to those with full training as clinical psychologists. However, psychologists who had made significant research contributions to the clinical area were exempted from some of the training requirements.

## Bylaws: Section on Clinical Child Psychology of the Division of Clinical Psychology, American Psychological Association (1962)

*"Membership*

1. The membership of the Section shall consist of two classes: Member and Affiliate.

2. To qualify for the status of Member an individual shall be a member of the Division and of the APA who has an interest in the scientific or professional aspects of clinical work with children. A Member shall be entitled to all the rights and privileges of the Section.

3. To qualify for the status of Affiliate an individual shall be a member of the APA who has an interest in the scientific or professional aspects of clinical work with children. A Member shall be entitled to all the rights and privileges of the Section.

4. An Affiliate who becomes a member of the Division shall automatically become a member of the Section.

5. If an Affiliate of the section represents himself as a member of the Division he shall be expelled from membership in the Section.

6. Election to membership shall be accomplished as follows:

   a) Application shall be made to the Secretary-Treasurer of the Section, who may devise a special form for this purpose. The applicant shall state that he is a member in good standing of the APA and indicate whether he is a member of the Division.

   b) The Secretary-Treasurer shall examine all applications and submit these to the Executive Council for action.

   c) All members shall be elected by a majority vote of the members present and voting at the annual business meeting of the Section, on nomination of the Executive Council.

   d) The Secretary-Treasurer shall notify new Members and Affiliates of their election immediately after the annual meeting and this notice shall specifically indicate the class of membership to which the individual has been elected. Such election shall not be effective until the payment of such Section dues as may be in effect at the time of election.

7. Any member who wishes to resign his membership in the Section shall indicate his intention in writing to the Secretary-Treasurer. Any member who is in arrears of effective dues for a period of two years shall be presumed to have resigned from the Section."

Source: Archives of the History of American Psychology, University of Akron.

*Author's note*: Only one part of these Section 1 bylaws has been reproduced, the part pertaining to membership (at that time a significant concern of the Division). Since then, the rules on membership in all sections have been made less restrictive, so that the sections function more as interest groups than does the division.

## Section 4 Bylaws

"A number of Division 12 Members and Fellows worked to develop a Section focusing on women's concerns within Clinical Psychology. Bylaws were written, a petition proposed and signatures gathered for charter membership. At its winter meeting [January 11–12, 1980, Washington, DC], the Executive Board of Division 12 approved the establishment of a Section on Clinical Psychology of Women and designated it as Section IV of Division 12. The purpose of the Section as stated in its bylaws is: to promote the general objectives of the American Psychological Association, to encourage the evolution and development of a specialty of Clinical Psychology as a science and profession and (a) to increase scientific understanding of those aspects of clinical psychology that pertain to women; (b) to promote the development of models for the delivery of service to women; (c) to increase the quality of educational and training opportunities for women in clinical psychology; (d) to advocate on behalf of women clinical psychologists with respect to the formation of policies of the Division; and (e) to develop the subspecialty of Clinical Psychology of Women."

Source: Sobel, S. B., & Strickland, B. (1980). Division 12 establishes a section on clinical psychology of women. *The Clinical Psychologist, 33*(3), 1.

# Officers of the Division of Clinical Psychology and Related Organizations

AMERICAN ASSOCIATION OF CLINICAL PSYCHOLOGISTS

1917–1918   Chair: J. E. Wallace Wallin
Secretary: Leta S. Hollingworth
1918–1919   Chair: J. E. Wallace Wallin
Secretaries: Leta S. Hollingworth/R. H. Gault

CLINICAL SECTION, AMERICAN PSYCHOLOGICAL ASSOCIATION

1919–1920   Chair: F. N. Maxfield
Secretary: Leta S. Hollingworth
1920–1921   Chairs: F. N. Maxfield/David Mitchell
Secretary: Augusta F. Bronner
1921–1922   Chair: F. N. Maxfield
Secretaries: Augusta Bronner/Clara H. Town
Executive Committee: Thomas H. Haines, Rudolf Pintner,
F. L. Wells, Guy M. Whipple, Helen T. Woolley
1922–1923   Chair: F. L. Wells
Secretary: Clara H. Town
Executive Committee: Leta S. Hollingworth, F. N. Maxfield,
Rudolf Pintner, F. L. Wells, Guy M. Whipple, Helen T.
Woolley
1923–1924   Chair: David Mitchell
Secretary: E. A. Doll

1924–1925   Chairs: David Mitchell/Arnold L. Gesell
            Secretary: E. A. Doll
1925–1926   Chairs: David Mitchell/Helen T. Woolley
            Secretary: C. S. Berry
            Executive Committee: Samuel Heckman, Bertha M. Luckey
1926–1927   Chair: Augusta F. Bronner
            Secretaries: C. S. Berry/Mabel Fernald
1927–1928   Chairs: Augusta F. Bronner/David Mitchell
            Secretary: Augusta F. Bronner
            Executive Committee: H. H. Young, Mabel R. Fernald
1928–1929   Chair: H. H. Young [no meeting]
            Secretary: C. S. Berry
            Executive Committee: John E. Anderson, F. N. Maxfield,
               Louise Poull
1929–1930   Chairs: H. H. Young/S. I. Franz [no meeting]
1930–1931   Chairs: S. I. Franz/Frederick Kuhlmann
            Secretaries: James B. Miner/Luton Ackerson
            Executive Committee: T. G. Hegge, F. N. Maxfield, M. R.
               Trabue
1931–1932   Chairs: Frederick Kuhlmann/J.B. Miner
            Secretary: Luton Ackerson
1932–1933   Chairs: F. Kuhlmann/E. A. Doll
            Secretary: Luton Ackerson
            Executive Committee: T. G. Hegge, F. N. Maxfield, Richard
               H. Paynter, M. R. Trabue
1933–1934   Chair: E. A. Doll
            Secretary: Luton Ackerson
            Executive Committee: H. J. Baker, Richard Paynter
1934–1935   Chair: Clara H. Town
            Secretary: Edward B. Greene
            Executive Committee: H. Meltzer
1935–1936   Chair: Martin L. Reymert
            Executive Committee: Rose G. Anderson
1936–1937   Chair: Gertrude H. Hildreth
            Executive Committee: E. A. Doll


CLINICAL SECTION, AMERICAN ASSOCIATION FOR APPLIED
PSYCHOLOGY

1937–1938   Vice Presidents: F. N. Maxfield/Andrew W. Brown
            Secretary: C. M. Louttit

Executive Committee: Andrew W. Brown, Edward B.
Greene, Gertrude H. Hildreth, C. M. Louttit, F. N.
Maxfield, Catharine Cox Miles

1938–1939 Vice President: E. A. Doll
Secretary: Elaine F. Kinder
Executive Committee: Gertrude H. Hildreth, F. Kuhlmann,
J. B. Miner
Representive to Board of Governors: A. W. Brown
Representatives to Board of Editors: E. A. Doll, C. M. Louttit,
Bertha M. Luckey, F. L. Wells
Representative to Board of Affiliates: J. J. B. Morgan

1939–1940 Vice President: E. A. Doll
Secretary: Elaine F. Kinder
Executive Committee: Carney Landis, J. B. Miner, J. E. W.
Wallin
Representative to Board of Governors: A. W. Brown
Representative to Board of Editors: Gertrude Hildreth

1940–1941 Vice President: F. Kuhlmann
Secretary: Elaine F. Kinder
Members at Large: Carney Landis, J. B. Miner, Carl R.
Rogers, J. E. W. Wallin
Representative to Board of Governors: A. W. Brown

1941–1942 Vice Presidents: F. Kuhlmann/F. N. Maxfield/Carl R. Rogers
Secretary-Treasurer: Elaine F. Kinder
Members at Large: C. H. Calhoon, Mabel R. Fernald,
Gertrude Hildreth, George A. Kelly, Carney Landis, James
B. Miner, Carl R. Rogers
Representative to Board of Governors: A. W. Brown
Representatives to Board of Editors: E. A. Doll, Bertha M.
Luckey, Garry C. Myers, Wilda M. Rosebrook, Laurance F.
Shaffer
Representative to Board of Affiliates: Robert Bernreuter
Editor, *Newsletter*: Gertrude Hildreth

1942–1943 Vice President: Carl R. Rogers
Secretary-Treasurer: Gertrude H. Hildreth
Members at Large: A. W. Brown, C. H. Calhoon, Mabel R.
Fernald, George A. Kelly, Carney Landis, James B. Miner,
Carl R. Rogers
Representatives to Board of Editors: Edgar A. Doll, Gertrude
Hildreth, Bertha M. Luckey, Garry C. Myers, Wilda M.
Rosebrook, Laurance F. Shaffer

Representatives to Board of Affiliates: Robert Bernreuter,
Bertha M. Luckey

Editors, *Newsletter*: Gertrude Hildreth, Carl R. Rogers

1943–1944   Vice President: Carl R. Rogers

Secretary-Treasurer: Gertrude H. Hildreth

Members at Large: A. W. Brown, James B. Miner, Carl R.
Rogers, C. H. Calhoon, Mabel R. Fernald, George A. Kelly

Representatives to Board of Editors: E. A. Doll, C. M. Louttit,
Marie Skodak, Bertha M. Luckey, Garry C. Myers, Wilda
M. Rosebrook, Laurance F. Shaffer

Representative to Board of Affiliates: Robert Bernreuter

1944–1945   Vice Presidents: Carl R. Rogers/Bertha M. Luckey

Secretary-Treasurer: Frank P. Bakes

Members at Large: C. H. Calhoon, Mabel R. Fernald, George
A. Kelly, James B. Miner, Carl R. Rogers,

Representatives to Board of Editors: E. A. Doll, Bertha M.
Luckey, Garry C. Myers, Wilda M. Rosebrook, Laurance F.
Shaffer

Representative to Board of Affiliates: Robert Bernreuter

1945–1946   Vice President: Robert A. Brotemarkle

Secretary: Frank P. Bakes

Members at Large: A. W. Brown, C. H. Calhoon, Mabel R.
Fernald, George A. Kelly, Carney Landis, J. B. Miner, Carl
R. Rogers, Florence M. Teagarden

Representative to Board of Governors: Florence Teagarden

Representatives to Board of Editors: E. A. Doll, Gertrude
Hildreth, C. M. Louttit, Bertha M. Luckey

Representatives to Board of Affiliates: Robert Bernreuter,
Gordon L. Riley

## DIVISION OF CLINICAL AND ABNORMAL PSYCHOLOGY (DIVISION 12), AMERICAN PSYCHOLOGICAL ASSOCIATION

1945–1946   Chair: E. A. Doll

Secretary: Frank P. Bakes

Representatives to APA Council: E. A. Doll, Gertrude
Hildreth, Carl R. Rogers

1946–1947   President: Laurance F. Shaffer

President-elect: David Shakow

Secretary: David Rapaport

Representatives to APA Council: E. A. Doll, David
Rapaport, L. F. Shaffer, David Shakow, David Wechsler
1947–1948 President: David Shakow
President-elect: David Wechsler
Secretary: David Rapaport
Members at Large: Norman Cameron, Bertha M. Luckey,
Saul Rosenzweig
Representatives to APA Council: Samuel J. Beck, William A.
Hunt, C. M. Louttit, David Rapaport, David Shakow,
David Wechsler
Editor, *Newsletter*, Vol. 1: David Rapaport
1948–1949 President: David Wechsler
President-elect: Carl R. Rogers
Secretary: David Rapaport
Members at Large: Norman Cameron, David Shakow
Representatives to APA Council: Margaret Brenman, Robert
C. Challman, William A. Hunt, C. M. Louttit, David
Rapaport, L. F. Shaffer
Editors, *Newsletter*, Vol. 2: David Rapaport, Anne Roe, David
Wechsler
1949–1950 President: Carl R. Rogers
President-elect: Norman Cameron
Secretary-Treasurer: Anne Roe
Members at Large: David Shakow, Ruth S. Tolman
Representatives to APA Council: Margaret Brenman, Harold
M. Hildreth, E. Lowell Kelly/Robert C. Challman, C. M.
Louttit, Saul Rosenzweig, L. F. Shaffer
Editors, *Newsletter*, Vol. 3: Harry V. McNeill, Anne Roe, Carl
R. Rogers
1950–1951 President: Norman Cameron
President-elect: Samuel J. Beck
Secretaries: Anne Roe/Harry V. McNeill
Members at Large: Starke R. Hathaway, Ruth S. Tolman
Representatives to APA Council: Margaret Brenman, Robert
E. Harris Harold M. Hildreth, Jean Walker Macfarlane,
Saul Rosenzweig, L. F. Shaffer
Editors, *Newsletter*, Vol. 4: Norman A. Cameron, Harry V.
McNeill, Anne Roe
1951–1952 President: Samuel J. Beck
President-elect: O. Hobart Mowrer
Secretary-Treasurer: Ann Magaret
Members at Large: Starke R. Hathaway, Robert R. Holt

Representatives to APA Council: Robert E. Harris, Harold
M. Hildreth, Nicholas Hobbs, Jean W. Macfarlane, Ann
Magaret, Julian B. Rotter

Editors, *Newsletter*, Vol. 5: Samuel J. Beck, Ann Magaret

1952–1953   President: O. Hobart Mowrer
President-elect: William A. Hunt
Past President: Samuel J. Beck
Secretary-Treasurer: Anne Magaret
Members at Large: Robert R. Holt, James G. Miller
Representatives to APA Council: Robert E. Harris, Nicholas
Hobbs, Jean W. Macfarlane, Ann Magaret, Ruth S. Tolman,
Joseph Zubin

Editors, *Newsletter*, Vol. 6: Ann Magaret, O. Hobart Mowrer

1953–1954   President: William A. Hunt
President-elect: Harold M. Hildreth
Past President: O. Hobart Mowrer
Secretary-Treasurer: Ann Magaret Garner
Members at Large: George S. Klein, James G. Miller
Representatives to APA Council: Ann M. Garner, Nicholas
Hobbs, Victor C. Raimy, Anne Roe, Ruth Tolman, Joseph
Zubin

Editors, *Newsletter*, Vol. 7: Ann M. Garner, William A. Hunt

1954–1955   President: Harold M. Hildreth
President-elect: Jean W. Macfarlane
Past President: William A. Hunt
Secretary-Treasurer: Helen D. Sargent
Members at Large: George S. Klein, Roy Schafer
Representatives to APA Council: Robert R. Holt, Victor C.
Raimy, Anne Roe, Helen D. Sargent, Ruth S. Tolman,
Joseph Zubin

Editors, *Newsletter*, Vol. 8: Harold M. Hildreth, Helen D.
Sargent

## Division of Clinical Psychology (Division 12), American Psychological Association

1955–1956   President: Jean W. Macfarlane
President-elect: George A. Kelly
Past President: Harold M. Hildreth
Secretary-Treasurer: Helen D. Sargent
Members at Large: Samuel B. Kutash, Roy Schafer

Representatives to Council: John E. Bell, Sol L. Garfield, Robert R. Holt, Victor C. Raimy, Anne Roe, Helen D. Sargent, Robert I. Watson

Editors, *Newsletter*, Vol. *9*: Jean W. Macfarlane, Helen D. Sargent

1956–1957 President: George A. Kelly

President-elect: Anne Roe

Past President: Jean W. Macfarlane

Secretary-Treasurer: Helen D. Sargent/Ivan N. Mensh

Members at Large: Helen D. Sargent, Edward Joseph Shoben, Jr.

Representatives to APA Council: John E. Bell, Sol L. Garfield, Florence C. Halpern, Robert R. Holt, Samuel B. Kutash, Ivan N. Mensh, Robert I. Watson

Editors, *Newsletter*, Vol. *10*: George A. Kelly, Helen D. Sargent/Ivan M. Mensh/Elizabeth Baker Wolf

1957–1958 President: Anne Roe

President-elect: James G. Miller

Past President: George A. Kelly

Secretary-Treasurer: Ivan N. Mensh

Members at Large: Thomas W. Richards, Edward Joseph Shoben, Jr.

Representatives to APA Council: John E. Bell, Sol L. Garfield, Ann M. Garner, Florence L. Halpern, Samuel B. Kutash, Ivan N. Mensh Robert I. Watson

Editor, *Newsletter*, Vol. *11*: Elizabeth B. Wolf

1958–1959 President: James G. Miller

President-elect: E. Lowell Kelly

Past President: Anne Roe

Secretary-Treasurer: Ivan N. Mensh

Members at Large: Boyd R. McCandless, Thomas W. Richards

Representatives to Council: Norman Garmezy, Ann M. Garner, Florence L. Halpern, Nicholas Hobbs, E. Lowell Kelly, Samuel B. Kutash, Ivan N. Mensh, Victor C. Raimy

Editor, *Newsletter*, Vol. *12*: Elizabeth B. Wolf

1959–1960 President: E. Lowell Kelly

President-elect: Nicholas Hobbs

Past President: James G. Miller

Secretary-Treasurer: Ivan N. Mensh

Representatives to APA Council: Ann M. Garner, Harrison
G. Gough, Nicholas Hobbs, E. Lowell Kelly, Ivan N.
Mensh, Victor C. Raimy, Anne Roe
Editors, *Newsletter*, Vol. 13: Elizabeth B. Wolf/D. Craig
Affleck

1960–1961 President: Nicholas Hobbs
President-elect: Robert R. Holt
Past President: E. Lowell Kelly
Secretary-Treasurer: Sol L. Garfield
Representatives to APA Council: Edward S. Bordin, Sol L.
Garfield, Harrison G. Gough, Nicholas Hobbs, Robert R.
Holt, E. Lowell Kelly, Victor C. Raimy, Anne Roe/James
G. Miller, William U. Snyder
Editor, *Newsletter*, Vol. 14: D. Craig Affleck

1961–1962 President: Robert R. Holt
President-elect: Victor Raimy
Past President: Nicholas Hobbs
Secretary-Treasurer: Sol L. Garfield
Representatives to APA Council: Edward S. Bordin, Sol L.
Garfield, Nicholas Hobbs, Robert R. Holt, Paul E. Meehl,
Eliot H. Rodnick, William U. Snyder
Editor, *Newsletter*, Vol. 15: D. Craig Affleck

1962–1963 President: Victor C. Raimy
President-elect: Starke R. Hathaway
Past President: Robert R. Holt
Secretary-Treasurer: Sol L. Garfield
Representatives to APA Council: Edward S. Bordin, Sol L.
Garfield, Starke R. Hathaway, Robert R. Holt, Victor C.
Raimy, Eliot H. Rodnick, William U. Snyder
Editors, *Newsletter*, Vol. 16, D. Craig Affleck/Leonard Haber

1963–1964 President: Starke R. Hathaway
President-elect: Sol L. Garfield
Past President: Victor C. Raimy
Secretary-Treasurer: Florence C. Halpern
Section Representatives: Sol Gordon (1), Theodore H. Blau
(2)
Representatives to APA Council: George W. Albee, Norman
L. Farberow, Florence L. Halpern, Molly Harrower, Starke
R. Hathaway, Victor C. Raimy, Hans H. Strupp
Editor, *Newsletter*, Vol. 17: Leonard Haber

1964–1965 President: Sol L. Garfield
President-elect: Ivan N. Mensh

Past President: Starke R. Hathaway
Secretary-Treasurer: Florence Halpern
Section Representatives: Sol Gordon (1), Theodore H. Blau
    (2)
Representatives to APA Council: George W. Albee, Norman
    Farberow, Florence Halpern, Molly Harrower Starke R.
    Hathaway
Editor, *Newsletter*, Vol. *18*: Leonard Haber

1965–1966 President: Ivan N. Mensh
President-elect: George W. Albee
Past President: Sol L. Garfield
Secretary-Treasurer: Florence Halpern
Section Representatives: Sol Gordon (1), Theodore H. Blau
    (2)
Representatives to APA Council: George W. Albee, Norman
    Farberow, Sol L. Garfield, Florence Halpern, Molly
    Harrower, Ivan N. Mensh
Editor, *Newsletter*, Vol. *19*: Leonard Haber

1966–1967 President: George W. Albee
President-elect: Florence Halpern
Past President: Ivan N. Mensh
Secretary-Treasurer: Norman Farberow
Section Representatives: Lovick C. Miller (1), Theodore H.
    Blau (2), Frederick Kanfer (3)
Representatives to APA Council: Irwin A. Berg, Hedda
    Bolgar, Gordon F. Derner, Joseph B. Margolin, Ivan N.
    Mensh, Alan O. Ross
Editor, *The Clinical Psychologist*, Vol. *20*: Donald K. Freedheim

1967–1968 President: Florence Halpern
President-elect: J. McV. Hunt
Past President: George W. Albee
Secretary-Treasurer: Norman L. Farberow
Section Representatives: Lovick C. Miller (1), Frederick
    Kanfer (3)
Representatives to APA Council: Irwin A. Berg, Hedda
    Bolgar, Gordon Derner, J. McV. Hunt, Joseph B. Margolin,
    Alan O. Ross
Editor, *The Clinical Psychologist*, Vol. *21*: Donald K. Freedheim

1968–1969 President: J. McV. Hunt
President-elect: Alan O. Ross
Past President: Florence Halpern
Secretary-Treasurer: Norman L. Farberow

Section Representatives: Lovick C. Miller (1), Frederick
Kanfer (3)
Representatives to APA Council: Irwin A. Berg, Hedda
Bolgar, Gordon Derner, Norman L. Farberow, Joseph B.
Margolis, Alan O. Ross
Editor, *The Clinical Psychologist*, Vol. 22, Donald K. Freedheim
1969–1970 President: Alan O. Ross
President-elect: Julian B. Rotter
Past President: J. McV. Hunt
Secretary-Treasurer: William Schofield
Section Representatives: Paul Dingman (1), Frederick Kanfer
(3)
Representatives to APA Council: Florence Halpern, J. McV.
Hunt, Edwin S. Shneidman, Leonard P. Ullman, Carl N.
Zimet
Editor, *The Clinical Psychologist*, Vol. 23: Norman A. Milgram
1970–1971 President: Julian B. Rotter
President-elect: Norman L. Farberow
Past President: Alan O. Ross
Secretary-Treasurer: William Schofield
Section Representatives: Charlotte H. Altman (1), Frederick
Kanfer (3)
Representatives to APA Council: Norman L. Farberow, Jules
D. Holzberg, Leonard Krasner, Edwin S. Shneidman,
Leonard P. Ullman, Carl N. Zimet
Editor, *The Clinical Psychologist*, Vol. 24: Norman A. Milgram
1971–1972 President: Norman L. Farberow
President-elect: Edwin S. Shneidman
Past President: Julian B. Rotter
Secretary-Treasurer: William Schofield
Section Representatives: Charlotte H. Altman (1), Paul M.
Lehrer (3)
Representatives to APA Council: Allan G. Barclay, Jules D.
Holzberg Frederick H. Kanfer, L, Krasner, Leonard P.
Ullman, Carl N. Zimet
Editor, *The Clinical Psychologist*, Vol. 25: Norman A. Milgram
1972–1973 President: Edwin S. Shneidman
Presidents-elect: Jules Holzberg/Theodore H. Blau
Past President: Norman L. Farberow
Secretary-Treasurer: Allan G. Barclay
Section Representatives: Charlotte H. Altman (1), Gerald C.
Davison (3)

Representatives to APA Council: George W. Albee, Allan G. Barclay, Theodore H. Blau, Sol L. Garfield, Florence C. Halpern, [Jules Holzberg], Frederick H. Kanfer, Leonard Krasner

Editor, *The Clinical Psychologist*, Vol. 26: Jerome H. Resnick

1973–1974 President: Theodore H. Blau
President-elect: Hans H. Strupp
Past President: Edwin S. Shneidman
Secretary-Treasurer: Allan G. Barclay
Section Representatives: Logan Wright (1), Steven G. Goldstein (2), Gerald C. Davison (3)
Representatives to APA Council: George W. Albee, Allan G. Barclay, Theodore H. Blau, Gordon F. Derner, Sol L. Garfield, Florence Halpern, Frederick H. Kanfer, Julian B. Rotter
Editor, *The Clinical Psychologist*, Vol. 27: Jerome H. Resnick

1974–1975 President: Hans H. Strupp
President-elect: Gordon F. Derner
Past President: Theodore H. Blau
Secretary-Treasurer: Allan G. Barclay
Section Representatives: Logan Wright (1), Steven Goldstein (2), Gordon Paul (3)
Representatives to APA Council: George W. Albee, Theodore H. Blau, Gordon F. Derner, Florence C. Halpern, Alan O. Ross, Julian B. Rotter
Editor, *The Clinical Psychologist*, Vol. 28: Jerome H. Resnick

1975–1976 President: Gordon Derner
President-elect: Max Siegel
Past President: Hans H. Strupp
Secretary-Treasurer: Allan G. Barclay
Section Representatives: Logan Wright (1), Steven Goldstein (2), Gordon Paul (3)
Representatives to APA Council: George Albee, Allan G. Barclay, Theodore Blau, Gordon F. Derner, Raymond D. Fowler, Sol L. Garfield, Florence Halpern, Arthur L. Kovacs, Peter Nathan, Alan O. Ross, Julian Rotter
Editor, *The Clinical Psychologist*, Vol. 29: Jerome H. Resnick

1976–1977 President: Max Siegel
President-elect: Norman Garmezy
Past President: Gordon Derner
Secretary-Treasurer: Allan G. Barclay

Section Representatives: Albert Cain (1), Steven G. Goldstein
(2), Gordon Paul (3)

Representatives to APA Council: Norman Abeles, Allan G.
Barclay, Gerald C. Davison, Gordon Derner, Raymond D.
Fowler, Arthur L. Kovacs, Peter Nathan, Alan O. Ross

Editor, *The Clinical Psychologist*, Vol. 30: Jerome H. Resnick

1977–1978    President: Norman Garmezy
President-elect: Nicholas A. Cummings
Past President: Max Siegel
Secretary-Treasurer: Allan G. Barclay
Section Representatives: Albert Cain (1), C. Eugene Walker
(2), Gordon Paul (3)

Representatives to APA Council: Norman Abeles, Allan G.
Barclay, Gerald C. Davison, Herbert Dorken, Raymond D.
Fowler, Arthur Kovacs, Peter E. Nathan, Jerome H.
Resnick, Alan O. Ross

Editor, *The Clinical Psychologist*, Vol. 31: Jerome H. Resnick

1978–1979    President: Nicholas A. Cummings
President-elect: Seymour B. Sarason
Past President: Norman Garmezy
Secretary-Treasurer: Allan G. Barclay
Section Representatives: Albert C. Cain (1), C. Eugene
Walker (2), Frederick H. Kanfer (3)

Representives to APA Council: Norman Abeles, Patrick
DeLeon, Herbert Dorken, Jerome H. Resnick, Max Siegel,
Suzanne B. Sobel, Bonnie R. Strickland

Editor, *The Clinical Psychologist*, Vol. 32: Sandra L. Harris

1979–1980    President: Seymour B. Sarason
President-elect: Allan G. Barclay
Past President: Nicholas A. Cummings
Secretary-Treasurer: Lee B. Sechrest
Section Representatives: Theodore H. Blau (1), C. Eugene
Walker (2), Frederick H. Kanfer (3)

Representatives to APA Council: Norman Abeles, Thomas J.
Boll, Patrick H. DeLeon, Herbert Dorken, Marvin Metsky,
Stanley Moldawsky, Jeanne S. Phillips, Jerome H. Resnick,
Max Siegel, Suzanne Sobel, Bonnie R. Strickland

Editor, *The Clinical Psychologist*, Vol. 33: Sandra L. Harris

1980–1981    President: Allan G. Barclay
President-elect: Logan Wright
Past President: Seymour B. Sarason
Secretary: Lee B. Sechrest

Section Representatives: Theodore H. Blau (1), Tom W. Patterson (2), Frederick H. Kanfer (3), Suzanne B. Sobel (4)

Representatives to APA Council: Thomas J. Boll, Patrick H. DeLeon, Marvin Metsky, Stanley Moldawsky, Jeanne S. Phillips, Jerome H. Resnick, Max Siegel, Bonnie R. Strickland

Editor, *The Clinical Psychologist*, Vol. 34: Sandra L. Harris

1981–1982 President: Logan Wright
President-elect: Bonnie R. Strickland
Past President: Allan G. Barclay
Secretary: Lee B. Sechrest
Treasurer: Laura C. Toomey
Section Representatives: Theodore H. Blau (1), Tom W. Patterson (2), Leonard H. Ullman (3), Suzanne B. Sobel (4), Phyllis Magrab (5)

Representatives to APA Council: Thomas J. Boll, Patrick DeLeon, Rachel T. Hare-Mustin, Sandra L. Harris, Marvin Metsky, Stanley Moldawsky, Peter E. Nathan, Jeanne S. Phillips, Jerome H. Resnick, Max Siegel, Bonnie R. Strickland, Carl N. Zimet

Editor, *The Clinical Psychologist*, Vol. 35: Samuel M. Turner

1982–1983 President: Bonnie R. Strickland
President-elect: Peter E. Nathan
Past President: Logan Wright
Secretary: Jeanne S. Phillips
Treasurer: Laura C. Toomey
Section Representatives: Donald K. Routh (1), Tom W. Patterson (2), Sandra Harris (3), Suzanne B. Sobel (4), Phyllis Magrab (5)

Representatives to APA Council: Allan G. Barclay, Rachel T. Hare-Mustin, Marvin Metsky, Peter E. Nathan, Logan Wright, Carl N. Zimet

Editor, *The Clinical Psychologist*, Vol. 36, Samuel M. Turner

1983–1984 President: Peter E. Nathan
President-elect: Lee B. Sechrest
Past President: Bonnie R. Strickland
Secretary: Jeanne S. Phillips
Treasurer: Laura C. Toomey
Section Representatives: Donald K. Routh (1), David J. Schroeder (2), Frederick H. Kanfer (3), Elaine Blechman (4), Phyllis Magrab (5)

Representatives to APA Council: Allan G. Barclay, Rachel T. Hare-Mustin, Peter E. Nathan, Bonnie R. Strickland, Logan Wright, Carl N. Zimet

Editor, *The Clinical Psychologist*, Vol. *37*: Samuel M. Turner

1985    President: Lee B. Sechrest
President-elect: Jules Barron
Past President: Peter E. Nathan
Secretary: Russell L. Adams
Treasurer: Laura C. Toomey
Section Representatives: Donald K. Routh (1), David J. Schroeder (2), Frederick H. Kanfer (3), Elaine Blechman (4), Phyllis Magrab (5)
Representatives to APA Council: Allan G. Barclay, Jerome H. Resnick, George Stricker, Bonnie R. Strickland, Diane J. Willis, Rogers H. Wright
Editor, *The Clinical Psychologist*, Vol. *38*: Lawrence Cohen

1986    President: Jules Barron
President-elect: Patrick H. DeLeon
Past President: Lee B. Sechrest
Secretary: Russell L. Adams
Treasurer: Laura C. Toomey
Section Representatives: June M. Tuma (1), David J. Schroeder (2), Linda Craighead (3), Gloria Gottsegen (4), Donald K. Routh (5)
Representatives to APA Council: Morris Goodman, Rachel T. Hare- Mustin, Jerome H. Resnick, Charles D. Spielberger, George Stricker, Rogers H. Wright
Editor, *The Clinical Psychologist*, Vol. *39*: Lawrence Cohen

1987    President: Patrick H. DeLeon
President-elect: Rogers H. Wright
Past President: Jules Barron
Secretary: Russell L. Adams
Treasurer: Laura C. Toomey
Section Representatives: June M. Tuma (1), Linda Craighead (3), Gloria Gottsegen (4), Donald K. Routh (5), Russell Jones (6)
Representatives to APA Council: Rachel T. Hare-Mustin, Jerome H. Resnick, George Stricker, Samuel M. Turner, Diane J. Willis, Rogers H. Wright
Editor, *The Clinical Psychologist*, Vol. *40*: Lawrence Cohen

1988    President: Rogers H. Wright
President-elect: Charles D. Spielberger

Past President: Patrick H. DeLeon
Secretary: Carolyn S. Schroeder
Treasurer: Laura C. Toomey
Section Representatives: June M. Tuma (1), Linda Craighead
(3), Gloria Gottsegen (4), Donald K. Routh (5), Samuel M.
Turner (6), Arthur Teicher (7)
Representatives to APA Council: Allan G. Barclay, Thomas J.
Boll, Rachel T. Hare-Mustin, George Stricker, Samuel
Turner, Diane J. Willis, Rogers Wright
Editors, *Clinical Psychology Review*, Vol. *8*, Alan S. Bellack,
Michel Hersen
Editor, *The Clinical Psychologist*, Vol. *41*: Gerald P. Koocher
1989 President: Charles D. Spielberger
President-elect: Norman Abeles
Past President: Rogers H. Wright
Secretary: Carolyn S. Schroeder
Treasurer: Laura M. Toomey
Section Representatives: Gerald P. Koocher (1), W. Edward
Craighead (3), Judith Worell (4), Sheila Eyberg (5), Russell
T. Jones (6), Arthur Teicher (7)
Representatives to APA Council: Norman Abeles, Allan G.
Barclay, Thomas J. Boll, Bonnie R. Strickland, Diane J.
Willis
Editors, *Clinical Psychology Review*, Vol. *9*: Alan S. Bellack,
Michel Hersen
Editor, *The Clinical Psychologist*, Vol. *42*: Gerald P. Koocher
1990 President: Norman Abeles
President-elect: Jerome Resnick
Past President: Charles D. Spielberger
Secretary: June M. Tuma
Treasurer: Laura M. Toomey
Section Representatives: Gerald P. Koocher (1), W. Edward
Craighead (3), Judith Worell (4), Sheila Eyberg (5), Russell
T. Jones (6), Arthur Teicher (7)
Representatives to Council: Norman Abeles, Allan G.
Barclay, Thomas J. Boll, Bonnie Strickland, Diane J. Willis
Editors, *Clinical Psychology Review*, Vol. *10*: Alan S. Bellack,
Michel Hersen
Editor, *The Clinical Psychologist*, Vol. *43/Clinical Psychology
Bulletin*: Gerald P. Koocher
1991 President: Jerome H. Resnick
President-elect: George Stricker

Past President: Norman Abeles

Secretary: June M. Tuma

Treasurer: Gerald P. Koocher

Section Representatives: Donald K. Routh (1), W. Edward Craighead (3), Judith Worell (4), Sheila Eyberg (5), Russell T. Jones (6), Jules Barron (7)

Representatives to APA Council: Norman Abeles, Lynn P. Rehm, Bonnie R. Strickland, Jan Wollersheim, Rogers H. Wright

Editors, *Clinical Psychology Review*, Vol. 11: Alan S. Bellack, Michel Hersen

Editor, *The Clinical Psychologist*, Vol. 44/*Clinical Psychology Bulletin*: Ronald Blount

1992   President: George Stricker

President-elect: David H. Barlow

Past President: Jerome H. Resnick

Secretary: June M. Tuma

Treasurer: Gerald P. Koocher

Section Representatives: Sheila Eyberg (1), Barry A. Edelstein (3), Violet Franks (4), Carolyn S. Schroeder (5), Bernadette Gray-Little (6)

Representatives to APA Council: Karen Calhoun, Lynn P. Rehm, Laura C. Toomey, Jan Wollersheim, Rogers H. Wright

Editors, *Clinical Psychology Review*, Vol. 12: Alan S. Bellack, Michel Hersen

Editor, *The Clinical Psychologist*, Vol. 45/*Clinical Psychology Bulletin*: Ronald Blount

1993   President: David H. Barlow

President-elect: Martin E. P. Seligman

Past President: George Stricker

Secretary: Donald K. Routh

Treasurer: Gerald P. Koocher

Section Representatives: Sheila Eyberg (1), Barry A. Edelstein (3), Violet Franks (4), Carolyn S. Schroeder (5), Bernadette Gray-Little (6)

Representatives to APA Council: Norman Abeles, Karen Calhoun, Charles D. Spielberger, Laura C. Toomey

Editor, *The Clinical Psychologist*, Vol. 46: Ronald Blount

## SECTION ON CLINICAL CHILD PSYCHOLOGY
## (SECTION 1, DIVISION 12)

1962–1963  Chair: Alan O. Ross
Chair-elect: Lovick C. Miller
Editor, *Newsletter*, Vol. 1: Allan G. Barclay
1963–1964  Chair: Lovick C. Miller
Chair-elect: Theodore Leventhal
Secretary-Treasurer: Allan G. Barclay
Representative to Division 12: Sol Gordon
Editor, *Newsletter*, Vol. 2: Allan G. Barclay
1964–1965  Chair: Theodore Leventhal
Chair-elect: S. Thomas Cummings
Secretary-Treasurer: Allan G. Barclay
Representative to Division 12: Sol Gordon
Editor, *Newsletter*, Vol. 3: Allan G. Barclay
1965–1966  Chair: S. Thomas Cummings
Chair-elect: Sebastiano G. Santostefano
Past Chair: Theodore Leventhal
Secretary-Treasurer: Charlotte Altman
Representative to Division 12: Sol Gordon
Editor, *Newsletter*, Vol. 4: Martin R. Gluck
1966–1967  Chair: Sebastiano G. Santostefano
Chair-elect: Zanwil Sperber
Past Chair: S. Thomas Cummings
Secretary-Treasurer: Charlotte H. Altman
Representative to Division 12: Lovick C. Miller
Editor, *Newsletter*, Vol. 5: Martin R. Gluck
1967–1968  Chair: Zanwil Sperber
Chair-elect: Charlotte H. Altman
Past Chair: Sebastiano G. Santostefano
Secretary-Treasurer: Mark Rudnick
Representative to Division 12: Lovick C. Miller
Editor, *Newsletter*, Vol. 6: Martin R. Gluck
1968–1969  Chair: Charlotte H. Altman
Chair-elect: Allan G. Barclay
Past Chair: Zanwil Sperber
Secretary-Treasurer: Mark Rudnick
Representative to Division 12: Lovick C. Miller
Editor, *Newsletter*, Vol. 7: Gertrude J. Williams
1969–1970  Chair: Allan G. Barclay
Chair-elect: Sol Gordon

Past Chair: Charlotte H. Altman
Secretary-Treasurer: Bettie Arthur
Representative to Division 12: Paul R. Dingman
Editor, *Newsletter*, Vol. *8*: Gertrude J. Williams

1970–1971 Chair: Sol Gordon
Chair-elect: Paul R. Dingman
Past Chair: Allan G. Barclay
Secretary-Treasurer: K. Gerald Marsden
Representative to Division 12: Charlotte H. Altman
Editor, *Newsletter*, Vols. *9, 10*: Gertrude J. Williams

1971–1972 Chair: Paul R. Dingman
Chair-elect: Erwin Friedman
Past Chair: Sol Gordon
Secretary-Treasurer: K. Gerald Marsden
Representative to Division 12: Charlotte H. Altman
Editor, *Journal of Clinical Child Psychology*, Vol. *1*: Gertrude J.
Williams (first issue "Winter 1971–1972")

1972–1973 President: Erwin Friedman [Note: The position title was
changed from "chair" to "president" at this point.]
President-elect: Marilee Fredericks
Past President: Paul R. Dingman
Secretary-Treasurer: K. Gerald Marsden
Representative to Division 12: Charlotte H. Altman
Editor, *Journal of Clinical Child Psychology*, Vol. *2*: Gertrude J.
Williams

1973–1974 President: Marilee Fredericks
President-elect: Milton F. Shore
Past President: Erwin Friedman
Secretary-Treasurer: Loretta K. Cass
Representative to Division 12: Logan Wright
Editor, *Journal of Clinical Child Psychology*, Vol. *3*: Gertrude J.
Williams

1974–1975 President: Milton F. Shore
President-elect: Gertrude J. Williams
Past President: Marilee Fredericks
Secretary-Treasurer: Loretta K. Cass
Representative to Division 12: Logan Wright
Editor, *Journal of Clinical Child Psychology*, Vol. *4*: Gertrude J.
Williams

1975–1976 President: Gertrude J. Williams
President-elect: Lee Salk
Past President: Milton F. Shore

Secretary-Treasurer: Loretta K. Cass
Representative to Division 12: Logan Wright
Editors, *Journal of Clinical Child Psychology*, Vol. 5: Gertrude J.
    Williams/Barbara Ellis Long/Diane J. Willis

1976–1977   President: Lee Salk
President-elect: Paul Wohlford
Past President: Gertrude J. Williams
Secretary-Treasurer: Donald K. Routh
Representative to Division 12: Albert C. Cain
Editor, *Journal of Clinical Child Psychology*, Vol. 6: Diane J.
    Willis

1977–1978   President: Paul Wohlford
President-elect: Gerald P. Koocher
Past President: Lee Salk
Secretary-Treasurer: Donald K. Routh
Representative to Division 12: Albert C. Cain
Editor, *Journal of Clinical Child Psychology*, Vol. 7: Diane J.
    Willis

1978–1979   President: Gerald P. Koocher
President-elect: Donald K. Routh
Past President: Paul Wohlford
Secretary-Treasurer: Lenore B. Behar
Representative to Division 12: Albert C. Cain
Editor, *Journal of Clinical Child Psychology*, Vol. 8: Diane J.
    Willis

1979–1980   President: Donald K. Routh
President-elect: June M. Tuma
Past President: Gerald P. Koocher
Secretary-Treasurer: Lenore B. Behar
Representative to Division 12: Theodore H. Blau
Editor, *Journal of Clinical Child Psychology*, Vol. 9: Diane J.
    Willis

1980–1981   President: June M. Tuma
President-elect: Carolyn S. Schroeder
Past President: Donald K. Routh
Secretary-Treasurer: Lenore B. Behar
Representative to Division 12: Theodore H. Blau
Editor, *Journal of Clinical Child Psychology*, Vol. 10: Diane J.
    Willis

1981–1982   President: Carolyn S. Schroeder
President-elect: Diane J. Willis
Past President: June M. Tuma

Secretary-Treasurer: Lenore B. Behar
Representative to Division 12: Theodore H. Blau
Editor, *Journal of Clinical Child Psychology*, Vol. *11*: June M. Tuma

1982–1983   President: Diane J. Willis
President-elect: Lenore B. Behar
Past President: Carolyn S. Schroeder
Secretary: Sheila Eyberg
Treasurer: Martha Perry
Representative to Division 12: Donald K. Routh
Editor, *Journal of Clinical Child Psychology*, Vol. *12*: June M. Tuma

1984   President: Lenore B. Behar [Note: Terms of office changed to the calendar year at this point.]
President-elect: Herbert C. Quay
Past President: Diane J. Willis
Secretary: Sheila Eyberg
Treasurer: Martha Perry
Members at Large: Alan E. Kazdin, Annette M. La Greca, Anthony Mannarino
Representative to Division 12: Donald K. Routh
Editor, *Journal of Clinical Child Psychology*, Vol. *13*: June M. Tuma

1985   President: Herbert C. Quay
President-elect: James H. Johnson
Past President: Lenore B. Behar
Secretary: Sheila Eyberg
Treasurer: Martha Perry
Members at Large: Alan E. Kazdin, Annette M. La Greca, Anthony Mannarino
Representative to Division 12: Donald K. Routh
Editor, *Journal of Clinical Child Psychology*, Vol. *14*: June M. Tuma

1986   President: James H. Johnson
President-elect: Sheila Eyberg
Past President: Herbert C. Quay
Secretary: Jan Culbertson
Treasurer: Martha Perry
Members at Large: Annette M. La Greca, Anthony Mannarino, Thomas H. Ollendick
Representative to Division 12: June M. Tuma

Editor, *Journal of Clinical Child Psychology*, Vol. *15*: June M. Tuma

Editor, *Newsletter*: Diane J. Willis

1987 President: Sheila Eyberg

President-elect: Russell A. Barkley

Past President: James H. Johnson

Secretary: Jan L. Culbertson

Treasurer: Martha Perry

Members at Large: Anthony Mannarino, Thomas H. Ollendick, Michael C. Roberts

Representative to Division 12: June M. Tuma

Editor, *Journal of Clinical Child Psychology*, Vol. *16*: Donald K. Routh

Editor, *Newsletter*: Diane J. Willis

1988 President: Russell A. Barkley

President-elect: Richard R. Abidin

Past President: Sheila Eyberg

Secretary: Jan L. Culbertson

Treasurer: Jean Elbert

Members at Large: A. J. Finch, Jr., Thomas H. Ollendick, Michael C. Roberts

Representative to Division 12: June M. Tuma

Editor, *Journal of Clinical Child Psychology*, Vol. *17*: Donald K. Routh

Editor, *Newsletter*: Diane J. Willis

1989 President: Richard R. Abidin

President-elect: Jan L. Culbertson

Past President: Russell A. Barkley

Secretary: Susan B. Campbell

Treasurer: Jean Elbert

Members at Large: A. J. Finch, Jr., Michael C. Roberts, C. Eugene Walker

Representative to Division 12: Gerald P. Koocher

Editor, *Journal of Clinical Child Psychology*, Vol. *18*: Donald K. Routh

Editor, *Newsletter*: Wendy Stone

1990 President: Jan L. Culbertson

President-elect: Thomas H. Ollendick

Past President: Richard R. Abidin

Secretary: Susan B. Campbell

Treasurer: Jean Elbert

Members at Large: Marilyn Erickson, A. J. Finch, Jr., C. Eugene Walker

Representative to Division 12: Gerald P. Koocher

Editor, *Journal of Clinical Child Psychology*, Vol. *19*: Donald K. Routh

Editor, *Newsletter*: Wendy Stone

1991 President: Thomas H. Ollendick

President-elect: Annette M. La Greca

Past President: Jan L. Culbertson

Secretary: Susan B. Campbell

Treasurer: Jean Elbert

Members at Large: Richard R. Abidin, Marilyn Erickson, C. Eugene Walker

Representative to Division 12: Donald K. Routh

Editor, *Journal of Clinical Child Psychology*, Vol. *20*: Donald K. Routh

Editor, *Newsletter*: Wendy Stone

1992 President: Annette M. La Greca

President-elect: Michael C. Roberts

Past President: Thomas H. Ollendick

Secretary: Susan B. Campbell

Treasurer: Jean Elbert

Members at Large: Richard R. Abidin, Marilyn Erickson, Wendy Stone

Representative to Division 12: Sheila Eyberg

Editor, *Journal of Clinical Child Psychology*, Vol. *21*: Jan L. Culbertson

Editor, *Newsletter*: Toni Eisenstadt

1993 President: Michael C. Roberts

President-elect: A. J. Finch, Jr.

Past President: Annette M. La Greca

Secretary: Susan B. Campbell

Treasurer: Jean Elbert

Members at Large: Richard R. Abidin, Wendy Stone, Kenneth J. Tarnowski

Representative to Division 12: Sheila Eyberg

Editor, *Journal of Clinical Child Psychology*, Vol. *22*: Jan L. Culbertson

Editor, *Newsletter*: Toni Eisenstadt

## Psychologists Interested in the Advancement of Psychotherapy (Section 2, Division 12)

1963–1964   President: Eugene T. Gendlin
             Vice President: Leonard Pearson
             Secretary: Carl N. Zimet
             Treasurer: Carl E. Morgan
             Representative to Division 12: Theodore H. Blau
             Editor, *Psychotherapy*, Vol. 1: Eugene T. Gendlin
             Editor, *Bulletin*: Marjorie Creelman
1964–1965   President: Leonard Pearson
             President-elect: Hans H. Strupp
             Secretary: Marjorie Creelman
             Treasurer: Carl E. Morgan
             Executive Board: Jules Barron, Arthur Burton, Erika Chance,
                 Reuben Fine, Victor C. Raimy, William U. Snyder
             Representative to Division 12: Theodore H. Blau
             Editor, *Psychotherapy*, Vol. 2: Eugene T. Gendlin
             Editor, *Bulletin*: Marjorie Creelman
1965–1966   President: Hans H. Strupp
             President-elect: Reuben Fine
             Past President: Leonard Pearson
             Secretary: Marjorie Creelman
             Treasurers: Carl E. Morgan/Ronald Fox
             Executive Board: Jules Barron, Charlotte B. Buhler, Arthur
                 Burton, Erika Chance, Jack D. Krasner, Harold Lindner,
                 William U. Snyder, Fred E. Spaner
             Editor, *Psychotherapy*, Vol. 3: Eugene T. Gendlin
             Editor, *Bulletin*: Vin Rosenthal
1966–1967   President: Reuben Fine
             President-elect: Fred Spaner
             Past President: Hans H. Strupp
             Secretary: Nancy Orlinsky
             Treasurer: Ronald Fox
             Representative to Division 12: Theodore H. Blau
             Executive Board: Jules Barron, Lawrence Bookbinder,
                 Charlotte Buhler, Robert Harper, Jack Krasner, Harold
                 Lindner, Leonard Pearson, Vin Rosenthal
             Editor, *Psychotherapy*, Vol. 4: Eugene T. Gendlin
             Editor, *Bulletin*: Vin Rosenthal

CORRESPONDING COMMITTEE OF FIFTY

1961–1962   Chair: Roger Bibace
            Steering Committee: David Bingham, Mary Engel, Edward
               Strain
      1963   Co-Chairs: Alvin Burstein, J. R. Newbrough
            Editor, *Newsletter*, Vol. 1: Allen E. Bergin
      1964   Co-Chairs: Allan Barclay, Donald Kausch, David McDonald
            Editor, *Newsletter*, Vol. 2: Allen E. Bergin
      1965   Chair: Allan Barclay
            Editor, *Newsletter*, Vol. 3: Stuart Wilson
      1966   Chair: Irwin H. Cohen
            Editor, *Newsletter*, Vol. 4: Stuart Wilson
      1967   Chair: Mark H. Lewin
      1968   Chair: Mark H. Lewin
            Editor, *Newsletter*, Vol. 5: C. Eugene Walker
      1969   Chair: Mark H. Lewin
            Editor, *Newsletter*, Vol 6: C. Eugene Walker
      1970   Chair: C. Eugene Walker
            Editor, *Newsletter*, Vol. 7: Steven G. Goldstein
      1971   Chair: C. Eugene Walker
            Editor, *Newsletter*, Vol. 8: Steven G. Goldstein/Frederic
               Weizmann
      1972   Chair: C. Eugene Walker
            Editor, *Newsletter*, Vol. 9: Frederic Weizmann
      1973   Chair: C. Eugene Walker
            Editor, *Newsletter*, Vol. 10: Frederic Weizmann


SECTION ON CONTINUING PROFESSIONAL DEVELOPMENT
(SECTION 2, DIVISION 12)

1973–1974   President-elect: C. Eugene Walker
            Secretary-Treasurer: Frederic Weizmann
            Representative to Division 12: Steven G. Goldstein
1974–1975   President: C. Eugene Walker
            President-elect: George Albee
            Secretary-Treasurer: Frederic Weizmann
            Representative to Division 12: Steven G. Goldstein
            Editor, *Newsletter*: Carl B. Dodrill
1975–1976   President: George Albee
            Secretary-Treasurer: Frederic Weizmann

Representative to Divison 12: Steven G. Goldstein

Editor, *Newsletter*: Carl B. Dodrill [Note: The *Newsletter* was evidently discontinued at this point.]

1976–1977 President: Allan G. Hedberg
Secretary-Treasurer: Frederic Weizmann
Representative to Divison 12: Steven G. Goldstein

1977–1978 President: Robert Wildman
Secretary-Treasurer: Wayne Hodges
Representative to Division 12: C. Eugene Walker

1978–1979 President: Tom W. Patterson
President-elect: John W. Baker, II
Secretary-Treasurer: Wayne Hodges
Representative to Division 12: C. Eugene Walker

1979–1980 President: John W. Baker, II
President-elect: Edmund J. Phillips
Secretary-Treasurer: Wayne Hodges
Representative to Division 12: C. Eugene Walker

1980–1981 President: Edmund J. Phillips
President-elect: David J. Schroeder
Past President: John W. Baker, II
Secretary-Treasurer: Michael G. McKee
Representative to Division 12: Tom W. Patterson

1981–1982 President: David J. Schroeder
President-elect: Larry E. Beutler
Past President: Edmund J. Phillips
Secretary-Treasurer: Michael G. McKee
Representative to Division 12: Tom W. Patterson

1982–1983 President: Larry E. Beutler
President-elect: Michael G. McKee
Past President: David J. Schroeder
Secretary-Treasurer: Michael G. McKee
Representative to Division 12: Tom W. Patterson

1983–1984 President: Michael G. McKee
President-elect: Bobby L. Gant
Past President: Larry E. Beutler
Secretary-Treasurer: Janet R. Matthews
Representative to Division 12: David J. Schroeder

1984–1985 President: Bobby L. Gant
President-elect: Jeanne Fish
Past President: Michael G. McKee
Secretary-Treasurer: Janet R. Matthews
Representative to Division 12: David J. Schroeder

1985–1986   President: Jeanne Fish
            Past President: Bobby L. Gant
            Representative to Division 12: David J. Schroeder

## SECTION ON CLINICAL GEROPSYCHOLOGY (SECTION 2, DIVISION 12)

1993   Organizing Committee: Barry Edelstein, Dolores
       Gallagher-Thompson, Margaret Gatz, Alfred Kaszniak,
       George Niederehe, Michael A. Smyer, George Stricker,
       Linda Teri

## SECTION FOR THE DEVELOPMENT OF CLINICAL PSYCHOLOGY AS AN EXPERIMENTAL–BEHAVIORAL SCIENCE/SECTION FOR A SCIENCE OF CLINICAL PSYCHOLOGY (SECTION 3, DIVISION 12)

1965   Organizing Committee: Albert Bandura, Cyril M. Franks,
       Arnold Goldstein, Frederick H. Kanfer, Leonard Krasner,
       Peter Lang, Robert Rosenthal, Kurt Salzinger, Irwin
       Sarason
1966   Chair: Leonard Krasner
1966–1967   Chair: Leonard P. Ullman
            Chair-elect: Arnold Goldstein
            Past Chair: Leonard Krasner
            Secretary-Treasurer: Kenneth Heller
            Representative to Division 12: Frederick H. Kanfer
            Editor, *Newsletter*: Stanley Feldstein
1967–1968   Chair: Arnold Goldstein
            Chair-elect: Richard S. Lazarus
            Past Chair: Leonard P. Ullman
            Secretary-Treasurer: Kenneth Heller
            Representative to Division 12: Frederick H. Kanfer
            Editor, *Newsletter*: Stanley Feldstein
1968–1969   Chair: Richard S. Lazarus
            Chair-elect: Bertram Cohen
            Past Chair: Arnold Goldstein
            Secretary-Treasurer: Kenneth Heller
            Representative to Division 12: Frederick H. Kanfer
            Editor, *Newsletter*: Stanley Feldstein
1969–1970   Chair: Bertram Cohen

Chair-elect: Brendan Maher
Past Chair: Richard S. Lazarus
Secretary-Treasurer: Peter E. Nathan
Representative to Division 12: Frederick H. Kanfer
Editor, *Newsletter*: Stanley Feldstein
1970–1971  Chair: Brendan Maher
Chair-elect: Walter Mischel
Past Chair: Bertram Cohen
Secretary-Treasurer: Peter E. Nathan
Representative to Division 12: Frederick H. Kanfer
Editor, *Newsletter*: Stanley Feldstein
1971–1972  Chair: Walter Mischel
Chair-elect: Gordon L. Paul
Past Chair: Brendan Maher
Secretary-Treasurer: Donna M. Gelfand
Representative to Division 12: Paul M. Lehrer
Editor, *Newsletter*: Stanley Feldstein
1972–1973  Chair: Gordon L. Paul
Chair-elect: Peter J. Lang
Past Chair: Walter Mischel
Secretary-Treasurer: K. Daniel O'Leary
Representative to Division 12: Gerald C. Davison
Editor, *Newsletter*: Michael J. Mahoney
1973–1974  Chair: Peter J. Lang
Chair-elect: Cyril M. Franks
Past Chair: Gordon L. Paul
Secretary-Treasurer: Loren Chapman
Representative to Division 12: Gerald C. Davison
Editor, *Newsletter*: Michael J. Mahoney
1974–1975  Chair: Cyril M. Franks
Chair-elect: Loren Chapman
Past Chair: Peter J. Lang
Secretary-Treasurer: Richard McFall
Representative to Division 12: Gordon L. Paul
Editor, *Newsletter*: Michael J. Mahoney
1975–1976  Chair: Loren Chapman
Chair-elect: Peter E. Nathan
Past Chair: Cyril M. Franks
Secretary-Treasurer: Richard McFall
Representative to Division 12: Gordon L. Paul
Editor, *Newsletter*: Rafael Klorman
1976–1977  President: Peter E. Nathan

President-elect: David H. Barlow
Past President: Loren Chapman
Secretary-Treasurer: Rosemery O. Nelson
Representative to Division 12: Gordon L. Paul
Editor, *Newsletter*: Rafael Klorman

1977–1978   President: David H. Barlow
President-elect: K. Daniel O'Leary
Past President: Peter E. Nathan
Secretary-Treasurer: Rosemery O. Nelson
Representative to Division 12: Frederick H. Kanfer
Editor, *Newsletter*: Rafael Klorman

1978–1979   President: K. Daniel O'Leary
President-elect: Rosemery O. Nelson
Past President: David H. Barlow
Secretary-Treasurer: G. Alan Marlatt
Representative to Division 12: Frederick Kanfer
Editor, *Newsletter*: G. Alan Marlatt

1979–1980   President: Rosemery O. Nelson
President-elect: Alan O. Ross
Past President: K. Daniel O'Leary
Secretary-Treasurer: G. Alan Marlatt
Representative to Division 12: Frederick H. Kanfer
Editor, *Newsletter*: G. Alan Marlatt

1980–1981   President: Alan O. Ross
President-elect: Leonard D. Eron
Past President: Rosemery O. Nelson
Secretary-Treasurer: W. Edward Craighead
Representative to Division 12: Frederick H. Kanfer
Editor, *Newsletter*: G. Alan Marlatt

1981–1982   President: Leonard D. Eron
President-elect: Donna M. Gelfand
Past President: Alan O. Ross
Secretary-Treasurer: W. Edward Craighead
Representative to Division 12: Leonard P. Ullman
Editor, *Newsletter*: William Hay

1982–1983   President: Donna M. Gelfand
President-elect: W. Edward Craighead
Past President: Leonard D. Eron
Secretary-Treasurer: Kelly D. Brownell
Representative to Division 12: Sandra L. Harris
Editor, *Newsletter*: William Hay

1983–1984   President: W. Edward Craighead

President-elect: G. Terence Wilson
Past President: Donna M. Gelfand
Secretary-Treasurer: Kelly D. Brownell
Representative to Division 12: Frederick H. Kanfer
Editor, *Newsletter*: Rolf Peterson

1984–1985 President: G. Terence Wilson
President-elect: G. Alan Marlatt
Past President: W. Edward Craighead
Secretary-Treasurer: Karen L. Bierman
Representative to Division 12: Frederick H. Kanfer
Editor, *Newsletter*: Rolf Peterson

1985–1986 President: G. Alan Marlatt
President-elect: Philip C. Kendall
Past President: G. Terence Wilson
Secretary-Treasurer: Karen L. Bierman
Representative to Division 12: Linda Craighead
Editor, *Newsletter*: Larry Grimm

1986–1987 President: Philip C. Kendall
President-elect: Neil S. Jacobson
Past President: G. Alan Marlatt
Secretary-Treasurer: Paul A. Lehrer
Representative to Division 12: Linda Craighead
Editor, *Newsletter*: Larry Grimm

1987–1988 President: Neil S. Jacobson
President-elect: Lynn P. Rehm
Past President: Philip C. Kendall
Secretary-Treasurer: Paul A. Lehrer
Representative to Division 12: Linda Craighead
Editor, *Newsletter*: Larry Grimm

1988–1989 President: Lynn C. Rehm
President-elect: Richard McFall
Past President: Neil S. Jacobson
Secretary-Treasurer: Paul A. Lehrer
Representiatve to Division 12: W. Edward Craighead
Editor, *Newsletter*: Larry Grimm

1989–1990 President: Richard McFall
President-elect: Karen S. Calhoun
Past President: Lynn P. Rehm
Secretary-Treasurer: Paul A. Lehrer
Representative to Division 12: W. Edward Craighead
Editor, *Newsletter*: Larry Grimm

1991    President: Karen S. Calhoun [Note: Terms of office changed
            to the calendar year at this point.]
        President-elect: Richard Bootzin
        Past President: Richard McFall
        Secretary-Treasurer: Laura L. Carstensen
        Representative to Division 12: W. Edward Craighead
        Editor, *Newsletter*: Robert Klepac
1992    President: Richard Bootzin
        President-elect: Thomas Oltmanns
        Past President: Karen S. Calhoun
        Secretary-Treasurer: Laura L. Carstensen
        Representative to Division 12: Barry A. Edelstein
        Editor, *Newsletter*: Robert Klepac
1993    President: Thomas Oltmanns
        President-elect: Laura L. Carstensen
        Past President: Richard Bootzin
        Secretary-Treasurer: Ian H. Gotlib
        Representative to Division 12: Robert Klepac
        Editor, *Newsletter*: Robert Klepac

## SECTION ON CLINICAL PSYCHOLOGY OF WOMEN (SECTION 4, DIVISION 12)

1980–1981    President: Rachel T. Hare-Mustin
            President-elect: Elaine Blechman
            Secretary: Carole A. Rayburn
            Treasurer: Patricia A. Wisocki
            Representative to Division 12: Suzanne B. Sobel
    1982    President: Elaine Blechman [Note: Terms of office changed
                to the calendar year at this point.]
            President-elect: Sandra L. Harris
            Past President: Rachel T. Hare-Mustin
            Secretary: Carole A. Rayburn
            Treasurer: Patricia A. Wisocki
            Representative to Division 12: Suzanne B. Sobel
            Editors, *Newsletter*: Nancy Beakel, Judith Todd
    1983    President: Sandra L. Harris
            President-elect: Carole A. Rayburn
            Past President: Elaine Blechman
            Secretary: Carole Rayburn
            Treasurer: Lenore B. Behar

Representative to Division 12: Suzanne B. Sobel
Editor, *Newsletter*: Judith Todd

1984   President: Carole A. Rayburn
President-elect: Judith Worell
Past President: Sandra L. Harris
Secretary: Violet Franks
Treasurer: Lenore B. Behar
Representative to Division 12: Elaine Blechman
Editor, *Newsletter*: Judith Todd

1985   President: Carole A. Rayburn
President-elect: Judith Worell
Past President: Sandra L. Harris
Secretary: Violet Franks
Treasurer: Lenore B. Behar
Representative to Division 12: Elaine Blechman
Editor, *Clinical Psychology of Women*: Asuncion M. Austria

1986   President: Judith Worell
President-elect: Julia A. Sherman
Past President: Carole A. Rayburn
Secretary: Violet Franks
Treasurer: Violet Franks
Representative to Division 12: Gloria B. Gottsegen
Editor, *Clinical Psychology of Women*: Asuncion M. Austria

1987   President: Judith Worell
President-elect: Julia A. Sherman
Past President: Carole A. Rayburn
Secretary: Frances M. Culbertson
Treasurer: Violet Franks
Representative to Division 12: Gloria B. Gottsegen
Editor, *Clinical Psychology of Women*: Asuncion M. Austria

1988   President: Julia A. Sherman
President-elect: Iris E. Fodor
Past President: Judith Worell
Secretary: Frances M. Culbertson
Treasurer: Gloria Gottsegen
Representative to Division 12: Gloria B. Gottsegen
Editor, *Clinical Psychology of Women*: Asuncion M. Austria

1989   President: Iris E. Fodor
President-elect: Violet Franks
Past President: Julia A. Sherman
Secretary: Frances M. Culbertson
Treasurer: Gloria Gottsegen

Representative to Division 12: Judith Worell
Editor, *Clinical Psychology of Women*: Asuncion M. Austria
1990   President: Violet Franks
President-elect: Frances M. Culbertson
Secretary: Janet Matthews
Treasurer: Gloria Gottsegen
Representative to Division 12: Judith Worell
Editor, *Clinical Psychology of Women*: Asuncion M. Austria
1991   President: Frances M. Culbertson
President-elect: Jacqueline Bouhoutsos
Past President: Violet Franks
Secretary: Janet R. Matthews
Treasurer: Gloria B. Gottsegen
Representative to Division 12: Judith Worell
Editor, *Clinical Psychology of Women*: Violet Franks
1992   Presidents: Jacqueline Bouhoutsos/Frances M. Culbertson
President-elect: Asuncion M. Austria
Past President: Frances M. Culbertson
Secretary: Janet R. Matthews
Treasurer: Michael Gottlieb
Representative to Division 12: Violet Franks
Editor, *Clinical Psychology of Women*: Mary Anne Siderits
1993   President: Asuncion M. Austria
President-elect: Gloria Gottsegen
Past President: Frances M. Culbertson
Secretary: Janet Matthews
Treasurer: Michael Gottlieb
Representative to Division 12: Violet Franks
Editor, *Clinical Psychology of Women*: Mary Anne Siderits

## SOCIETY OF PEDIATRIC PSYCHOLOGY (ORIGINALLY PART OF SECTION 1; SINCE 1980, SECTION 5, DIVISION 12)

1968–1970   Chair: Logan Wright
Chair-elect: Lee Salk
Secretary: Dorothea M. Ross
Editor, *Pediatric Psychology*: G. Gail Gardner
1970–1971   President: Lee Salk
President-elect: David Rigler
Past President: Logan Wright
Secretary-Treasurer: Donald K. Routh

Editor, *Pediatric Psychology*: G. Gail Gardner
1971–1972 Presidents: David Rigler/Lee Salk
President-elect: Arthur N. Wiens
Secretary-Treasurer: Donald K. Routh
Council Members: Allan G. Barclay, Marilyn
Erickson/David Rigler, Arthur Wiens
Editor, *Newsletter*: Allan G. Barclay/Diane J. Willis
1972–1973 President: Arthur N. Wiens
President-elect: Donald K. Routh
Past President: Lee Salk
Secretary-Treasurer: David A. Vore
Council Members: Allan G. Barclay, Milton F. Shore, Diane J.
Willis
Editor, *Newsletter*: Diane J. Willis
1973–1974 President: Donald K. Routh
President-elect: David A. Vore
Past President: Arthur N. Wiens
Secretary-Treasurer: Thomas J. Kenny
Council Member: Diane J. Willis
Editor, *Newsletter*: Diane J. Willis
1974–1975 President: David A. Vore
President-elect: Diane J. Willis
Past President: Donald K. Routh
Secretary-Treasurer: Carolyn S. Schroeder
Council Members: Donald K. Freedheim, H. Elizabeth King,
Diane J. Willis
Editor, *Newsletter*: Diane J. Willis
1975–1976 President: Thomas J. Kenny
President-elect: Diane J. Willis
Past President: David A. Vore
Secretary-Treasurer: Carolyn S. Schroeder
Council Members: Donald K. Freedheim, H. Elizabeth King,
June M. Tuma
Editors, *Journal of Pediatic Psychology*, Vol. 1: Diane J.
Willis/Donald K. Routh
1976–1977 President: Diane J. Willis
President-elect: Carolyn S. Schroeder
Past President: Thomas J. Kenny
Secretary-Treasurer: Larry M. Raskin
Council Members: Donald K. Freedheim, H. Elizabeth King,
June M. Tuma
Editor, *Journal of Pediatric Psychology*, Vol. 2: Donald K. Routh

1977–1978  President: Carolyn S. Schroeder
President-elect: H. Elizabeth King
Past President: Diane J. Willis
Secretary-Treasurer: Larry M. Raskin
Council Members: Thomas J. Kenny, June M. Tuma
Editor, *Journal of Pediatric Psychology*, Vol. 3: Donald K. Routh

1978–1979  President: H. Elizabeth King
President-elect: June M. Tuma
Past President: Carolyn S. Schroeder
Secretary-Treasurer: Philip W. Davidson
Council Members: Dennis D. Drotar, Phyllis R. Magrab,
Arlene Schaefer
Editor, *Journal of Pediatric Psychology*, Vol. 4: Donald K. Routh

1979–1980  President: June M. Tuma
President-elect: Phyllis R. Magrab
Past President: H. Elizabeth King
Secretary-Treasurer: Philip W. Davidson
Council Members: Dennis D. Drotar, Sheila Eyberg, Gary B.
Mesibov
Editor, *Journal of Pediatric Psychology*, Vol. 5: Donald K. Routh

1980–1981  President: Phyllis R. Magrab
President-elect: Dennis D. Drotar
Past President: June M. Tuma
Secretary-Treasurer: Georgette M. Psarras
Council Members: Sheila M. Eyberg, Gary B. Mesibov,
Michael C. Roberts
Editor, *Journal of Pediatric Psychology*, Vol. 6: Donald K. Routh

1981–1982  President: Dennis D. Drotar
President-elect: Gary B. Mesibov
Past President: Phyllis R. Magrab
Secretary-Treasurer: Georgette M. Psarras
Council Member: Michael C. Roberts
Representative to Division 12: Phyllis R. Magrab
Editor, *Journal of Pediatric Psychology*, Vol. 7: Donald K. Routh

1982–1983  President: Gary B. Mesibov
President-elect: Sheila M. Eyberg
Past President: Dennis D. Drotar
Secretary-Treasurer: Georgette Psarras Constantinou
Council Members: Dennis C. Harper, Michael C. Roberts,
Brian Stabler
Representative to Division 12: Phyllis R. Magrab

Editor, *Journal of Pediatric Psychology*, Vol. *8*: Gerald P.
  Koocher

Editor, *Newsletter*: Michael C. Roberts

1984  President: Sheila M. Eyberg [Note: Terms of office changed
    to the calendar year at this point.]

President-elect: Michael C. Roberts

Past President: Gary B. Mesibov

Secretary-Treasurer: Sue White

Council Members: Dennis C. Harper, Annette M. La Greca,
  Brian Stabler

Representative to Division 12: Phyllis R. Magrab

Editor, *Journal of Pediatric Psychology*, Vol. *9*: Gerald P.
  Koocher

Editor, *Newsletter*: Brian Stabler

1985  President: Michael C. Roberts

President-elect: Dennis C. Harper

Past President: Sheila M. Eyberg

Secretary-Treasurer: Sue White

Members at Large: Georgette Psarras Constantinou, Annette
  M. La Greca, Brian Stabler

Representative to Division 12: Phyllis R. Magrab

Editor, *Journal of Pediatric Psychology*, Vol. *10*: Gerald P.
  Koocher

Editor, *Newsletter*: Elizabeth Robinson

1986  President: Dennis C. Harper

President-elect: C. Eugene Walker

Past President: Michael C. Roberts

Secretary: J. Kenneth Whitt

Treasurer: Sue White

Members at Large: Debra Bendell, Georgette Psarras
  Constantinou, Annette M. La Greca

Representative to Division 12: Donald K. Routh

Editor, *Journal of Pediatric Psychology*, Vol. *11*: Gerald P.
  Koocher

Editor, *Newsletter*: Elizabeth Robinson

1987  President: C. Eugene Walker

President-elect: Annette M. La Greca

Past President: Dennis C. Harper

Secretary: J. Kenneth Whitt

Treasurer: Gerald P. Koocher

Members at Large: Debra Bendell, Georgette Psarras
  Constantinou, Jan L. Wallander

Representative to Division 12: Donald K. Routh
Editor, *Journal of Pediatric Psychology*, Vol. *12*: Gerald P.
  Koocher
Editor, *Newsletter*: Ronald Blount
1988   President: Annette M. La Greca
President-elect: Sue White
Past President: C. Eugene Walker
Secretary: J. Kenneth Whitt
Treasurer: Gerald P. Koocher
Member at Large: Terri Shelton
Representative to Division 12: Donald K. Routh
Editor, *Journal of Pediatric Psychology*, Vol. *13*: Michael C.
  Roberts
Editor, *Newsletter*: Ronald Blount
1989   President: Sue White
President-elect: Lawrence J. Siegel
Past President: Annette M. La Greca
Secretary: Jan L. Culbertson
Treasurer: Gerald P. Koocher
Members at Large: Terri L. Shelton, Jan L. Wallander
Representative to Division 12: Sheila M. Eyberg
Editor, *Journal of Pediatric Psychology*, Vol. *14*: Michael C.
  Roberts
Editor, *Newsletter*: Ronald Blount
1990   President: Lawrence J. Siegel
President-elect: Gerald P. Koocher
Past President: Sue White
Secretary: Jan L. Culbertson
Treasurer: Debra Bendell-Estroff
Members at Large: William A. Rae, Dennis C. Russo, Terri L.
  Shelton
Representative to Division 12: Sheila M. Eyberg
Editor, *Journal of Pediatric Psychology*, Vol. *15*: Michael C.
  Roberts
Editors, *Newsletter*: Mary C. Cerreto/Lawrence J. Siegel
1991   President: Gerald P. Koocher
President-elect: Jan L. Wallander
Past President: Lawrence J. Siegel
Secretary: Jan L. Culbertson
Treasurer: Debra Bendell Estroff
Members at Large: William A. Rae, Dennis C. Russo, Donald
  Wertlieb

Representative to Divison 12: Sheila M. Eyberg
Editor, *Journal of Pediatric Psychology*, Vol. *16*: Michael C.
  Roberts
Editor, *Progress Notes*: Lawrence J. Siegel
1992   President: Jan L. Wallander
President-elect: Suzanne B. Johnson
Past President: Gerald P. Koocher
Secretary: Terri L. Shelton
Treasurer: Debra Bendell Estroff
Members at Large: Dennis C. Russo, Conway F. Saylor,
  Donald Wertlieb
Representative to Division 12: Carolyn S. Schroeder
Editor, *Journal of Pediatric Psychology*, Vol. *17*: Michael C.
  Roberts
Editor, *Progress Notes*: Lawrence J. Siegel
1993   President: Suzanne B. Johnson
President-elect: Dennis C. Russo
Past President: Jan L. Wallander
Secretary: Terri L. Shelton
Treasurer: Melanie McGrath
Members at Large: Linda Hurley, Conway F. Saylor, Donald
  Wertlieb
Representative to Division 12: Carolyn S. Schroeder
Editor, *Journal of Pediatric Psychology*, Vol. *18*: Annette M. La
  Greca
Editor, *Progress Notes*: Lawrence J. Siegel


## Section on Ethnic Minority Clinical Psychology (Section 6, Division 12)

1986–1987   President: Gail E. Wyatt
President-elect: Lillian Comas-Diaz
Secretary: Elsie Go Lu
Treasurer: Medria Williams-Young
Representative to Division 12: Russell T. Jones
1988   President: Gail E. Wyatt [Note: Terms of office changed to
  the calendar year at this point.]
President-elect: Lillian Comas-Diaz
Secretary: Elsie Go Lu
Treasurer: Medria Williams-Young
Representative to Division 12: Russell T. Jones

1989   President: Lillian Comas-Diaz
       President-elect: Reiko H. True
       Past President: Gail E. Wyatt
       Secretary: Elsie Go Lu
       Treasurer: Medria Williams-Young
       Representative to Division 12: Russell T. Jones
1990   President: Reiko H. True
       Past President: Lillian Comas-Diaz
       Secretary: Elsie Go Lu
       Treasurer: Medria Williams-Young
       Representative to Division 12: Russell T. Jones
1991   President: Reiko H. True
       President-elect: Jean Lau Chin
       Past President: Lillian Comas-Diaz
       Secretary-Treasurer: Medria Williams-Young
       Representative to Division 12: Russell T. Jones
1992   President: Jean Lau Chin
       Past President: Reiko H. True
       Secretary: Steven Lopez
       Treasurer: Elsie Go Lu
       Representative to Division 12: Bernadette Gray-Little
1993   President: Vicki Mays
       President-elect: Lou Jenkins
       Past President: Jean Lau Chin
       Secretary: Felicisima Serafica
       Treasurer: Elsie Go Lu
       Representative to Division 12: Bernadette Gray-Little
       Newsletter: Jean Lau Chin

## SECTION ON THE THEORY AND PRACTICE OF GROUP PSYCHOTHERAPY (SECTION 7, DIVISION 12)

1988   President: Arthur Teicher
       President-elect: Jules Barron
       Secretary: David Hescheles
       Representative to Division 12: Arthur Teicher
1989   President: Arthur Teicher
       President-elect: Jules Barron
       Secretary: Gail Winbury
       Treasurer: Michael Andronico
       Representative to Division 12: Arthur Teicher

1990   President: Arthur Teicher
       President-elect: Jules Barron
       Secretary: Gail Winbury
       Treasurer: Michael Andronico
       Representative to Division 12: Arthur Teicher
1991   President: Arthur Teicher
       President-elect: Morris Goodman
       Secretary: Candace Nattland
       Treasurer: Michael Andronico
       Representative to Division 12: Jules Barron
       Editor, *Newsletter*: Irwin Kutash

# C

# Recipients of Awards of the Division of Clinical Psychology and Related Organizations

DIVISION OF CLINICAL PSYCHOLOGY (DIVISION 12), AMERICAN PSYCHOLOGICAL ASSOCIATION

*Award for Distinguished Contributions to the Science and Profession of Clinical Psychology*

1958   John G. Darley
       Frederic Lyman Wells
1959   Starke R. Hathaway
       David Shakow
1960   David Rapaport
       David Wechsler
1961   Samuel J. Beck
       Henry A. Murray
1962   Stanley D. Porteus
       Carl R. Rogers
1963   Edgar A. Doll
       Jean W. Macfarlane
1964   Norman A. Cameron
       Robert W. White
1965   George A. Kelly
       Bruno Klopfer
1966   Harold M. Hildreth (posthumous)
       Nicholas Hobbs
       Joseph Zubin (special award)

1967   William A. Hunt
       Paul E. Meehl
1968   Jerry W. Carter, Jr.
       Julian B. Rotter
1969   Noble H. Kelley
       Seymour Sarason
1970   John E. Bell
       R. Nevitt Sanford
1971   Rollo R. May
       Silvan S. Tomkins
1972   E. Lowell Kelly
       Anne Roe
1973   Florence C. Halpern
       J. McV. Hunt
1974   Robert R. Holt
       Evelyn Hooker
1975   Gardner Lindzey
       O. Hobart Mowrer
1976   Sol L. Garfield
       Eliot H. Rodnick
1977   Norman Farberow
       Edwin S. Shneidman
1978   Erich Fromm
       Bernard Kalinkowitz
       Sheldon Korchin
       Benjamin B. Wolman
1979   Bruno Bettelheim
       Erik Erikson
1980   Molly Harrower
       Karen Machover
1981   Hans H. Strupp
       Carl N. Zimet
1982   Alan O. Ross
       Janet T. Spence
1983   Joseph D. Matarazzo (scientific award)
       Jack Wiggins, Jr. (professional award)
1984   Mary D. S. Ainsworth (scientific award)
       Louis Cohen (professional award)
1985   Harold L. Raush (professional award)
       Saul Rosenzweig (scientific award)
1986   Lester Luborsky (scientific award)
       Jeanne Phillips (professional award)

1987   Robert A. Harper (professional award)
       Morris B. Parloff (scientific award)
       Oscar A. Parsons (scientific award)
       Robert D. Weitz (professional award)
1988   Ronald E. Fox
       Norman Garmezy
       Frank J. Sullivan (public service award)
1989   Patrick H. DeLeon
       Charles D. Spielberger
1990   Herman Feifel (scientific award)
       Rogers H. Wright (professional award)
1991   [no awards]
1992   Jules Barron (special posthumous award)
       Alan E. Kazdin (scientific award)
       Donald K. Routh (professional award)
1993   K. Daniel O'Leary (scientific award)
       Robert J. Resnick (professional award)

## SECTION ON CLINICAL CHILD PSYCHOLOGY (SECTION 1, DIVISION 12)

*Distinguished Professional Contribution Award*

1978   Nicholas Hobbs
1979   Lee Salk
1980   Alan O. Ross
1981   Milton F. Shore
1982   Herbert E. Rie
1983   Ann Magaret Garner
1984   Gerald P. Koocher
1985   Gertrude J. Williams
1986   Charles Wenar
1987   Gerald R. Patterson
1988   Urie Bronfenbrenner
1989   Donald K. Routh
1990   Virginia I. Douglas
1991   Herbert C. Quay
1992   Norman Garmezy
1993   Thomas M. Achenbach

*Student Research Award*

1986   Nirmala Rao
1987   Thomas V. Sayger
1988   Paul Frick
1989   Jeremy S. Stock
1990   Mary Anne G. Christ
1991   Lisa A. Moore
1992   Daniel W. Hoover
1993   Kate Keenan

*Other award*

1992   Donald K. Routh (scholarly contributions as editor)

# SECTION FOR THE DEVELOPMENT OF CLINICAL PSYCHOLOGY AS AN EXPERIMENTAL–BEHAVIORAL SCIENCE/SECTION FOR A SCIENCE OF CLINICAL PSYCHOLOGY (SECTION 3, DIVISION 12)

*Distinguished Scientist Award*

1971   David Shakow
1972   Albert Bandura
1973   Leonard P. Ullman
1974   Norman Garmezy
1975   Joseph Zubin
1976   Paul E. Meehl
1977   Gordon L. Paul
1978   Walter Mischel
1979   Hans H. Strupp
1980   Peter J. Lang
1981   Sol L. Garfield
1982   Gerald R. Patterson
1983   Sarnoff A. Mednick
1984   S. J. Rachman
1985   K. Daniel O'Leary
1986   Martin E. P. Seligman
1987   G. Terence Wilson
1988   Hans J. Eysenck
1989   David Barlow
1990   John Teasdale
1991   John M. Neale
1992   Loren Chapman

1993   Edna Foa

*Outstanding Dissertation Award*

1975   Joan Huser Liem
1976   Arne Gray
1977   Sandra M. Levy
1978   Orcena E. Lyle
1979   Edmund F. Chaney
1980   Robert E. Drake
1981   Richard C. Delaney
1982   [no award]
1983   Judith A. Turner
1984   Keith H. Nuechterlein
1985   Anne D. Simons
1986   J. Gayle Beck
1987   James C. Overholser
1988   Joyce Hopkins
1989   Linda K. Forsberg
1990   Michael Cook
1991   Janet S. Klosko
1992   Sharon Zeitlin
1993   Howard Berenbaum

*Poster Award*

1991   Julie Babcock
1992   Steve Ilardi
       Sheila Mulvaney


# SECTION ON CLINICAL PSYCHOLOGY OF WOMEN (SECTION 4, DIVISION 12)

*Distinguished Contribution Award*

1986   Elaine Blechman
       Frances M. Culbertson

*Other award*

1993   David H. Barlow (special award)

## SOCIETY OF PEDIATRIC PSYCHOLOGY (ORIGINALLY PART OF SECTION 1; AS OF 1980, SECTION 5, DIVISION 12)

*Distinguished Contribution Award*

1977   Lee Salk
1978   Logan Wright
1979   Dorothea Ross
1980   Arthur N. Wiens
1981   Donald K. Routh
1982   Diane J. Willis
1983   Thomas J. Kenny
1984   Carolyn S. Schroeder
1985   Phyllis R. Magrab

*[Renamed] Distinguished Service Award*

1986   June M. Tuma
1987   Gerald P. Koocher
1988   [no award]
1989   Dennis D. Drotar
1990   Gary B. Mesibov
1991   Annette M. La Greca
1992   Brian Stabler

*[Renamed] Lee Salk Distinguished Service Award*

1993   Michael C. Roberts

*Significant Research Contribution Award*

1986   John J. Spinetta
1988   Lizette Peterson
1991   Barbara Melamed
1993   Dennis D. Drotar

*Student Research Award*

1977   Barry Golinko
1982   Sandra Shaheen
1984   Ann V. Deaton
1986   David O'Grady
1988   Karen E. Smith

1990   Leilani Greening
       Lenora G. Knapp
1991   Lucretia Mann
1992   Jacqueline Hutchinson
1993   Wendy B. Schuman

*Presidential Award*

1989   Logan Wright
       Lee Salk
       Dorothea Ross
       Diane J. Willis
       Phyllis R. Magrab
       Donald K. Routh

*Other awards*

1977   Arthur Wiens (special award)
1986   Gerald P. Koocher (scholarly contributions as editor)
1992   Michael C. Roberts (scholarly contributions as editor)

# D

# *Alphabetical List of Officers and Awardees*

Abeles, Norman (1928–), Ph.D. (counseling psychology), University of Texas, 1958, licensed, ABPP–CO, Fellow of Division 12.

Abidin, Richard Robert (1938–), Ed.D. (school psychology), Rutgers University, 1964, licensed, ABPP–CL, Fellow of Divison 12.

Achenbach, Thomas M. (1940–), Ph.D. (general psychology), University of Minnesota, 1966, licensed, Fellow of Division 12.

Ackerson, Luton A. (1892–), Ph.D., Columbia University, 1927, Fellow of Division 12.

Adams, Russell Lee (1941–), Ph.D. (educational psychology), University of Texas, 1967, licensed, ABPP–CL, Fellow of Division 12.

Affleck, Dean Craig (1928–), Ph.D., Northwestern University, 1954, licensed, ABPP–CL, Fellow of APA.

Ainsworth, Mary Dinsmore Salter (1913–), Ph.D. (personality psychology), University of Toronto, 1939, licensed, ABPP–CL, Fellow of Division 12.

Albee, George W. (1921–), Ph.D. (clinical psychology), University of Pittsburgh, 1949, licensed, ABPP–CL, Fellow of Division 12.

Altman, Charlotte Hall (1908–), Ph.D. (clinical psychology), University of Chicago, 1954, licensed, ABPP–CL, Fellow of Division 12.

Anderson, John Edward (1893–1966), Ph.D., Harvard University, 1917, Fellow of APA.

Anderson, Rose Gustava (1893–1978), Ph.D. (clinical psychology), Columbia University, 1925, licensed, ABPP–CL, Fellow of Division 12.

Andronico, Michael Paul (1936–), Ph.D. (clinical psychology), Rutgers University, 1963, licensed.

Arthur, Bettie (1924–), Ph.D. (clinical psychology), University of Michigan, 1958, licensed.

Austria, Asuncion C. Miteria, Ph.D. (clinical psychology), Northwestern University, 1970, licensed.

Babcock, Julie, graduate student, University of Washington.

Baker, Harry Jay (1889–), Ph.D. (educational psychology), University of Michigan, 1920, licensed, ABPP–CL, Fellow of APA.

Baker, John William, II (1940–), Ph.D. (clinical psychology), West Virginia University, 1967, licensed, ABPP–CL.

Bakes, Frank P. (1902–1983), Ph.D., University of Iowa, 1938, ABPP–CL, Fellow of Division 12.

Bandura, Albert (1925–), Ph.D. (clinical psychology), University of Iowa, 1952, Fellow of APA.

Barclay, Allan G. (1930–), Ph.D. (clinical psychology), Washington University, 1960, licensed, ABPP–CL, Fellow of Division 12.

Barkley, Russell A. (1949–), Ph.D. (clinical psychology), Bowling Green State University, 1977, licensed, ABPP–CL.

Barlow, David Harrison (1942–), Ph.D. (clinical psychology), University of Vermont, 1969, licensed, ABPP–CL, Fellow of Division 12.

Barron, Jules (1923–1991), Ph.D. (clinical psychology), New York University, 1952, licensed, ABPP–CL, Fellow of Division 12.

Beakel, Nancy Grauer (1936–), Ph.D. (clinical psychology), U.C.L.A., 1970, licensed.

Beck, J. Gayle, Ph.D. (clinical psychology), State University of New York at Albany, 1984.

Beck, Samuel Jacob (1896–), Ph.D., Columbia University, 1932, ABPP–CL, Fellow of Division 12.

Behar, Lenore Marylyn Balsam (1938–), Ph.D. (clinical psychology), Duke University, 1963, licensed, Fellow of APA.

Bell, John Elderkin (1913–), Ed.D. (clinical psychology), Columbia University, 1942, ABPP–CL, Fellow of Division 12.

Bellack, Alan Scott (1944–), Ph.D. (clinical psychology), Pennsylvania State University, 1970, licensed, Fellow of Division 12.

Bendell, Roberta Debra (married name: Bendell-Estroff) (1940–), Ph.D. (school psychology), University of Kansas, 1975, licensed.

Berenbaum, Howard (1960–), Ph.D. (clinical psychology), Indiana University, 1987.

Berg, Irwin August (1913–), Ph.D. (physiological psychology), University of Michigan, 1942, ABPP–CO, Fellow of Division 12.

Bergin, Allen E. (1934–), Ph.D. (clinical psychology), Stanford University, 1960, licensed, ABPP–CL, Fellow of Division 12.

Bernreuter, Robert Gibbon (1901–), Ph.D. (general psychology), Stanford University, 1931, licensed, ABPP–CL, Fellow of APA.

Berry, Charles Scott (1875–1960), Ph.D., Harvard University, 1907, certified by APA as a consulting psychologist, Fellow of APA.

Bettelheim, Bruno (1903–1990), Ph.D., University of Vienna, 1938, ABPP–CL, Fellow of Division 12.

Beutler, Larry Edward (1941–), Ph.D. (clinical psychology), University of Nebraska, 1970, licensed, ABPP–CL, Fellow of Division 12.

Bibace, Roger (1926–), Ph.D. (clinical psychology), Clark University, 1956, licensed.

Bierman, Karen Leah (1953–), Ph.D. (clinical psychology), U.C.L.A., 1980, licensed.

Bingham, David Starr (1926–), Ph.D., University of Connecticut, 1957.

Blau, Theodore Hertzl (1928–), Ph.D. (clinical psychology), Pennsylvania State University, 1951, licensed, ABPP–CL, Fellow of Division 12.

Blechman, Elaine Ann (1943–), Ph.D. (clinical psychology), U.C.L.A., 1971, licensed, Fellow of Division 12.

Blount, Ronald (1953–), Ph.D. (clinical psychology), West Virginia University, 1985.

Bolgar, Hedda Bekker (1909–), Ph.D. (developmental psychology), University of Vienna, 1934, licensed, ABPP–CL, Fellow of Division 12.

Boll, Thomas Jeffrey (1942–), Ph.D. (clinical psychology), Marquette University, 1967, licensed, ABPP–CL, Fellow of Division 12.

Bookbinder, Lawrence Joseph (1930–), Ph.D. (clinical psychology), Northwestern University, 1959, licensed, Fellow of APA.

Bootzin, Richard R. (1940–), Ph.D. (clinical psychology), Purdue University, 1969, licensed, Fellow of Division 12.

Bordin, Edward S. (1913–), Ph.D., Ohio State University, 1942, licensed, ABPP–CO, Fellow of Division 12.

Bouhoutsos, Jacqueline C. (1924–), Ph.D. (clinical psychology), University of Innsbruck, 1956, licensed, Fellow of Division 12.

Brenman, Margaret (married name: Brenman-Gibson) (1918–), Ph.D. (clinical psychology), University of Kansas, 1942, licensed, ABPP–CL, Fellow of Division 12.

Bronfenbrenner, Urie (1917–), Ph.D. (developmental psychology), University of Michigan, 1942, ABPP–CL, Fellow of APA.

Bronner (Healy), Augusta Fox (1881–1966), Ph.D., Columbia University, 1914.

Brotemarkle, Robert Archibald (1892–1972), Ph.D., University of Pennsylvania, 1923.

Brown, Andrew Wilson (1890–1946), Ph.D., Columbia University, 1926.

Brownell, Kelly D. (1951–), Ph.D. (clinical psychology), Rutgers University, 1977, licensed, Fellow of APA.

Buhler, Charlotte Malachowski (1893–1974), Ph.D., University of Munich, 1918, ABPP–CL, Fellow of APA.

Burstein, Alvin G. (1931–), Ph.D. (clinical psychology), University of Chicago, 1959, licensed, ABPP–CL, Fellow of Division 12.

Burton, Arthur (1914–), Ph.D., University of California, Berkeley, 1940, licensed, Fellow of Division 12.

Cain, Albert Clifford (1933–), Ph.D. (clinical psychology), University of Michigan, 1962, licensed, Fellow of Division 12.

Calhoon, Clair Henry (1900–), Ph.D. (clinical psychology), Ohio State University, 1930, licensed, ABPP–CL, Fellow of Division 12.

Calhoun, Karen S. (1943–), Ph.D. (clinical psychology), Louisiana State University, 1971, licensed.

Cameron, Norman Alexander (1896–1975), Ph.D. University of Michigan, 1927, ABPP–CL, Fellow of APA.

Campbell, Susan B. (1942–), Ph.D. (developmental psychology), McGill University, 1969, licensed, Fellow of Division 12.

Carstensen, Laura L. (1953–), Ph.D. (clinical psychology), West Virginia University, 1983, licensed.

Carter, Jerry Williams, Jr. (1908–), Ph.D. (experimental psychology), Indiana University, 1938, ABPP–CL, Fellow of Division 12.

Cass, Loretta Kekeisen (1912–), Ph.D. (clinical psychology), Ohio State University, 1950, licensed, ABPP–CL, Fellow of Division 12.

Cerreto, Mary C. (1951–), Ph.D. (clinical psychology), University of Washington, 1976, licensed, Fellow of APA.

Challman, Robert Chester (1906–), Ph.D., Stanford University, 1935, licensed, ABPP–CL, Fellow of Division 12.

Chance, Erika (1919–), Ph.D., Stanford University, 1953, licensed.

Chaney, Edmund F. (1948–), Ph.D. (clinical psychology), University of Washington, Seattle, 1976, licensed.

Chapman, Loren James (1927–), Ph.D. (clinical psychology), Northwestern University, 1954, licensed, Fellow of Division 12.

Chin, Jean Lau (1944–), Ed.D. (school psychology), Columbia University, 1974, licensed.

Christ, Mary Anne G. (1961–), Ph.D. (clinical psychology), University of Georgia, 1992.

Cohen, Bertram David (1923–), Ph.D. (clinical psychology), University of Iowa, 1949, licensed, ABPP–CL, Fellow of Division 12.

Cohen, Irwin H. (1931–), Ph.D. (clinical psychology), Michigan State University, 1960, licensed, ABPP–CL.

Cohen, Lawrence H. (1950–), Ph.D. (clinical psychology), Florida State University, 1977, licensed, Fellow of Division 12.

Cohen, Louis David (1912–), Ph.D. (clinical psychology), Duke University 1949, licensed, ABPP–CL, Fellow of Division 12.

Comas-Diaz, Lillian, Ph.D. (clinical psychology), University of Massachusetts, 1979, licensed, Fellow of APA.

Cook, Michael (1955–), Ph.D. (animal behavior), University of Wisconsin, Madison, 1988.

Craighead, Linda Wilcoxon (1950–), Ph.D. (clinical psychology), Pennsylvania State University, 1976, licensed.

Craighead, W. Edward (1942–), Ph.D. (clinical psychology), University of Illinois, 1970, licensed, Fellow of Division 12.

Creelman, Marjorie Broer (1908–), Ph.D. (clinical psychology), Case Western Reserve University, 1954, licensed.

Culbertson, Frances Jody Mitchell (1921–), Ph.D. (social psychology), University of Michigan, 1955, licensed, ABPP–S, Fellow of Division 12.

Culbertson, Janet L. (1949–), Ph.D. (school psychology), University of Tennessee, 1978, licensed, Fellow of APA.

Cummings, Nicholas Andrew (1924–), Ph.D. (clinical psychology), Adelphi University, 1958, licensed, Fellow of Division 12.

Cummings, S. Thomas (1921–), Ph.D. (clinical psychology), University of Pittsburgh, 1950, licensed, ABPP–CL, Fellow of Division 12.

Darley, John Gordon (1910–), Ph.D. (general psychology), University of Minnesota, 1937, ABPP–CO, Fellow of APA.

Davidson, Philip William (1941–), Ph.D. (experimental psychology), George Washington University, 1970, licensed.

Davison, Gerald C. (1939–), Ph.D. (clinical psychology), Stanford University, 1965, licensed, Fellow of Division 12.

Deaton, Ann Virginia (1957–), Ph.D. (clinical psychology), University of Texas, 1983, licensed.

Delaney, Richard C. (1948–), Ph.D. (clinical psychology), University of Illinois-Chicago Circle, 1977, licensed, ABPP–CN.

DeLeon, Patrick Henry (1943–), Ph.D. (clinical psychology), Purdue University, 1969, licensed, ABPP–CL, Fellow of Division 12.

Derner, Gordon Frederick (1915–1983), Ph.D., Columbia University, 1950, ABPP–CL, Fellow of Division 12.

Dingman, Paul R. (1920–), Ph.D. (clinical psychology), Clark University, 1950, licensed, ABPP–CL, Fellow of Division 12.

Dodrill, Carl B. (1943–), Ph.D. (clinical psychology), Purdue University, 1970, licensed, ABPP–CL, Fellow of APA.

Doll, Edgar Arnold (1889–1969), Ph.D., Princeton, 1920, Fellow of APA.

Dorken, Herbert, (1925–), Ph.D. (clinical psychology), University of Montreal, 1951, licensed, ABPP–CL, Fellow of Division 12.

Douglas, Virginia Isabel Baker (1927–), Ph.D., University of Michigan, 1959.

Drake, Robert E., Jr., Ph.D. (clinical psychology), Duke University, 1977.

Drotar, Dennis D. (1945–), Ph.D. (clinical psychology), University of Iowa, 1970, licensed, Fellow of Division 12.

Edelstein, Barry Allen (1945–), Ph.D. (clinical psychology), Memphis State University, 1975, licensed, Fellow of APA.

Eisdorfer, Carl (1930–), Ph.D. (general psychology), New York University, 1959, licensed, Fellow of Division 12.

Eisenstadt, Toni H., Ph.D., Department of Clinical and Health Psychology, University of Florida.

Elbert, Jean (1943–), Ph.D. (learning disabilities), Northwestern University, 1979.

Engel, Mary Susan (1930–), Ph.D. (clinical psychology), George Peabody College, 1956.

Erickson, Marilyn Ann T. (1936–), Ph.D. (developmental psychology), University of Washington, 1961, licensed, Fellow of Division 12.

Erikson, Erik Homburger (1902–), LL.D., Harvard University, 1978.

Eron, Leonard David (1920–), Ph.D. (clinical psychology), University of Wisconsin, 1949, licensed, ABPP–CL, Fellow of Division 12.

Eyberg, Sheila, Ph.D. (clinical psychology), University of Oregon, 1972, licensed, Fellow of Division 12.

Eysenck, Hans Jurgen (1916–), Ph.D., University of London, 1940, Fellow of APA.

Farberow, Norman L. (1918–), Ph.D. (clinical psychology), U.C.L.A., 1950, licensed ABPP–CL, Fellow of Division 12.

Feifel, Herman (1915–), Ph.D. (personality psychology), Columbia University, 1948, licensed, ABPP–CL, Fellow of Division 12.

Feldstein, Stanley (1930–), Ph.D. (clinical psychology), Columbia University, 1960, licensed.

Fernald, Mabel Ruth (1883–1952), Ph.D., University of Chicago, 1910, ABPP–CL, Fellow of Division 12.

Finch, Alfred J., Jr. (1944–), Ph.D. (clinical psychology), University of Alabama, 1970, licensed, ABPP–CL, Fellow of Division 12.

Fine, Reuben (1914–), Ph.D. (clinical psychology), University of Southern California, 1948, licensed, ABPP–CL, Fellow of Division 12.

Fish, Jeanne Eloise (1929–), Ph.D. (clinical psychology), University of Kansas, 1960 licensed, ABPP–CL.

Foa, Edna B. (1937–), Ph.D. (personality psychology), University of Missouri, 1970, licensed.

Fodor, Iris Elaine Goldstein (1935–), Ph.D. (clinical psychology), Boston University, 1965, licensed, ABPP–CL, Fellow of Division 12.

Forsberg, Linda K., Ph.D. (clinical psychology), Wayne State University, 1985.

Fowler, Raymond D., Jr. (1930–), Ph.D. (clinical psychology), Pennsylvania State University, 1957, licensed, ABPP–CL, Fellow of Division 12.

Fox, Ronald Ernest (1936–), Ph.D. (clinical psychology), University of North Carolina at Chapel Hill, 1962, licensed, ABPP–CL, Fellow of Division 12.

Franks, Cyril Maurice (1923–), Ph.D. (experimental psychology), University of London, 1954, licensed, Fellow of Division 12.

Franks, Violet (1926–), Ph.D. (experimental psychology), University of London, 1959, licensed, Fellow of APA.

Franz, Shepherd Ivory (1874–1933), Ph.D., Columbia University, 1899.

Fredericks, Marilee (1928–), Ph.D. (educational psychology), University of Oregon, 1957, licensed, ABPP–CL.

Freedheim, Donald K. (1932–), Ph.D. (clinical psychology), Duke University, 1960, licensed, Fellow of Division 12.

Frick, Paul J., Ph.D. (clinical psychology), University of Georgia.

Friedman, Erwin (1925–), Ph.D., University of Budapest, 1949, licensed, Fellow of Division 12.

Fromm, Erich (1900–1980), Ph.D., Heidelberg, 1922, licensed, ABPP–CL.

Gant, Bobby L. (1951–), Ph.D. (counseling psychology), University of Missouri, 1977, licensed.

Gardner, Grace Gail (1938–1984), Ph.D., Columbia University, 1966, licensed.

Garfield, Sol Louis (1918–), Ph.D. (general psychology), Northwestern University, 1942, licensed, ABPP–CL, Fellow of Division 12.

Garmezy, Norman (1918–), Ph.D. (clinical psychology), University of Iowa, 1950, licensed, ABPP–CL, Fellow of Division 12.

Gatz, Margaret J. (1944–), Ph.D. (clinical psychology), Duke University, 1972, licensed, Fellow of Division 12.

Gault, Robert Harvey (1874–?), Ph.D., University of Pennsylvania, 1905, Fellow of APA.

Gelfand, Donna Mae Larsen (1937–), Ph.D. (clinical psychology), Stanford University, 1961, Fellow of Division 12.

Gendlin, Eugene T. (1926–), Ph.D., University of Chicago, 1958, licensed, Fellow of APA.

Gesell, Arnold Lucius (1880–1961), Ph.D., Clark University, 1906, certified by APA as a consulting psychologist.

Gluck, Martin Richard (1927–), Ph.D. (clinical psychology), University of Pittsburgh, 1953, licensed, ABPP–CL, Fellow of Division 12.

Goldstein, Arnold P. (1933–), Ph.D. (clinical psychology), Pennsylvania State University, 1959, licensed, Fellow of APA.

Goldstein, Steven George (1939–), Ph.D. (clinical psychology), Purdue University, 1967, licensed, ABPP–CL, Fellow of Division 12.

Golinko, Barry E. (1947–), Ph.D. (clinical psychology), Wayne State University, 1977, licensed.

Goodman, Morris (1925–), Ph.D. (clinical psychology), Case Western Reserve University, 1951, licensed, ABPP–CL, Fellow of Division 12.

Gordon, Sol (1923–), Ph.D., University of London, 1953, Fellow of Division 12.

Gotlib, Ian H. (1951–), Ph.D. (clinical psychology), University of Waterloo, Ontario, 1981, licensed.

Gottlieb, Michael C. (1943–), Ph.D. (counseling psychology), Texas Tech University, 1972, licensed.

Gottsegen, Gloria Behar (1930–), Ph.D. (educational psychology), New York University, 1967, licensed, Fellow of Division 12.

Gough, Harrison Gould (1921–), Ph.D. (clinical psychology), University of Minnesota, 1949, licensed, Fellow of APA.

Gray, Arne L. (1944–), Ph.D. (clinical psychology), University of Waterloo, 1974, licensed.

Gray-Little, Bernadette (1944–), Ph.D. (clinical psychology), St. Louis University, 1970, licensed.

Greene, Edward Barrows (1895–1981), Ph.D., Columbia University, 1929.

Greening, Leilani (1959–), Ph.D. (clinical psychology), Southern Illinois University, 1989.

Grimm, Laurence George, Ph.D. (clinical psychology), University of Illinois, 1979, licensed.

Haber, Leonard (1933–), Ph.D. (clinical psychology), Adelphi University, 1960, licensed.

Haines, Thomas Harvey (1871–1951), Ph.D., Harvard University, 1901, Fellow of APA.

Halpern, Florence Cohn (1900–1981), Ph.D., New York University, 1951.

Hare-Mustin, Rachel T. (1928–), Ph.D. (clinical psychology), Temple University, 1969, licensed, ABPP–CL, Fellow of Division 12.

Harper, Dennis C. (1942–), Ph.D. (educational psychology), University of Iowa, 1972, licensed, Fellow of APA.

Harper, Robert Allan (1915–), Ph.D. (social psychology), Ohio State University, 1942, licensed, Fellow of Division 12.

Harris, Sandra Lee (1942–), Ph.D. (clinical psychology), State University of New York, Buffalo, 1970, Fellow of Division 12.

Harrower, Molly (1906–), Ph.D. (experimental psychology), Smith College, 1934, licensed, ABPP–CL, Fellow of Division 12.

Hathaway, Starke Rosecrans (1903–1984), Ph.D., University of Minnesota, 1932, licensed, ABPP–CL, Fellow of Division 12.

Hay, William M., Ph.D., University of North Carolina, Greensboro, 1977, licensed.

Heckman, Samuel B. (1870–?), Ph.D., University of Pennsylvania, 1906, certified by APA as a consulting psychologist, Fellow of APA.

Hedberg, Allan G. (1937–), Ph.D. (clinical psychology), Queens University, 1969, licensed.

Hegge, Thorleif Gruner (1889–), Ph.D., University of Copenhagen, 1918.

Heller, Kenneth (1933–), Ph.D. (clinical psychology), Pennsylvania State University, 1959, licensed, Fellow of Division 12.

Hersen, Michel (1940–), Ph.D. (clinical psychology), State University of New York, Buffalo, 1966, licensed, Fellow of Division 12.

Hescheles, David Robert (1942–), Psy.D. (school psychology), Rutgers University, 1975, licensed.

Hildreth, Gertrude Howell (1898–1984), Ph.D., Columbia University, 1925.

Hildreth, Harold Mowbray (1906–1965), Ph.D., Syracuse University, 1935.

Hobbs, Nicholas (1915–1983), Ph.D., Ohio State University, 1946.

Hodges, Wayne B. (1945–), Psy.D. (clinical psychology), Baylor University, 1975, licensed.

Hollingworth, Leta Stetter (1886–1939), Ph.D. (educational psychology), Columbia University, 1916, certified by APA as a consulting psychologist.

Holt, Robert R. (1917–), Ph.D. (general psychology), Harvard University, 1944, licensed, ABPP–CL, Fellow of Division 12.

Holzberg, Jules Donald (1915–1973), Ph.D., New York University, 1949, Fellow of Division 12.

Hooker, Evelyn (1907–), Ph.D. (experimental psychology), Johns Hopkins University, 1932, licensed, ABPP–CL, Fellow of Division 12.

Hoover, Daniel W. (1961–), Ph.D. (clinical psychology), University of Kentucky, 1991.

Hopkins, Joyce (1950–), Ph.D. (clinical psychology), University of Pittsburgh, 1987.

Hunt, Joseph McVicker (1906–1991), Ph.D. (experimental psychology), Cornell University, 1933, ABPP–CL, Fellow of Division 12.

Hunt, William Alvin (1903–1986), Ph.D., Harvard University, 1931.

Hurley, Linda K. (1951–), Ph.D. (clinical psychology), American University, 1986, licensed.

Hutchinson, Jacqueline (1957–), Ph.D. (applied developmental psychology), University of Maryland, Baltimore County, 1990.

Ilardi, Steve, graduate student, Duke University.

Jacobson, Neil S. (1949–), Ph.D. (clinical psychology), University of North Carolina, Chapel Hill, 1977, licensed, Fellow of Division 12.

Jenkins, Louis E. Ph.D. (clinical psychology), Pennsylvania State University, 1973, licensed.

Johnson, James Harmon (1943–), Ph.D. (clinical psychology), Northern Illinois University, 1976.

Johnson, Suzanne Taffel Bennett (1948–), Ph.D. (clinical psychology), State University of New York, Stony Brook, 1974, licensed, Fellow of Division 12.

Jones, Russell Thomas, Ph.D. (clinical psychology), Pennsylvania State University, 1976, Fellow of Division 12.

Kalinkowitz, Bernard N. (1915–1992), Ph.D. (clinical psychology), New York University, 1948, licensed, Fellow of Division 12.

Kanfer, Frederick H. (1925–), Ph.D. (clinical psychology), Indiana University, 1953, ABPP–CL, Fellow of Division 12.

Kaszniak, Alfred W. (1949–), Ph.D. (clinical psychology), University of Illinois, 1976, licensed.

Kausch, Donald F. (1931–), Ph.D. (clinical psychology), University of Nebraska, 1962, licensed, ABPP–CL.

Kazdin, Alan E. (1945–), Ph.D. (clinical psychology), Northwestern University, 1970, licensed, Fellow of Division 12.

Keenan, Kate, Graduate Student in clinical psychology, University of Pittsburgh.

Kelley, Noble H. (1901–), Ph.D. (general psychology), University of Iowa, 1936, licensed, ABPP–CL, Fellow of Division 12.

Kelly, Everett Lowell (1905–1986), Ph.D., Stanford University, 1930.

Kelly, George Alexander (1905–1967), Ph.D., University of Iowa, 1931, licensed, ABPP–CL, Fellow of Division 12.

Kendall, Philip C. (1950–), Ph.D. (clinical psychology), Virginia Commonwealth University, 1977, licensed, Fellow of Division 12.

Kenny, Thomas J. (1932–), Ph.D. (counseling psychology), Catholic University of America, 1969, licensed, Fellow of Division 12.

Kinder, Elaine Flitner (1890–), Ph.D., Johns Hopkins University, 1925.

King, Harriette Elizabeth (1946–), Ph.D. (clinical psychology), University of Georgia, 1972, licensed.

Klein, George Stuart (1917–1971), Ph.D., Columbia University, 1942, licensed, ABPP- CL, Fellow of Division 12.

Klepac, Robert K. (1943–), Ph.D. (clinical psychology), Kent State University, 1969, licensed.

Klopfer, Bruno (1900–1971), Ph.D., University of Munich, 1922.

Klorman, Rafael (1945–), Ph.D. (clinical psychology), University of Wisconsin, 1972, licensed.

Klosko, Janet S., Ph.D. (clinical psychology), State University of New York, Albany, 1988.

Knapp, Lenora G. (1961–), Ph.D. (clinical psychology), University of Alabama, 1990.

Koocher, Gerald Paul (1947–), Ph.D. (clinical psychology), University of Missouri, Columbia, 1972, licensed, ABPP–CL, Fellow of Division 12.

Korchin, Sheldon J. (1921–1989), Ph.D., Harvard University, 1946.

Kovacs, Arthur Leonard (1931–), Ph.D. (clinical psychology), University of Michigan, 1958, licensed, ABPP–CL, Fellow of Division 12.

Krasner, Jack Daniel (1921–), Ph.D. (general psychology), New York University, 1952, licensed, Fellow of Division 12.

Krasner, Leonard (1924–), Ph.D. (clinical psychology) Columbia University, 1950, licensed, ABPP–CL, Fellow of APA.

Kuhlmann, Frederick (1876–1941), Ph.D. Clark University, 1903

Kutash, Irwin L. (1945–), Ph.D. (clinical psychology), Adelphi University, 1972, licensed, ABPP–CL.

Kutash, Samuel B. (1912–), Ph.D., New York University, 1944, ABPP–CL.

La Greca, Annette Marie (1950–), Ph.D. (clinical psychology), Purdue University, 1978, licensed, Fellow of Division 12.

Landis, Carney (1897–1962), Ph.D., University of Minnesota, 1924, Fellow of APA.

Lang, Peter John (1930–), Ph.D. (clinical psychology), University of Buffalo, 1958, licensed, Fellow of Division 12.

Lazarus, Richard Stanley (1922–), Ph.D. (experimental psychology) University of Pittsburgh, 1948, licensed, ABPP–CL, Fellow of APA.

Lehrer, Paul Michael (1941–), Ph.D. (clinical psychology), Harvard University, 1969, licensed, Fellow of APA.

Leventhal, Theodore (1924–), Ph.D. (clinical psychology), University of Kansas, 1953, licensed.

Levy, Sandra M. (1943–), Ph.D. (clinical psychology), Indiana University, 1975, licensed.

Liem, Joan Huser (1946–), Ph.D. (clinical psychology), Boston University, 1973, licensed.

Lindner, Harold (1923–), Ph.D. (clinical psychology), University of Maryland, 1951, licensed, ABPH-CH, Fellow of APA.

Lindzey, Gardner Edmond (1920–), Ph.D. (general psychology) Harvard University, 1949, Fellow of Division 12.

Long, Barbara Ellis (1923–), Ph.D. (clinical psychology), Union Graduate School, 1973, licensed, Fellow of APA.

Lopez, Steven (1953–), Ph.D. (clinical psychology), U.C.L.A., 1983, licensed.

Louttit, Chauncey McKinley (1901–1956), Ph.D. (comparative psychology), Yale University, 1928, Fellow of APA.

Lu, Elsie Go (1938–), Ph.D. (clinical psychology), U.C.L.A., 1966, licensed.

Luborsky, Lester Bernard (1920–), Ph.D. (general psychology), Duke University, 1945, licensed, ABPP–CL, Fellow of Division 12.

Luckey, Bertha Musson (1890–1966), Ph.D., University of Gottingen, 1966, certified by APA as a consulting psychologist.

Lyle, Orcena E., Ph.D. (clinical psychology), University of Minnesota, 1972, licensed.

Macfarlane, Jean Walker (1894–1989), Ph.D., University of California, Berkeley, 1922.

Machover, Karen Alper (1902–), M.A. (clinical psychology), New York University, 1929, licensed, ABPP–CL.

Magaret, Ann (married name: Garner) (1916–), Ph.D. (clinical psychology), Stanford University, 1941, licensed, ABPP–CL, Fellow of Division 12.

Magrab, Phyllis R. (1940–), Ph.D., University of Maryland, 1969, licensed, Fellow of Division 12.

Maher, Brendan Arnold (1924–), Ph.D. (clinical psychology), Ohio State University, 1954, licensed, ABPP–CL, Fellow of Division 12.

Mahoney, Michael J. (1946–), Ph.D. (general psychology), Stanford University, 1972, licensed, Fellow of Division 12.

Mann, Lucretia (1952–), graduate student, Department of Clinical and Health, Psychology University of Florida.

Mannarino, Anthony P. (1950–), Ph.D. (clinical psychology), Ohio State University, 1975, licensed.

Margolin, Joseph Bernard (1921–), Ph.D. (social psychology), New York University, 1954, licensed, ABPP–CL, Fellow of Divison 12.

Marlatt, Gordon Alan (1941–), Ph.D. (clinical psychology), Indiana University, 1968, licensed, Fellow of Division 12.

Marsden, Kenneth Gerald (1935–), Ed.D., Harvard University, 1967.

Matarazzo, Joseph Dominic (1925–), Ph.D. (clinical psychology), Northwestern University, 1952, licensed, ABPP–CL, Fellow of Division 12.

Matthews, Janet R. (1944–), Ph.D. (clinical psychology), University of Mississippi, 1976, licensed, Fellow of APA.

Maxfield, Francis Norton (1877–1945), Ph.D., University of Pennsylvania, 1912.

May, Rollo Reese (1909–), Ph.D., Columbia University, 1949, licensed, ABPP–CL, Fellow of Division 12.

Mays, Vickie M., Ph.D. (clinical psychology), University of Massachusetts, 1979.

McCandless, Boyd Rowden (1915–1975), Ph.D. (developmental psychology), University of Iowa, 1941, licensed, ABPP–CL, Fellow of APA.

McDonald, David G. (1933–), Ph.D. (clinical psychology), Washington University, 1959.

McFall, Richard M. (1939–), Ph.D. (clinical psychology), Ohio State University, 1965, licensed.

McGrath, Melanie L., Ph.D. (clinical psychology), University of Mississippi, 1990, licensed.

McKee, Michael G. (1931–), Ph.D. (clinical psychology), University of California, Berkeley, 1960, licensed.

McNeill, Harry V. (1906–), Ph.D., University of Louvain, Belgium, 1933.

Mednick, Sarnoff A. (1928–), Ph.D. (clinical psychology), Northwestern University, 1954.

Meehl, Paul Everett (1920–), Ph.D. (clinical psychology), University of Minnesota, 1945, licensed, ABPP–CL, Fellow of Division 12.

Melamed, Barbara G. (1943–), Ph.D. (clinical psychology), University of Wisconsin, 1969, licensed, Fellow of Division 12.

Meltzer, Hyman (1899–), Ph.D. (clinical psychology), Columbia University, 1925, licensed, ABPP–CL, Fellow of Division 12.

Mensh, Ivan Norman (1915–), Ph.D. (clinical psychology), Northwestern University, 1948, licensed, ABPP–CL, Fellow of Division 12.

Mesibov, Gary B. (1945–), Ph.D. (social psychology), Brandeis University, 1974, licensed, Fellow of Division 12.

Metsky, Marvin (1922–), Ph.D. (clinical psychology), New York University, 1953, licensed, ABPP–CL.

Miles, Catharine Cox (1890–), Ph.D., Stanford University, 1925, licensed, ABPP–CL, Fellow of APA.

Milgram, Norman Alvin (1931–), Ph.D. (clinical psychology), Boston University, 1958, ABPP–CL, Fellow of Division 12.

Miller, James Grier (1916–), Ph.D. (general psychology), Harvard University, 1943, ABPP–CL, Fellow of Division 12.

Miller, Lovick C. (1923–), Ph.D. (clinical psychology), Harvard University, 1953, licensed, ABPP–CL, Fellow of Divison 12.

Miner, James Burt (1873–1943), Ph.D., Columbia University, 1903, certified by APA as a consulting psychologist, Fellow of APA.

Mischel, Walter (1930–), Ph.D. (clinical psychology), Ohio State University, 1956, Fellow of APA.

Mitchell, David (1884–1956), Ph.D. (psychology), University of Pennsylvania, 1913, certified by APA as a consulting psychologist.

Moldawsky, Stanley (1925–), Ph.D. (clinical psychology), University of Iowa, 1951, licensed, ABPP–CL, Fellow of Division 12.

Moore, Lisa A. (1960–), Ph.D. (clinical psychology), Texas A&M University.

Morgan, Carl E. (1925–), Ph.D. (clinical psychology), University of Houston, 1956, licensed, ABPP–CL.

Morgan, John Jacob Brooke (1888–1945), Ph.D., Columbia University, 1916.

Mowrer, Orval Hobart (1907–1982), Ph.D., Johns Hopkins University, 1932, ABPP–CL, Fellow of Division 12.

Mulvaney, Sheila, graduate student, University of Arizona.

Murray, Henry Alexander (1893–1988), Ph.D. (biochemistry), University of Cambridge, 1927.

Myers, Garry Cleveland (1884–?), Ph.D., Columbia University, 1913, certified by APA as a consulting psychologist, Fellow of APA.

Nathan, Peter E. (1935–), Ph.D. (clinical psychology), Washington University, 1962, licensed, Fellow of Division 12.

Nattland, Candice, Psy.D. (professional psychology), Rutgers University, 1984, licensed.

Neale, John M. (1943–), Ph.D. (clinical psychology), Vanderbilt University, 1969.

Nelson, Rosemery O. (1945–), Ph.D. (clinical psychology), State University of New York, Stony Brook, 1972, licensed, Fellow of Division 12.

Newbrough, J. R. (1934–), Ph.D. (clinical psychology), University of Utah, 1959, licensed, Fellow of Division 12.

Niederehe, George (1945–), Ph.D. (clinical psychology), University of Chicago, 1976, licensed.

Nuechterlein, Keith H., Ph.D. (clinical psychology), University of Minnesota, 1979.

O'Grady, David D. (1952–), Ph.D. (clinical psychology), California School of Professional Psychology, Berkeley, 1983, licensed.

O'Leary, Keith Daniel (1940–), Ph.D. (clinical psychology), University of Illinois, 1967, licensed, Fellow of Division 12.

Ollendick, Thomas H. (1945–), Ph.D. (clinical psychology), Purdue University, 1971, licensed, Fellow of Division 12.

Oltmanns, Thomas Frederich (1949–), Ph.D. (clinical psychology), State University of New York, Stony Brook, 1976, licensed, Fellow of Division 12.

Orlinsky, Nancy (1932–), Ph.D. (clinical psychology), University of Chicago, 1962, licensed.

Overholser, James Carter (1957–), Ph.D. (clinical psychology), Ohio State University, 1986, licensed.

Parloff, Morris B. (1918–), Ph.D. (clinical psychology), Case Western Reserve University, 1953, licensed, Fellow of Division 12.

Parsons, Oscar A. (1920–), Ph.D. (clinical psychology), Duke University, 1954, licensed, ABPP–CL, Fellow of Division 12.

Patterson, Gerald Roy (1926–), Ph.D. (counseling psychology), University of Minnesota, 1956, Fellow of Division 12.

Patterson, Tommy Wayne (1931–), Ph.D. (clinical psychology), University of Nebraska, 1963, licensed, ABPP–CL.

Paul, Gordon Lee (1935–), Ph.D. (clinical psychology), University of Illinois, 1964, licensed, Fellow of Division 12.

Paynter, Richard Henry, Jr. (1890–1972), Ph.D., Columbia University, 1917.

Pearson, Leonard (1926–), Ph.D. (clinical psychology), University of Chicago, 1956, licensed.

Perry, Martha A. (1940–), Ph.D. (clinical psychology), Syracuse University, 1970, licensed.

Peterson, Lizette (married name: Peterson-Homer) (1951–), Ph.D. (clinical psychology), University of Utah, 1978, licensed, Fellow of APA.

Peterson, Rolf A. (1939–), Ph.D. (clinical psychology), University of Iowa, 1970, licensed, Fellow of Division 12.

Phillips, Edmund J. (1934–), Ph.D. (clinical psychology), Duquesne University, 1966, licensed, APBB-CL.

Phillips, Jeanne Shirley (1929–), Ph.D. (clinical psychology), Washington University, 1957, licensed, ABPP–CL, Fellow of Division 12.

Pintner, Rudolf (1884–1942), Ph.D., University of Leipzig, 1913, certified by APA as a consulting psychologist.

Porteus, Stanley David (1883–1972), Sc.D., University of Hawaii, 1932, Fellow of APA.

Poull, Louise Elizabeth (1876–1958), Ph.D., Columbia University, 1922, certified by APA as a consulting psychologist.

Psarras, Georgette M. (married name: Georgette Psarras Constantinou).

Quay, Herbert Callister (1927–), Ph.D. (clinical psychology), University of Illinois, 1958, licensed, Fellow of Division 12.

Rachman, Stanley Jack, Ph.D., University of London, 1958.

Rae, William A. (1948–), Ph.D. (counseling psychology), University of Texas, 1975, licensed.

Raimy, Victor C. (1913–1987), Ph.D. (clinical psychology), Ohio State University, 1943, licensed, ABPP–CL, Fellow of Division 12.

Rao, Nirmala (1961–), Ph.D. (psychology), Tulane University, 1986.

Rapaport, David (1911–1960), Ph.D., Royal Hungarian Petrus Pazmany University, ABPP–CL, Fellow of Division 12.

Raskin, Larry Marvin (1940–), Ph.D. (experimental psychology), McGill University, 1966, licensed.

Raush, Harold L. (1921–), Ph.D. (clinical psychology), Stanford University, 1950, licensed, ABPP–CL, Fellow of APA.

Rayburn, Carole Ann (1938–), Ph.D. (educational psychology), Catholic University of America, 1969, licensed, Fellow of APA.

Rehm, Lynn Paul (1941–), Ph.D. (clinical psychology), University of Wisconsin, 1970, licensed, Fellow of Division 12.

Resnick, Jerome Howard (1936–), Ph.D. (clinical psychology), Syracuse University, 1964, licensed, Fellow of Division 12.

Resnick, Robert J. (1940–), Ph.D. (clinical psychology), University of Tennessee, 1968, licensed, ABPP–CL, Fellow of Division 12.

Reymert, Martin Luther (1883–1953), Ph.D., Clark University, 1917.

Richards, Thomas William (1907–), Ph.D. (clinical psychology), University of Pennsylvania, 1933, licensed, ABPP–CL, Fellow of Division 12.

Rie, Herbert Emanuel (1931–1982), Ph.D. (clinical psychology), Case Western Reserve University, 1959, licensed, ABPP–CL, Fellow of Division 12.

Rigler, David (1921–), Ph.D. (clinical psychology), University of Michigan, 1956, licensed, ABPP–CL, Fellow of APA.

Riley, Gordon Lee (1903–), Ph.D., Rutgers University, 1942, licensed, ABPP–CL, Fellow of Division 12.

Roberts, Michael Clark (1951–), Ph.D. (clinical psychology), Purdue University, 1978, licensed, Fellow of Division 12.

Robinson, Elizabeth Anne (1944–), Ph.D. (clinical psychology), University of South Carolina, 1977, licensed.

Rodnick, Eliot Herman (1911–), Ph.D. (experimental psychology), Yale University, 1936, licensed, ABPP–CL, Fellow of Division 12.

Roe, Anne (1904–1991), Ph.D., Columbia University, 1933, ABPP–CL, Fellow of Division 12.

Rogers, Carl Ransom (1902–1987), Ph.D. (clinical psychology), Columbia University, 1931, ABPP–CL, Fellow of Division 12.

Rosebrook, Wilda Mae (1894–), Ph.D., Ohio State University, 1931, ABPP–CO, Fellow of APA.

Rosenthal, Robert (1933–), Ph.D. (clinical psychology), U.C.L.A., 1956, ABPP–CL, Fellow of Division 12.

Rosenthal, Vin (1928–), Ph.D. (experimental psychology), Illinois Institute of Technology, 1955, licensed, ABPP–CL, Fellow of APA.

Rosenzweig, Saul (1907–), Ph.D. (clinical psychology), Harvard University, 1932, licensed, ABPP–CL, Fellow of Division 12.

Ross, Alan Otto (1921–), Ph.D. (clinical psychology), Yale University, 1953, licensed, APBB-CL, Fellow of Division 12.

Ross, Dorothea M., Ph.D. (personality and psychopathology), Stanford University, 1962.

Rotter, Julian B. (1916–), Ph.D., Indiana University, 1941, ABPP–CL, Fellow of Division 12.

Routh, Donald Kent (1937–), Ph.D. (clinical psychology), University of Pittsburgh, 1967, licensed, ABPP–CL, Fellow of Division 12.

Rudnick, Mark (1931–), Ph.D., University of Utah, 1960, licensed, ABPP–CL.

Russo, Dennis C., Ph.D. (educational psychology), University of California, Santa Barbara, 1975, licensed, Fellow of APA.

Salk, Lee (1926–1992), Ph.D. (clinical psychology), University of Michigan, 1954, licensed, Fellow of APA.

Salzinger, Kurt (1929–), Ph.D. (experimental psychology), Columbia University, 1954, licensed, Fellow of Division 12.

Sanford, R. Nevitt (1909–), Ph.D. (personality psychology), Harvard University, 1934, licensed, ABPP–CL, Fellow of Division 12.

Santostefano, Sebastiano G. (1929–), Ph.D. (clinical psychology), Pennsylvania State University, 1957, licensed, ABPP–CL, Fellow of Division 12.

Sarason, Irwin G. (1929–), Ph.D. (clinical psychology), Indiana University, 1955, licensed, Fellow of Division 12.

Sarason, Seymour Bernard (1919–), Ph.D., Clark University, 1942, licensed, ABPP–CL, Fellow of Divison 12.

Sargent, Helen Durham (1904–1959), Ph.D., Northwestern University, 1944.

Sayger, Thomas V. (1951–), Ph.D. (counseling psychology), Indiana State University, Terre Haute, 1987.

Saylor, Conway Fleming (1955–), Ph.D. (clinical psychology), Virginia Polytechnic Institute and State University, 1982, licensed.

Schaefer, Arlene Blackman (1943–), Ph.D. (developmental psychology), University of Rochester, 1972, licensed.

Schafer, Roy (1922–), Ph.D. (clinical psychology), Clark University, 1950, licensed, ABPP–CL, Fellow of APA.

Schofield, William (1921–), Ph.D. (clinical psychology), University of Minnesota, 1948, licensed, ABPP–CL, Fellow of Divison 12.

Schroeder, Carolyn Stineman (1939–), Ph.D. (clinical psychology), University of Pittsburgh, 1966, licensed, Fellow of Division 12.

Schroeder, David J. (1942–), Ph.D. (experimental psychology), University of Oklahoma, 1971, licensed.

Schuman, Wendy B., graduate student, University of Miami.

Sechrest, Lee Burton (1929–), Ph.D. (clinical psychology), Ohio State University, 1956, Fellow of Division 12.

Seligman, Martin E. P. (1942–), Ph.D. (experimental psychology), University of Pennsylvania, 1967, licensed, Fellow of Division 12.

Serafica, Felicisima C., Ph.D. (clinical psychology), Clark University, 1973, licensed.

Shaffer, Laurance Frederic (1903–1976), Ph.D., Columbia University, 1930, licensed, ABPP, CL, Fellow of Division 12.

Shaheen, Sandra Jean (1952–), Ph.D. (developmental psychology), Tufts University, 1984.

Shakow, David (1901–1981), Ph.D., Harvard University, 1942, ABPP–CL, Fellow of Division 12.

Shelton, Terri Lizabeth (1955–), Ph.D. (clinical psychology), Purdue University, 1983, licensed.

Sherman, Julia Ann (1934–), Ph.D. (clinical psychology), University of Iowa, 1957, licensed, ABPP–CL, Fellow of Division 12.

Shneidman, Edwin S. (1918–), Ph.D. (clinical psychology), University of Southern California, 1948, licensed, ABPP–CL, Fellow of Division 12.

Shoben, Edward Joseph, Jr. (1918–), Ph.D., University of Southern California, 1947, ABPP–CL, Fellow of Division 12.

Shore, Milton F. (1928–), Ph.D. (clinical psychology), Boston University, 1955, licensed, ABPP–CL, Fellow of Division 12.

Siderits, Mary Anne (1936–), Ph.D. (clinical psychology), University of Michigan, 1966, licensed.

Siegel, Lawrence Jeffrey (1948–), Ph.D. (clinical psychology), Case Western Reserve University, 1975, licensed, Fellow of Division 12.

Siegel, Max (1918–1988), Ph.D. (clinical psychology), New York University, 1951, licensed, ABPP–CL, Fellow of Division 12.

Simons, Anne Dickinson (1952–), Ph.D. (clinical psychology), Washington University, 1982.

Skodak, Marie (married name, Marie Skodak Crissey) (1910–), Ph.D. (developmental psychology), University of Iowa, 1938, licensed, ABPP–S, Fellow of Division 12.

Smith, Karen E. (1958–), Ph.D. (clinical psychology), University of Alabama–Birmingham, 1987.

Snyder, William Ulrich (1915–), Ph.D. (clinical psychology), Ohio State University, 1943, licensed ABPP–CL, Fellow of Division 12.

Sobel, Suzanne Barbara (1943–), Ph.D. (clinical psychology), University of Tennessee, 1971, licensed, Fellow of Division 12.

Spaner, Fred E. (1918–), Ph.D., Purdue University, 1950, licensed, ABPP–CL, Fellow of Division 12.

Spence, Janet A. Taylor (1923–), Ph.D. (clinical psychology), University of Iowa, 1949, Fellow of Division 12.

Sperber, Zanwil (1926–), Ph.D. (clinical psychology), University of Michigan, 1956, licensed, ABPP–CL, Fellow of Division 12.

Spielberger, Charles Donald (1927–), Ph.D. (clinical psychology), University of Iowa, 1954, licensed, ABPP–CL, Fellow of Division 12.

Spinetta, John J., Ph.D. (clinical psychology), University of Southern California, 1972, licensed, Fellow of Division 12.

Stabler, Brian (1944–), Ph.D. (school psychology), University of North Carolina, Chapel Hill, 1971, licensed.

Stock, Jeremy S., Ph.D. (clinical psychology), Catholic University of America.

Stone, Wendy Lee (1954–), Ph.D. (clinical psychology), University of Miami, 1981, licensed.

Strain, Edward Richard. (1925–), Ph.D. (clinical psychology), Duke University, 1952, licensed.

Stricker, George (1936–), Ph.D. (clinical psychology), University of Rochester, 1960, licensed, ABPP–CL, Fellow of Division 12.

Strickland, Bonnie Ruth (1936–), Ph.D. (clinical psychology), Ohio State University, 1962, licensed, ABPP–CL, Fellow of Division 12.

Strupp, Hans Hermann (1921–), Ph.D. (social psychology), George Washington University, 1954, licensed, ABPP–CL, Fellow of Division 12.

Sullivan, Frank J. (1940–), Ph.D. (experimental psychology), Catholic University of America, 1967.

Tarnowski, Kenneth John (1954–), Ph.D. (clinical psychology), University of South Carolina, 1984, licensed.

Teagarden, Florence Mabel (1887–1975), Ph.D. (clinical psychology), Columbia University, 1924, licensed, ABPP–CL, Fellow of Division 12.

Teasdale, John D.

Teicher, Arthur (1914–), Ph.D. (clinical psychology), New York University, 1952, licensed.

Todd, Judy L. (1944–), Ph.D. (clinical psychology), U.C.L.A., 1971, licensed.

Tolman, Ruth Sherman (1893–1957), Ph.D., University of California, Berkeley, 1937, ABPP–CL, Fellow of Division 12.

Tomkins, Silvan Solomon (1911–), Ph.D. (philosophy), University of Pennsylvania, 1934, licensed, ABPP–CL, Fellow of Division 12.

Toomey, Laura C. (1929–), Ph.D. (clinical psychology), University of Connecticut, 1961, licensed, Fellow of Division 12.

Town, Clara Harrison (1874–?), Ph.D., Pennsylvania, 1909.

Trabue, Marion Rex (1890–1972), Ph.D., Columbia University, 1915.

True, Reiko Homma (1933–), Ph.D. (clinical psychology), California School of Professional Psychology, San Francisco, 1976, licensed, Fellow of APA.

Tuma, June M. (1934–), Ph.D. (clinical psychology), Louisiana State University, 1965, licensed, ABPP–CL, Fellow of Division 12.

Turner, Judith Ann (1952–), Ph.D. (clinical psychology), U.C.L.A., 1974, licensed.

Turner, Samuel M. (1944–), Ph.D. (clinical psychology), University of Georgia, 1975, licensed, Fellow of Division 12.

Ullmann, Leonard P. (1930–), Ph.D. (clinical psychology), Stanford University, 1955, licensed, Fellow of Division 12.

Vore, David A. (1941–), Ph.D. (clinical psychology), Purdue University, 1969, licensed, ABPP–CL.

Walker, Clarence Eugene (1939–), Ph.D. (clinical psychology), Purdue University, 1965, licensed, Fellow of Division 12.

Wallander, Jan Lance (1953–), Ph.D. (clinical psychology), Purdue University, 1965, licensed, Fellow of Division 12.

Wallin, John Edward Wallace (1876–1969), Ph.D., Yale University, 1901, Fellow of Division 12.

Watson, Robert Irving, Sr. (1909–1980), Ph.D. (experimental psychology), Columbia University, 1938, ABPP–CL, Fellow of Division 12.

Wechsler, David (1896–1981), Ph.D., Columbia University, 1925, licensed, ABPP–CL, Fellow of Division 12.

Weitz, Robert D. (1912–), Ph.D. (clinical psychology), New York University, 1944, licensed, ABPP–CL, Fellow of Division 12.

Weizmann, Frederic (1939–), Ph.D. (clinical psychology), Ohio State University, 1966, licensed.

Wells, Frederic Lyman (1884–1964), Ph.D., Columbia University, 1906, certified by APA as a consulting psychologist, ABPP–CL, Fellow of Division 12.

Wenar, Charles (1922–), Ph.D. (developmental psychology), University of Iowa, 1951, licensed, ABPP–CL, Fellow of Division 12.

Wertlieb, Donald L. (1952–), Ph.D. (clinical-community psychology), Boston University, 1978, licensed.

Whipple, Guy Montrose (1876–1941), Ph.D., Cornell University, 1900.

White, Carol Sue (1945–), Ph.D. (experimental sensory psychology), Memphis State University, 1976, Fellow of APA.

White, Robert Winthrop (1904–), Ph.D. (personality psychology), Harvard University, 1932, ABPP–CL, Fellow of Division 12.

Whitt, James Kenneth (1946–), Ph.D. (clinical psychology), University of Texas, 1976, licensed.

Wiens, Arthur Nicholai (1926–), Ph.D. (clinical psychology), University of Portland, 1956, licensed, ABPP–CL, Fellow of Division 12.

Wiggins, Jack Gillmore, Jr. (1926–), Ph.D. (clinical psychology), Purdue University, 1952, licensed, Fellow of Division 12.

Wildman, Robert W., Sr. (1921–), Ph.D. (clinical psychology), Case Western Reserve University, 1960, licensed, Fellow of APA.

Williams, Gertrude Joanne Rubin (1927–1986), Ph.D. (experimental/clinical psychology), Washington University, 1958, licensed, ABPP–CL, Fellow of Division 12.

Williams, Medria W. (1949–), Ph.D. (clinical psychology), Columbia University, 1985, licensed.

Willis, Diane J. (1937–), Ph.D. (experimental psychology), University of Oklahoma, 1970, licensed, Fellow of Division 12.

Wilson, G. Terence (1944–), Ph.D. (clinical psychology), State University of New York, Stony Brook, 1971, licensed, Fellow of APA.

Wilson, Stuart (1934–), Ph.D. (clinical psychology), George Peabody College, 1962, licensed, ABPP–CL.

Winbury, Gail E., Psy.D. (clinical psychology), Massachusetts School of Professional Psychology, 1986.

Wisocki, Patricia A., Ph.D. (clinical psychology), Boston College, 1971, licensed, Fellow of Division 12.

Wohlford, Paul F. (1938–), Ph.D. (clinical psychology), Duke University, 1964, licensed, ABPP–CL.

Wolf, Elizabeth Baker (1917–), Ph.D., Western Reserve University, 1946, ABPP–CL, Fellow of Division 12.

Wollersheim, Janet Puccinelli (1936–), Ph.D. (clinical psychology), University of Illinois, 1968, licensed, Fellow of Division 12.

Wolman, Benjamin B. (1908–), Ph.D., University of Warsaw, 1935, licensed, Fellow of APA.

Woolley, Helen Bradford Thompson (1874–1947), Ph.D., University of Chicago, 1900, certified by APA as a consulting psychologist.

Worell, Judith Paula (1928–), Ph.D. (clinical psychology), Ohio State University, 1954, licensed, Fellow of Division 12.

Wright, Logan (1933–), Ph.D. (clinical psychology), George Peabody College for Teachers, 1964, licensed, ABPP–CL, Fellow of APA.

Wright, Rogers Hornsby (1927–), Ph.D., Northwestern University, 1955, licensed.

Wyatt, Gail Elizabeth (1944–), Ph.D. (educational psychology), U.C.L.A., 1973, licensed, Fellow of Division 12.

Young, Herman H. (1887–1931), Ph.D., Pennsylvania, 1916, certified by APA as a consulting psychologist.

Zeitlin, Sharon B.

Zimet, Carl Norman (1925–), Ph.D., Syracuse University, 1953, licensed, ABPP–CL, Fellow of Division 12.

Zubin, Joseph (1900–1990), Ph.D., Columbia University, 1932, licensed, ABPP–CL, Fellow of Division 12.

# References

Ainsworth, M. D. S. (1967). *Infancy in Uganda: Infant care and the growth of love.* Baltimore: Johns Hopkins University Press.

Ainsworth, M. D. S., Blehar, M. C., Waters, E., & Wall, S. (1978). Patterns of *attachment: A psychological study of the strange situation.* Hillsdale, NJ: Erlbaum.

Albee, G. W. (1968). Conceptual models and manpower requirements in psychology. *American Psychologist, 23,* 317–320.

Albee, G. W. (1970). The uncertain future of clinical psychology. *American Psychologist, 25,* 1071–1080.

Albee, G. W. (1977). Does including psychotherapy in health insurance represent a subsidy to the rich from the poor? *American Psychologist, 32,* 719–721.

APA Committee on Training Clinical Psychology. (1947). Recommended graduate training programs in clinical psychology. *American Psychologist, 2,* 539–558.

Bandura, A. (1977). Self-efficacy: Toward a unifying theory of behavioral change. *Psychological Review, 84,* 191–215.

Bandura, A., Ross, D., & Ross, S. (1961). Transmission of aggression through imitation of aggressive models. *Journal of Abnormal and Social Psychology, 63,* 575–582.

Barkley, R. A. (1990). *Attention-deficit hyperactivity disorder: A handbook for diagnosis and treatment.* New York: Guilford Press.

Barlow, D. H. (1981). On the relation of clinical research to clinical practice: Current issues, new directions. *Journal of Consulting and Clinical Psychology, 49,* 147–155.

Barlow, D. H. (1986). Causes of sexual dysfunction: The role of anxiety and cognitive interference. *Journal of Consulting and Clinical Psychology, 54,* 140–148.

Barron, J. (1986). Psychology as biography in the study of a person. *Psychotherapy in Private Practice, 4*(4), 1–15.

Beck, S. J. (1944). *Rorschach's test* (Vol. 1). *Basic processes.* New York: Grune & Stratton.

Beck, S. J. (1945). *Rorschach's test* (Vol. 2). *A variety of personality pictures.* New York: Grune & Stratton.

Beck, S. J. (1972). How the Rorschach came to America. *Journal of Personality Assessment, 36,* 105–108.

Bell, J. E. (1961). *Family group therapy.* Washington, DC: U.S. Government Printing Office (U.S. Public Health Service, Monograph No. 64).

Bellack, A. S. (1986). Schizophrenia: Behavior therapy's forgotten child. *Behavior Therapy, 17,* 199–214.

Benjamin, L. T., Jr. (1977). The Psychological Round Table: Revolution of 1936. *American Psychologist, 32*, 542–549.

Bettelheim, B. (1967). *The empty fortress.* New York: Free Press.

Beutler, L. E. (1979). Toward specific psychological therapies for specific conditions. *Journal of Consulting and Clinical Psychology, 47*, 882–897.

Beutler, L. E. (1983). *Eclectic psychotherapy.* New York: Pergamon Press.

Binet, A., & Simon, T. (1905). [A new method for the diagnosis of intellectual level of abnormal persons.] *Annee Psychologique, 11*, 191–244.

Blatt, B. (Ed.). (1968). [Special issue dedicated to J. E. W. Wallin.] *Journal of Education, 151*, 3–111.

Blechman, E. A., Olson, D. H., & Hellman, I. D. (1976). Stimulus control over family problem-solving behavior: The family Contract Game. *Behavior Therapy, 7*, 686–692.

Brennemann, J. (1933). Pediatric psychology and the child guidance movement. *Journal of Pediatrics, 2*, 1–26.

Breuer, J., & Freud, S. (1885/1986). *Studies in hysteria.* In The standard edition of the complete psychological works of Sigmund Freud, Vol. 2. London: Hogarth Press and the Institute of Psycho-Analysis.

Bronfenbrenner, U. (1970). *Two worlds of childhood: U.S.A. and U.S.S.R.* New York: Russell Sage Foundation.

Bronfenbrenner, U. (1979). *The ecology of human development.* Cambridge, MA: Harvard University Press.

Brotemarkle, R. A. (Ed.). (1931). *Clinical psychology: Studies in honor of Lightner Witmer.* Philadelphia: University of Pennsylvania Press.

Buck, J. N., Finley, C. B., Spelt, D. K., Rymarkiewiczowa, D., & Finger, F. W. (1946). The certification of clinical psychologists in Virginia. *American Psychologist, 1*, 395–398.

Buhler, C. (1971). Basic theoretical concepts of humanistic psychology. *American Psychologist, 26*, 378–386.

Burtt, H. E., & Pressey, S. L. (1957). Obituary: Henry Herbert Goddard: 1866–1957. *American Journal of Psychology, 70*, 656–657.

Cahan, E. D., & White, S. H. (1992). Proposals for a second psychology. *American Psychologist, 47*, 224–235.

Cain, A. C., Fast, I., & Erickson, M. E. (1964). Children's disturbed reactions to the death of a sibling. *American Journal of Orthopsychiatry, 34*, 741–752.

Cameron, N., & Magaret, A. (1957). *Behavior pathology.* Boston: Houghton Mifflin.

Carlson, H. S. (1978). The AASPB story: The beginnings and first 16 years of the American Association of State Psychology Boards, 1961–1977. *American Psychologist, 33*, 486–495.

Carroll, L. (1907). *Alice's adventures in Wonderland.* London: William Heinemann (Originally published 1886.)

Carter, J. W., Jr. (1950). The community health service program of the National Institute of Mental Health, U.S. Public Health Service. *Journal of Clinical Psychology, 6*, 112–117.

Cass, L., Cain, A., & Waite, R. (1970). American Association of Psychiatric Clinics for Children training standards for predoctoral internship in clinical child psychology. *Professional Psychology, 1,* 170–174.

Cattell, J. McK. (1890). Mental tests and measurements. *Mind, 15,* 373–381.

Cattell, J. McK. (1937). Retrospect: Psychology as a profession. *Journal of Consulting Psychology, 1,* 1–3.

Chapman, L. J., & Chapman, J. P. (1967). The genesis of popular but erroneous psychodiagnostic signs. *Journal of Abnormal Psychology, 72,* 193–204.

Committee on Certification of Consulting Psychologists Report for the Year 1926. (1927). *Psychological Bulletin, 24,* 148–149.

Cronbach, L. J. (1949). Statistical methods applied to Rorschach scores: A review. *Psychological Bulletin, 46,* 393–429.

Cronbach, L. J., & Meehl, P. E. (1955). Construct validity in psychological tests. *Psychological Bulletin, 52,* 281–302.

Cummings, N. (1985). An autobiography. *Psychotherapy in Private Practice, 3*(3), 3–8.

Cummings, N., & Follette, W. T. (1967). Psychiatric services and medical utilization in a prepaid health plan setting. *Medical Care, 5,* 25–35.

Dahlstrom, W. G., Meehl, P. E., & Schofield, W. (1986). Obituary: Starke Rosecrans Hathaway (1903–1984). *American Psychologist, 41,* 834–835.

David, H. P. (1962). New Jersey vignettes: Fifty years of state psychological services. *American Psychologist, 17,* 53–54.

Davison, G. C., Goldfried, M. R., & Krasner, L. (1970). A postdoctoral program in behavior modification: Theory and practice. *American Psychologist, 25,* 767–777.

DeLeon, P. H., VandenBos, G. R., & Bulatao, E. Q. (1991). Managed mental health care: A history of the federal policy initiative. *Professional Psychology: Research and Practice, 22,* 15–25.

Doll, E. A. (1920). The degree of Ph.D. and clinical psychology. *Journal of Applied Psychology, 4,* 88–90.

Doll, E. A. (1935). A genetic study of social maturity. *American Journal of Orthopsychiatry, 5,* 180–190.

Doll, E. A. (1946). Internship program at the Vineland laboratory. *Journal of Consulting Psychology, 10,* 184–190.

Doll, E. A., Phelps, W. M., & Melcher, R. T. (1932). *Mental deficiency due to birth injuries.* New York: Macmillan.

Douglas, V. I. (1972). Stop, look, and listen: The problem of sustained attention and impulse control in hyperactive and normal children. *Canadian Journal of Behavioral Science, 4,* 259–282.

Drake, R. E., Jr., & Wallach, M. A. (1979). Will mental patients stay in the community? A social psychological perspective. *Journal of Consulting and Clinical Psychology, 47,* 285–294.

Drotar, D. (1981). Psychological perspectives on chronic childhood illness. *Journal of Pediatric Psychology, 6,* 211–228.

Ekman, P., & Friesen, W. V. (1978). *Facial action and coding system.* Palo Alto, CA: Consulting Psychologists Press.

Elliott, R. M. (1956). Robert Mearns Yerkes: 1876–1956. *American Journal of Psychology, 69,* 487–494.

Epstein, S. (1979). Explorations in personality today and tomorrow: A tribute to Henry A. Murray. *American Psychologist, 34,* 649–653.

Epstein, S. (1980). The stability of behavior: II. Implications for psychological research. *American Psychologist, 35,* 790–806.

Erikson, E. (1950). *Childhood and society.* New York: Norton.

Exner, J. E., Jr. et al. (1989). *The Society for Personality Assessment: A history.* Hillsdale, NJ: Erlbaum.

Eyberg, S. M. (1978). Assessment of child behavior problems: The validation of a new inventory. *Journal of Clinical Child Psychology, 7,* 113–116.

Eysenck, H. J. (1949). Training in clinical psychology: An English point of view. *American Psychologist, 4,* 173–176.

Eysenck, H. J. (1952). The effects of psychotherapy: An evaluation. *Journal of Consulting Psychology, 16,* 319–324.

Feifel, H. (1969). Attitudes toward death: A psychological perspective. *Journal of Consulting and Clinical Psychology, 36,* 314–319.

Feifel, H., & Branscomb, A. B. (1973). Who's afraid of death? *Journal of Abnormal Psychology, 81,* 82–88.

Fernberger, S. W. (1932). The American Psychological Association: A historical summary, 1892–1930. *Psychological Bulletin, 29,* 1–89.

Fernberger, S. W. (1933). Obituary: Shepherd Ivory Franz (1874–1933). *Psychological Bulletin, 30,* 741–742.

Fine, R. (1982). On the history, theory, and future of nonmedical psychoanalysis. *Journal of Psychohistory, 9,* 501–527.

Fine, R. (1990). *The history of psychoanalysis* (rev. ed.). Northvale, NJ: Jason Aronson.

Fiske, D. W., Conley, J. J., & Goldberg, L. R. (1987). Obituary: E. Lowell Kelly (1905–1986). *American Psychologist, 42,* 511–512.

Flanagan, J. C. (1954). The critical incident technique. *Psychological Bulletin, 51,* 327–358.

Fox, R. E. (1982). The need for a reorientation of clinical psychology. *American Psychologist, 37,* 1051–1057.

Fox, R. E. (1986). Building a profession that is safe for practitioners: A personal perspective. *Psychotherapy in Private Practice, 4,* 3–12.

Frank, J. D. (1973). *Persuasion and healing.* Baltimore: Johns Hopkins University Press.

Fransella, F., & Bannister, D. (1977). *A manual for repertory grid technique.* London: Academic Press.

Franz, S. I. (1919). *Handbook of mental examination methods* (2nd ed.). New York: Macmillan.

Franz, S. I. (1923). *Nervous and mental re-education.* New York: Macmillan.

Franz, S. I., & Lashley, K. S. (1917). The retention of habits in the rat after destruction of the frontal portions of the cerebrum. *Psychobiology, 1,* 3–18.

Freud, S. (1927). *The problem of lay analysis.* New York: Brentano's.

Friedman, L. J. (1990). *Menninger: The family and the clinic.* New York: Knopf.

Galton, F. (1978). *Hereditary genius.* New York: St. Martin's Press. (Originally published 1896.)

Gardner, S., & Stevens, G. (1992). *Red Vienna and the golden age of psychology, 1918–1938*. New York: Praeger.

Garfield, S. L., & Bergin, A. E. (Eds.) (1978). *Handbook of psychotherapy and behavior change* (2nd ed.). New York: Wiley.

Garmezy, N., & Holzman, P. (1984). Obituary: David Shakow (1901–1981). *American Psychologist, 39,* 698–699.

Garmezy, N., & Rutter, M. (Eds.). (1983). *Stress, coping, and development in children.* New York: McGraw-Hill.

Gay, P. (1988). *Freud: A life for our times.* New York: W.W. Norton.

Gendlin, E. T. (1988). Obituary: Carl Rogers (1902–1987). *American Psychologist, 43,* 127–128.

Gesell, A. (1919). The field of clinical psychology as an applied science: A symposium. *Journal of Applied Psychology, 3,* 81–84.

Gibson, H. B. (1981). *Hans Eysenck: The man and his work.* London: Peter Owen.

Gill, M. M. (1961). In memoriam: David Rapaport, 1911–1960. *Journal of the American Psychoanalytic Association, 9,* 755–759.

Goddard, H. H. (1912). *The Kallakak family: A study in the heredity of feeblemindedness.* New York: Macmillan.

Goldstein, S. G. (1975). On being a divisional program chairperson: Or I loved you long distance, Junie Moon. *American Psychologist, 30,* 719–726.

Gordon, S. (1973). *The sexual adolescent: Communicating with teenagers about sex.* North Scituate, MA: Duxbury.

Gregg, A., et al. (1947). *The place of psychology in an ideal university.* Cambridge, MA: Harvard University Press.

Guthrie, R. V. (1976). *Even the rat was white: A historical view of psychology.* New York: Harper & Row.

Hale, N. G., Jr. (1971a). Introduction. In N. G. Hale, Jr. (Ed.), *James Jackson Putnam and psychoanalysis* (pp. 1–63). Cambridge, MA: Harvard University Press.

Hale, N. G., Jr. (1971b). *Freud and the Americans.* (Vol. 1). *The beginnings of psychoanalysis in the United States, 1876–1917.* New York: Oxford University Press.

Hall, C. S., & Lindzey, G. (1957). *Theories of personality.* New York: Wiley.

Halpern, F. (1973). *Survival: Black/white.* New York: Pergamon Press.

Hamlin, R. M., & Habbe, S. (1946). State psychological societies. *American Psychologist, 1,* 17–21.

Hare-Mustin, R. T. (1983). An appraisal of the relationship between women and psychotherapy: 80 years after the case of Dora. *American Psychologist, 38,* 593–601.

Hare-Mustin, R. T. (1987). A dual career life. *Psychotherapy in Private Practice, 5(2),* 45–49.

Harrower, M. R. (1948). The evolution of a clinical psychologist. *Canadian Journal of Psychology, 2,* 23–27.

Harris, S. L. (1976). *Teaching speech to a nonverbal child.* Lawrence, KS: H & H Enterprises.

Hathaway, S. R., & McKinley, J. C. (1940). A multiphasic personality schedule (Minnesota): I. Construction of the schedule. II. A differential study of hypochondriasis. *Journal of Psychology, 10,* 249–268.

Hathaway, S. R., & McKinley, J. C. (1942). *Minnesota Multiphasic Personality Inventory*. Minneapolis: University of Minnesota Press.

Healy, W. (1914). A pictorial completion test. *Psychological Review, 21,* 189–203.

Healy, W., & Bronner, A. F. (1926). *Delinquents and criminals: Their making and unmaking.* New York: Macmillan.

Hearst, E., & Capshew, J. H. (Eds.). (1988). *Psychology at Indiana University: A centennial review and compendium.* Bloomington: Indiana University Department of Psychology.

Heiser, K. F. (1945). Certification of psychologists in Connecticut. *Psychological Bulletin, 42,* 624–630.

Hildreth, G. H. (1930). *Psychological service for school problems.* Yonkers, NY: World Book Co.

Hobbs, N. (1948). The development of a code of ethical standards for psychology. *American Psychologist, 3,* 80–84.

Hobbs, N. (1966). Helping disturbed children: Psychological and ecological strategies. *American Psychologist, 21,* 1105–1115.

Hodges, W. F., & Weatherley, D. (1990). Obituary: Victor Raimy. *American Psychologist, 45,* 398.

Holt, R. R. (1985). The current status of psychoanalytic theory. *Psychoanalytic Psychology, 2,* 289–315.

Holzberg, J. D. (1952). The practice and problems of clinical psychology in a state psychiatric hospital. *Journal of Consulting Psychology, 16,* 98–103.

Huesmann, L. R., Eron, L. D., Lefkowitz, M. M., & Walder, L. O. (1984). The stability of aggression over time and generations. *Developmental Psychology, 20,* 1120–1134.

Hunt, J. McV. (1961). *Intelligence and experience.* New York: Ronald.

Hunt, J. McV. (1984). Obituary: Orbal Hobart Mowrer (1907–1982). *American Psychologist, 39,* 912–914.

Hunt, W. A. (1962). Obituary: Carney Landis: 1897–1962. *American Journal of Psychology, 75,* 506–509.

Hunt, W. A., & Landis, C. (1935). The overt behavior pattern in startle. *Journal of Experimental Psychology, 19,* 309–315.

Jacobson, E. (1929). *Progressive relaxation.* Chicago: University of Chicago Press.

Jacobson, N. (1989). The maintenance of treatment gains following social learning-based marital therapy. *Behavior Therapy, 20,* 325–336.

Jacobson, N., & Revenstorf, D. (1988). Statistics for assessing the clinical significance of psychotherapy techniques. *Behavioral Assessment, 10,* 133–145.

Jankowicz, A. D. (1987). Whatever became of George Kelly? *American Psychologist, 42,* 481–487.

Johnson, J. H. (1986). *Life events as stressors in childhood and adolescence.* Newbury Park, CA: Sage.

Jones, M. C. (1924a). A laboratory study of fear. *Pedagogical Seminary, 31,* 308–315.

Jones, M. C. (1924b). The elimination of children's fears. *Journal of Experimental Psychology, 7,* 382–390.

Jones, M. C. (1975). A 1924 pioneer looks at behavior therapy. *Journal of Behavior Therapy and Experimental Psychiatry, 6,* 181–187.

Jones, R. T. (1989). A salute to the founding mothers and fathers of clinical psychology. *The Clinical Psychologist, 42,* 19–28.

Kalinkowitz, B. (1978). Scientist-practitioner: The widening schism. *The Clinical Psychologist, 32,* 4–5.

Kazdin, A. E. (1978). *History of behavior modification: Experimental foundations of contemporary research.* Baltimore: University Park Press.

Kazdin, A. E. (1979). Fictions, factions, and functions of behavior therapy. *Behavior Therapy, 10,* 629–654.

Kelly, E. L., & Fiske, D. W. (1951). *The prediction of performance in clinical psychology.* Ann Arbor: University of Michigan Press.

Kelly, E. L., & Goldberg, L. (1959). Correlates of later performance and specialization in psychology: A follow-up study of trainees assessed in the VA selection research project. *American Psychologist, 33,* 746–755.

Kelly, G. A. (1955). *The psychology of personal constructs.* New York: Norton.

Kiesler, C. A., & Pallak, M. S. (1980). The Virginia blues. *American Psychologist, 35,* 953–954.

Klopfer, B., & Kelley, D. (1942). *The Rorschach technique: A manual for a projective method of personality diagnosis.* Yonkers, NY: World Book Co.

Koocher, G. P., & O'Malley, J. E. (1981). *The Damocles syndrome.* New York: McGraw-Hill.

Korchin, S. J. (1980). Clinical psychology and minority problems. *American Psychologist, 35,* 262–269.

Korman, M. (1974). National conference on levels and patterns of professional training in psychology: The major themes. *American Psychologist, 29,* 441–449.

Korman, M. (Ed.). (1976). *Levels and patterns of professional training in psychology.* Washington, DC: American Psychological Association.

La Greca, A. M., Dandes, S. K., Wick, P., Shaw, K., & Stone, W. (1988). Development of the Social Anxiety Scale for Children. *Journal of Clinical Child Psychology, 17,* 84–91.

La Greca, A. M., Siegel, L., Wallander, J., & Walker, C. E. (Eds.). (1992). *Stress and coping in child health.* New York: Guilford Press.

Landis, C., & Hunt, W. A. (1939). *The startle pattern.* New York: Rinehart & Co.

Lang, P. J., & Lazovik, A. D. (1963). Experimental desensitization of a phobia. *Journal of Abnormal and Social Psychology, 66,* 519–525.

Laughlin, P. R., & Worley, J. L. (1991). Roles of the American Psychological Association and the Veterans Administration in the development of internships in psychology. *American Psychologist, 46,* 430–436.

Lazarus, R. S. (1949). The influence of color on the protocol of the Rorschach test. *Journal of Abnormal and Social Psychology, 44,* 508–516.

Lazarus, R. S. (1966). *Psychological stress and the coping process.* New York: McGraw-Hill.

Lazarus, R. S., & Folkman, S. (1984). *Stress, appraisal, and coping.* New York: Springer.

Levy, L. H. (1962). The skew in clinical psychology. *American Psychologist, 17,* 244–249.

Levy, L. H. (1984). The metamorphosis of clinical psychology: Toward a new charter as human services psychology. *American Psychologist, 39,* 486–494.

Lindzey, G. (Ed.). (1954). *Handbook of social psychology.* 2 Vols. Cambridge, MA: Addison-Wesley.

Loevinger, J. (1963). Conflict of commitment in clinical research. *American Psychologist, 18,* 241–251.

Louttit, C. M. (1936). *Clinical psychology: A handbook of children's behavior problems.* New York: Harper & Brothers.

Loyd, B. H., & Abidin, R. R. (1985). Revision of the Parenting Stress Index. *Journal of Pediatric Psychology, 10,* 169–177.

Macfarlane, J. W. (1938). *Studies in child guidance. I.* Washington, DC: Society for Research in Child Development.

Macfarlane, J. W. (1955). President's message. *Newsletter, Division of Clinical Psychology, 9*(1), 1.

Machover, K. (1949). *Personality projection in the drawing of the human figure.* Springfield, IL: Charles C Thomas.

Matarazzo, J. D. (1987). Obituary: William A. Hunt (1903–1986). *American Psychologist, 42,* 263–264.

Matarazzo, J. E., et al. (Eds.). (1984). *Behavioral health.* New York: Wiley.

May, R. (1950). *The meaning of anxiety.* New York: Ronald.

McCandless, B. R. (1957). Relations with pediatrics. *Newsletter, Division of Clinical Psychology, 11*(2), 8–9.

McCandless, B. R. (1968–1969). Points at issue between practical and academic school psychology. *Journal of School Psychology, 7*(2), 13–17.

McNeill, H. (1947). Freudians and Catholics. *Commonweal, 46,* 350–353.

McReynolds, P. (1987). Lightner Witmer: Little-known founder of clinical psychology. *American Psychologist, 42,* 849–858.

Mednick, S. A., Parnas, J., & Schulsinger, F. (1987). The Copenhagen High Risk Project. *Schizophrenia Bulletin, 13,* 485–495.

Meehl, P. E. (1954). *Clinical versus statistical prediction.* Minneapolis: University of Minnesota Press.

Meehl, P. E. (1962). Schizotaxia, schizotypy, and schizophrenia. *American Psychologist, 17,* 827–838.

Melamed, B. G., & Siegel, L. J. (1975). Reduction of anxiety in children facing hospitalization and surgery by use of filmed modeling. *Journal of Consulting and Clinical Psychology, 43,* 511–521.

Meltzer, H. (1966). Psychology of the scientist: XVII. Research has a place in private practice. *Psychological Reports, 19,* 463–472.

Miller, J. G. (1978). *Living systems.* New York: McGraw-Hill.

Miller, L. C., Barrett, C. L., Hampe, E., & Noble, H. (1972). Comparison of reciprocal inhibition, psychotherapy, and waiting list control for phobic children. *Journal of Abnormal Psychology, 79,* 269–279.

Mischel, W. (1958). Preference for delayed and immediate reinvorcement: An experimental study of a cultural observation. *Journal of Abnormal and Social Psychology, 56,* 57–61.

Mischel, W. (1968). *Personality and assessment.* New York: Wiley.

Mitchell, D. (1919). The clinical psychologist. *Journal of Abnormal Psychology, 14,* 325–332.

Mitchell, D. (1931). Private practice. In R. A. Brotemarkle (Ed.), *Clinical psychology: Studies in honor of Lightner Witmer* (pp. 177–190). Philadelphia: University of Pennsylvania Press.

Morgan, C., & Murray, H. A. (1935). A method for investigating phantasies: The Thematic Apperception Test. *Archives of Neurology and Psychiatry, 34,* 289- 306.

Mowrer, O. H., & Mowrer, W. M. (1938). Enuresis: A method for its study and treatment. *American Journal of Orthopsychiatry, 8,* 436–459.

Murray, H. A. (1935). Psychology and the university. *Archives of Neurology and Psychiatry* (Chicago), *34,* 803–817.

Murray, H. A. (1938). *Explorations in personality.* New York: Oxford University Press.

Murray, H. A. (1940). What should psychologists do about psychoanalysis? *Journal of Abnormal and Social Psychology, 35,* 150–175.

Murray, H. A. (1956). Morton Prince: Sketch of his life and work. *Journal of Abnormal and Social Psychology, 51,* 291–295.

Murray, H., & Morgan, C. (1938). *Explorations in personality.* New York: Oxford University Press.

Mussen, P., & Eichorn, D. (1988). Obituary: Mary Cover Jones (1896–1987). *American Psychologist, 43,* 818.

Napoli, D. S. (1981). *Architects of adjustment: The history of the psychological profession in the United States.* Port Washington, NY: Kennikat Press.

Nathan, P. E. (1987). Rutgers: The Center of Alcohol Studies. *British Journal of Addictions, 82,* 833–840.

Nelson, R. O. (1983). Behavioral assessment: Past, present, and future. *Behavioral Assessment, 5,* 195–206.

Ochroch, R., & Kalinkowitz, B. N. (1982). Obituary: Florence Halpern (1900–1981). *American Psychologist, 37,* 1396.

Office of Strategic Services Assessment Staff (1948). *Assessment of men.* New York: Rinehart.

*Oxford book of carols.* (1928). Oxford, U.K.: Oxford University Press.

Patrick, C. J., & Iacono, W. G. (1989). False positive outcomes and methodological issues in research on polygraph testing. *Psychophysiology, 26,* S2.

Patterson, G. R. (1974). Interventions for boys with conduct problems: Multiple settings, treatments, and criteria. *Journal of Consulting and Clinical Psychology, 42,* 471–481.

Paul, G. L. (1966). *Insight versus desensitization in psychotherapy: An experiment in anxiety reduction.* Stanford, CA: Stanford University Press.

Pearson, L. (1961). Letter to the editor. *Newsletter, Division of Clinical Psychology, 14*(3), 15.

Perlman, J., Folsom, E., & Campion, D. (Eds.) (1981). *Walt Whitman: The measure of his song.* Minneapolis, MN: Holy Cow! Press.

Peterson, L. et al. (1984). Comparison of three modeling procedures on the presurgical and postsurgical reactions of children. *Behavior Therapy, 15,* 197- 203.

Poffenberger, A. T. (1938). The training of a clinical psychologist. *Journal of Consulting Psychology, 2,* 1–6.

Poffenberger, A. T. (1940). Leta Stetter Hollingworth: 1886–1939. *American Journal of Psychology, 53,* 299–301.

Pope, K. S., & Bouhoutsos, J. C. (1986). *Sexual intimacy between psychotherapists and patients*. New York: Columbia University Press.

Porteus, S. D. (1965). *Porteus Maze Tests: Fifty years' application*. Palo Alto, CA: Pacific Books.

Prince, M. (1908). *The dissociation of a personality*. New York: Longmans, Green.

Purtscher, N. (1947). *Doctor Mesmer: An historical study*. London: J. Westhouse.

Raimy, V. C. (Ed.). (1950). *Training in clinical psychology*. New York: Prentice-Hall.

Rapaport, D. (1944). The psychologist in the private mental hosptial. *Journal of Consulting Psychology, 8*, 298–301.

Rapaport, D. (1951). *Organization and pathology of thought*. New York: Columbia University Press.

Rapaport, D., Gill, M. M., & Schafer, R. (1945). *Diagnostic psychological testing*. Vol. 1. Chicago: Yearbook.

Rapaport, D., Gill, M. M., & Schafer, R. (1946). *Diagnostic psychological testing*. Vol. 2. Chicago: Yearbook.

Raush, H. L. (1974). Research, practice, and accountability. *American Psychologist, 29*, 678–681.

Reisman, J. M. (1991). *A history of clinical psychology* (2nd ed.). New York: Hemisphere Publishing Corporation.

Report of the Committee on Training in Clinical Psychology of the American Psychological Association Submitted at the Detroit Meeting of the American Psychological Association, September 9–13, 1947. (1947). Recommended graduate training program in clinical psychology. *American Psychologist, 2*, 539–558.

Rie, H. E., & Rie, E. D. (Eds.). (1980). *Handbook of minimal brain dysfunctions: A critical view*. New York: Wiley.

Roberts, M. C., Fanurik, D., & Wilson, D. R. (1988). A community program to reward children's use of seat belts. *Journal of Community Psychology, 16*, 395–407.

Robinson, F. G. (1992). *Love's story told: A life of Henry A. Murray*. Cambridge, MA: Harvard University Press.

Robyak, J. E., & Goodyear, R. K. (1984). Graduate school origins of diplomates and fellows in professional psychology. *Professional Psychology: Research and Practice, 15*, 379–387.

Roe, A. (1953) *The making of a scientist*. New York: Dodd, Mead.

Rogers, C. R. (1942). *Counseling and psychotherapy*. Boston: Houghton Mifflin.

Rogers, C. R. (1951). Where are we going in clinical psychology? *Journal of Consulting Psychology, 15*, 171–177.

Rogers, C. R. (1951). *Client centered therapy*. Boston: Houghton Mifflin.

Rogers, C. R. (1974). In retrospect: Forty-six years. *American Psychologist, 29*, 115–123.

Rorschach, H. (1921). *Psychodiagnostik*. Bern: Huber.

Ross, A. O. (1959). *The practice of clinical child psychology*. New York: Grune & Stratton.

Rotter, J. B. (1954). *Social learning and clinical psychology*. Englewood Cliffs, NJ: Prentice-Hall.

Rotter, J. B. (1966). Generalized expectancies for internal versus external control of reinforcement. *Psychological Monographs, 80* (Whole No. 609).

Rotter, J. B. (1973). The future of clinical psychology. *Journal of Consulting and Clinical Psychology, 40,* 313–321.

Routh, D. K. (1969). Graduate training in pediatric psychology: The Iowa program. *Pediatric Psychology, 1*(1), 5–6.

Routh, D. K. (1982). Intellectual progeny of Seashore and Spence: Iowa psychologists. In D. K. Routh (Ed.), *Learning, speech, and the complex effects of punishment: Essays honoring George J. Wischner* (pp. 213–230). New York: Plenum.

Routh, D. K. (1984). When was the first psychology clinic in Iowa founded? *Iowa Psychologist, 29,* No. 5, 3–7.

Routh, D. K. (Ed.). (1988). *Handbook of pediatric psychology.* New York: Guilford Press.

Routh, D. K., Patton, L., & Sanfilippo, M. D. (1991). Celebrating 20 years of the *Journal of Clinical Child Psychology:* From advocacy to scientific research and back again. *Journal of Clinical Child Psychology, 20,* 2–6.

Rubenstein, E. A., & Parloff, M. B. (Eds.). (1959). *Research in psychotherapy: Proceedings of a conference.* Washington, DC: American Psychological Association.

Ruckmick, C. A. (1942). Obituary: Guy Montrose Whipple: 1876–1941. *American Journal of Psychology, 55,* 132–134.

Salk, L. (1992). *Familyhood: Nurturing the values that matter.* New York: Simon & Schuster.

Santostefano, S. (1978). *A biodevelopmental approach to clinical child psychology: Cognitive controls and cognitive control therapy.* New York: Wiley.

Sarason, S. B. (1983). School psychology: An autobiographical fragment. *Journal of School Psychology, 21,* 285–295.

Sarason, S. B. (1988). *The making of an American psychologist: An autobiography.* San Francisco: Jossey-Bass.

Schafer, R. (1954). *Psychoanalytic interpretation in Rorschach testing.* New York: Grune & Stratton.

Schroeder, D. J., & Fish, J. E. (1987). A brief history of Section II: Continuing Professional Development. *The Clinical Psychologist, 40*(1), 16.

Sears, R. R. (1946). Graduate training facilities. I. General information. II. Clinical psychology. *American Psychologist, 1,* 135–150.

Sears, R. R. (1947). Clinical training facilities: 1947. *American Psychologist, 2,* 199–205.

Seligman, M. E. P. (1975). *Helplessness: On depression, development, and death.* San Francisco: W. H. Freeman.

Shaffer, L. F. (1947). The problem of psychotherapy. *American Psychologist, 2,* 459–467.

Shaffer, L. F. (1964). Obituary: Frederic Lyman Wells: 1884–1964. *American Journal of Psychology, 77,* 679–682.

Shields, S. A. (1975). Ms. Pilgrim's progress: The contributions of Leta Stetter Hollingworth to the psychology of women. *American Psychologist, 30,* 852–859.

Shneidman, E. S. (1985). *Definition of suicide.* New York: Wiley.

Skodak, M. (1939). Children in foster homes: A study of mental development. *University of Iowa Studies in Child Welfare, 16,* No. 1.

Smith, M. B., & Anderson, J. W. (1989). Obituary: Henry A. Murray (1893–1988). *American Psychologist, 44*, 1153–1154.

Snyder, C. R., Shenkel, R., & Lowey, C. R. (1977). Acceptance of personality interpretations: The "Barnum effect" and beyond. *Journal of Consulting and Clinical Psychology, 45*, 104–114.

Sobel, S. B., & Strickland, B. (1980). Division 12 establishes a section on clinical psychology of women. *The Clinical Psychologist, 33*(3), 1.

Spence, J. T. (1971). What can you say about a twenty-year old theory that won't die? *Journal of Motor Behavior, 3*, 193–203.

Spence, K. W., & Taylor, J. T. (1953). The relation of conditioned response strength to anxiety in normal, neurotic, and psychotic subjects. *Journal of Experimental Psychology, 45*, 265–272.

Spielberger, C. D. (1989). Report of the Treasurer, 1988. Turning the deficit around: Better days ahead. *American Psychologist, 44*, 987–992.

Spielberger, C. D., Gorsuch, R., & Lushene, R. (1970). *Manual for the State-Trait Anxiety Inventory.* Palo Alto, CA: Consulting Psychologists Press.

Spinetta, J. J., Rigler, D., & Karon, M. (1974). Personal space as a measure of a dying child's isolation. *Journal of Consulting and Clinical Psychology, 42*, 751–756.

Stabler, B., & Underwood, L. E. (Eds.). (1986). *Slow grows the child.* Hillsdale, NJ: Erlbaum.

Stevenson, G. S., & Smith, G. (1934). *Child guidance clinics: A quarter century of development.* New York: Commonwealth Fund.

Stricker, G. (1973). The doctoral dissertation in clinical psychology. *Professional Psychology, 4*, 72–78.

Stricker, G. (1985). Obituary: Gordon F. Derner (1915–1983). *American Psychologist, 40*, 368–369.

Strickland, B. R. (1987). *The feminization of psychology: Problem and promise.* Paper presented at the meeting of the Association of Women in Psychology, Denver, Colorado.

Strupp, H. H. (1963). The outcome problem in psychotherapy revisited. *Psychotherapy, 1*, 1–13.

Strupp, H. (1991). Reflections on my career in clinical psychology. In C. E. Walker (Ed.), *The history of clinical psychology in autobiography* (Vol. 1, pp. 293–329). Pacific Grove, CA: Brooks/Cole.

Strupp, H., & Luborsky, L. (Eds.). (1962). *Research in psychotherapy.* Vol. 2. Washington, DC: American Psychological Association.

Symonds, J. P. (1946). Ten years of journalism in psychology, 1937–1946: First decade of the Journal of Consulting Psychology. *Journal of Consulting Psychology, 10*, 335–374.

Terman, L. M. (1925). *Genetic studies of genius.* Vol. 1. Stanford, CA: Stanford University Press.

Thorne, F. C. (1945). The field of clinical psychology: Past, present, and future. *Journal of Clinical Psychology, 1*, 1–20.

Thorne, F. C. (1976). Reflections on the golden age of Columbia University. *Journal of the History of the Behavioral Sciences, 12*, 159–165.

Tolman, R. (1943). Wartime organizational activities of women psychologists. *Journal of Consulting Psychology, 7*, 296–297.

Tomkins, S. S. (1962–1963). *Affect, imagery, consciousness* (Vols. 1 & 2). New York: Springer.

Tomkins, S. S. (1982). Personology is a complex, lifelong, never-ending enterprise. *Personality and Social Psychology Bulletin, 8*, 608–611.

Trow, W. C., & Carter, J. W., Jr. (1948). Progress report of the Committee on Psychological Service Centers. *American Psychologist, 3*, 57–58.

Twitmyer, E. B., & Nathanson, Y. S. (1932). *Correction of defective speech*. Philadelphia: Blakiston.

VandenBos, G. R. (1989). Loosely organized "organized psychology": 1988 executive officer's report. *American Psychologist, 44*, 979–986.

Viteles, M. S. (1932). *Industrial psychology*. New York: Norton.

Walker, C. E. (Ed.). (1991). *The history of clinical psychology in autobiography* (Vol. 1). Pacific Grove, CA: Brooks/Cole.

Wallin, J. E. W. (1919). The field of clinical psychology as an applied science: A symposium. *Journal of Applied Psychology, 3*, 87–95.

Wallin, J. E. W. (1955). *The odyssey of a psychologist*. Wilmington, DE: Author.

Wallin, J. E. W. (1961). A note on the origin of the APA clinical section. *American Psychologist, 16*, 256–258.

Wallin, J. E. W. (1966). A red-letter day in APA history. *Journal of General Psychology, 75*, 107–114.

Watson, J. B., & Rayner, R. (1920). Conditioned emotional reactions. *Journal of Experimental Psychology, 3*, 1–14.

Watson, R. I. (1956). Obituary: Lightner Witmer: 1867–1956. *American Journal of Psychology, 69*, 680–682.

Wechsler, D. (1939). *The measurement of adult intelligence*. Baltimore: Williams & Wilkins.

Wells, F. L. (1913). On formulation in psychoanalysis. *Journal of Abnormal Psychology, 8*, 217–227.

Wells, F. L. (1944). Diurnal behavior cycle in spiders. *Science, 99*, 513.

Wells, F. L., & Ruesch, J. (1945). *Mental examiners' handbook*. New York: Psychological Corporation.

Wenar, C. (1982). Developmental psychopathology: Its nature and models. *Journal of Clinical Child Psychology, 11*, 192–201.

Whipple, G. M. (1910). *Manual of mental and physical tests*. Vols. 1 & 2. Baltimore: Warwick & York.

White, R. W. (1952). *Lives in progress*. New York: Holt, Rinehart & Winston.

White, R. W. (1959). Motivation reconsidered: The concept of competence. *Psychological Review, 66*, 297–333.

White, S., Strom, G. A., Santilli, G., & Halpin, B. M. (1986). Interviewing young sexual abuse victims with the anatomically correct dolls. *Child Abuse and Neglect, 10*, 519–529.

Whitehorn, J. C. (1944). A century of psychiatric research in America. In J. K. Hall (Ed.), *One hundred years of American psychiatry* (pp. 167–193). New York: Columbia University Press.

Whitman, W. (1855). *Leaves of grass*. Portland, ME: T. B. Mosher.

Wiggins, J. G. (1976). The psychologist as a health professional in the health maintenance organization. *Professional Psychology, 7*, 9–13.

Witkin, H. A., Mensh, I. N., & Cates, J. (1972). Psychologists in medical schools. *American Psychologist, 27*, 434–440.

Witmer, L. (1896). Practical work in psychology. *Pediatrics, 2*, 462–471.

Witmer, L. (1897). The organization of practical work in psychology. *Psychological Review, 4*, 116.

Wolfle, H. M. (1948). Available internships in psychology. *American Psychologist, 3*, 95–97.

Wolpe, J. (1958). *Psychotherapy by reciprocal inhibition*. Stanford, CA: Stanford University Press.

Woodworth, R. S. (1917). *Personal Data Sheet*. Chicago: C. H. Stoelting.

Wrenn, R. L. (1992). Obituary: Anne Roe (1904–1991). *American Psychologist, 47*, 1052–1053.

Yerkes, R. M. (1907). *The dancing mouse*. New York: Macmillan.

Yerkes, R. M., Bridges, J. W., & Hardwick, R. S. (1915). *A point scale for measuring mental ability*. Baltimore: Warwick & York.

Yerkes, R. M., & Dodson, J. D. (1908). The relation of strength of stimulus to rapidity of habit formation. *Journal of Comparative Neurology and Psychology, 18*, 459–482.

Zimet, C. N. (1981). The clinical psychologist in the 1980's: Entitled or untitled? *The Clinical Psychologist, 35*, 12–14.

Zubin, J. (1954). Failures of the Rorschach technique. *Journal of Projective Techniques, 18*, 303–315.

# Index

271